DEFENCE REFORMS

A National Imperative

DEFENCE REFORMS

A National Imperative

Editors

Gurmeet Kanwal
Neha Kohli

idsa
INSTITUTE FOR DEFENCE STUDIES & ANALYSES
NEW DELHI

PENTAGON PRESS

Defence Reforms: A National Imperative
Editors: Gurmeet Kanwal and Neha Kohli

First Published in 2018

ISBN 978-93-86618-34-4

Published by
PENTAGON PRESS
206, Peacock Lane, Shahpur Jat
New Delhi-110049
Phones: 011-64706243, 26491568
Telefax: 011-26490600
email: rajan@pentagonpress.in
website: www.pentagonpress.in

In association with
Institute for Defence Studies and Analyses
No. 1, Development Enclave,
New Delhi-110010
Phone: +91-11-26717983
Website: www.idsa.in

Printed at Aegean Offset Printers, Greater Noida, U.P.

Contents

Preface

For many years after India's independence in 1947, the Higher Defence Organisation (HDO) handed down by Lord Mountbatten, the last British Viceroy and his Chief of Staff, Lord Ismay, remained almost entirely unchanged. The first instance of change came with the Sino-Indian Conflict of 1962 that aroused a new defence consciousness in the country after years of neglect. Thus, efforts to formalise defence planning began earnestly in 1964 when the first Five Year Defence Plan was drawn up. In 1965, a 'Planning Cell' was established in the Ministry of Defence (MoD). Unfortunately, while the threats and challenges to national security have grown manifold, the decision making and defence planning structures have not simultaneously evolved or kept pace. Rather, sporadic, piecemeal and ad hoc defence reforms were undertaken periodically, more often than not as reactions to occurrences, and not always with a view to address the root causes. For example, the Cabinet Committee on Security (CCS) was constituted only in the mid-1990s; till then, national security issues were being handled by the Cabinet Committee on Political Affairs (CCPA) in addition to its various other wide ranging responsibilities.

A major review of the management of national security was undertaken after the Kargil conflict of 1999 when the Kargil Review Committee (KRC), headed by the late K. Subrahmanyam, was appointed. The committee made several far-reaching recommendations on the development of India's nuclear deterrence, management of national security, intelligence reforms, border management, the defence budget, use of air power, counter-insurgency operations, integrated manpower policy, defence research and development (R&D), and even media relations. Subsequently, the Cabinet Committee on Security (CCS) appointed a Group of Ministers (GoM) headed by Deputy Prime Minister and Home Minister L.K. Advani to study the KRC report and recommend measures for its implementation. The GoM set up four task forces on intelligence reforms, internal security, border management, and higher defence management to undertake in-depth analyses of various facets of national security management. Based on the reports of these task forces, the GoM recommended sweeping reforms to the existing national security management system. The CCS accepted its recommendations in toto, except for that which recommended the creation of the post of a Chief of Defence Staff (CDS). While a large number of the recommendations that were approved by the CCS have been implemented, action on a few important ones has still not been taken.

In 2016-17, the Military Centre of the Institute for Defence Studies and Analyses (IDSA), New Delhi, undertook a research project to review the status of the defence reforms approved by the Vajpayee government after the Kargil conflict of 1999, with a view to recommending additional reforms that should be undertaken to improve functional efficiency. The major issues examined included the measures necessary to streamline defence planning; methods for optimising the defence budget; the ways and means for restructuring the MoD and the Services HQ to ensure smoother decision making and better integration; procedures for improving inter-ministerial coordination; and, other related issues.

The Military Centre organised a series of round-table discussions as part of the project, focussing especially on restructuring at the apex level, optimum utilisation of the defence budget, intelligence reforms, and inter-departmental coordination. Leading practitioners and government officials, both serving and retired, were invited to make presentations to the members of the Centre on the reforms recommended in their specific fields of expertise. The Military Centre also held in-house discussions on all aspects of defence planning and the reforms necessary to synergise decision making and improve the interface between the civilian bureaucracy and the armed forces. Eminent analysts were requested to examine key issues hampering the smooth management of national security and contribute short papers on their areas of expertise.

While conceptualising the project, it was decided to deal with the issues at the macro level. Based on the round-table discussions that followed, the papers were revised by the authors and have been compiled for publication in this anthology. The idea is to bring to the attention of not just the informed reader but also the wider public that pending defence reforms need to be undertaken urgently. It is also an attempt to engage with, and simultaneously inform, an interested readership on the intricacies of managing the complexities of national security in India.

Defence reforms are a vast and complex issue, and this compilation is by no means fully comprehensive. The Editors concede that it has not been possible to address many less important facets, despite the endeavour to speak to a wider audience, owing to limitations of time and space.

The Editors would like to thank Shri Jayant Prasad, Director General, IDSA, for his unstinting support to the project since its inception. Thanks also to Maj Gen Alok Deb (Retd.), Deputy Director General, IDSA, his predecessor Brig Rumel Dahiya (Retd.) and all the members of IDSA's Military Centre for their contribution to the project at several brainstorming sessions and their diligent reviews of the papers. Thanks are also due to the editorial team and, in particular to Natallia Khaniejo for her excellent and painstaking editing, and to Vivek Kaushik for his help in timely publication of this work.

Brig Gurmeet Kanwal (Retd.)
Distinguished Fellow, IDSA

Neha Kohli
Associate Editor
Journal of Defence Studies
IDSA

7 February 2018

About the Authors

Laxman Kumar Behera is Research Fellow at Institute for Defence Studies and Analyses (IDSA), New Delhi. His areas of specialisation include defence industry, arms spending and defence procurement.

Lt Gen Vinod Bhatia is Director, Centre for Joint Warfare Studies (CENJOWS), New Delhi. He is a former DGMO and was a member of the Sheketkar committee on Enhancing Combat Capability and Rebalancing the Defence Budget.

R. Chandrashekhar is a former member of the Armed Forces Headquarters Civil Service. He is a Senior Fellow at the Centre for Joint Warfare Studies (CENJOWS), New Delhi, and the author of *Rooks and Knights: Civil Military Relations in India* (2016).

Dr Monika Chansoria, presently a Senior Visiting Fellow at The Japan Institute of International Affairs (JIIA), Tokyo, is Senior Fellow and Head of the China-study programme at the Centre for Land Warfare Studies, New Delhi. She has authored five books on Asian security issues the latest of which is *China, Japan, and Senkaku Islands: Conflict in the East China Sea amid an American Shadow* (2017).

Amit Cowshish is a former Financial Advisor (Acquisition), Ministry of Defence. He has written extensively on defence expenditure and defence procurement.

Lt Gen Kamal Davar, a veteran of the 1965 and 1971 wars, is former GOC Ladakh and Corps Commander in Punjab. He raised the Defence Intelligence Agency (DIA) as its first Director General. He is a prolific writer on national security issues.

Brig Gurmeet Kanwal is Distinguished Fellow, Institute for Defence Studies and Analyses (IDSA), New Delhi and former Director, Centre for Land Warfare Studies (CLAWS), New Delhi.

Brig Narendra Kumar, a former infantryman, has extensive experience in counter-insurgency operations in Sri Lanka, Jammu and Kashmir and the north-east. He has served in a UN Mission in North Africa and with an Indian training team abroad. He is a former senior fellow at CLAWS held the Chair of Excellence.

Dr Anit Mukherjee is an Assistant Professor in the South Asia Programme at the S. Rajaratnam School of International Studies (RSIS), Nanyang Technological University and a Non-Resident Fellow at Brookings India.

Lt Gen (Dr) Anjan Mukherjee is former Director General, Financial Planning, Army HQ and Director General Artillery. He served as the Chief Investment officer and Joint MD of the Army Group Insurance Fund.

Maj Gen P.K. Mallick is a former Senior Directing Staff (SDS) at National Defence College, New Delhi. He has had immense experience in command, staff and instructional appointments in Indian Army.

Shruti Pandalai is an Associate Fellow working with the military centre at IDSA. Her research focuses on India's Foreign Policy and National Security Challenges. A former broadcast journalist, Shruti has also published extensively on the issue of Media and National Security.

Shakti Sinha is Director, Nehru Memorial Museum and Library, New Delhi. He has authored several book chapters and articles on strategic affairs, governance and political economy for Indian and international publications.

Col Rajneesh Singh was formerly a Research Fellow at the Institute for Defence Studies and Analyses (IDSA) where he worked on Higher Defence Management. An infantry officer, he is a PhD candidate at Jawaharlal Nehru University, New Delhi.

1

Introduction: The Need for Defence Reforms

Gurmeet Kanwal

South Asia is the second-most unstable region in the world and is closely vying with West Asia for the number one spot. Among the world's major democracies, India faces the most complex threats and challenges spanning the full spectrum of conflict from nuclear to sub-conventional. The key geo-strategic challenges in South Asia emanate from the ongoing conflict in Afghanistan and the Af-Pak border; unresolved territorial disputes between India and China, and India and Pakistan; and the almost unbridled march of radical extremism sweeping across the strategic landscape. The rising tide of Left-Wing Extremism (LWE) and the growing spectre of urban terrorism have also contributed towards vitiating India's security environment.

However, despite the prolonged exposure that security establishments have had in dealing with multifarious challenges, Indian defence planning has been retrospective instead of proactive, marked by knee-jerk reactions to emerging situations and haphazard single-service growth. The absence of a clearly enunciated National Security Strategy (NSS), poor civil-military relations, the failure to commit funds for modernisation on a long-term basis and sub-optimal inter-service prioritisation have severely handicapped defence planning. With a projected expenditure budget of US$ 100 billion for military modernisation over the next 10 years, it is now being realised that force structures need to be configured on an integrated tri-services basis to meet future threats and challenges.

Early Efforts towards Defence Reforms

For many years after independence, the Higher Defence Organisation (HDO) handed down by Lord Mountbatten and Lord Ismay remained almost completely unchanged. The Sino-Indian Conflict in 1962 aroused a new defence consciousness in the country after years of neglect, and efforts to formalise defence planning began earnestly in 1964. Various organisational changes were attempted:

- Defence requirements were assessed on a five-year basis and the First Defence Plan (1964-69) was drawn up.
- A Planning Cell was established in 1965 in the Ministry of Defence (MoD).
- The Second Defence Plan (1969-74) was instituted on a 'roll-on' basis. After a year was completed, an additional year was tagged at the other end so that the armed forces would always have a revised and updated five-year plan. This method was found to be impractical.
- In 1974, an Apex Group under the Union Minister for Planning suggested that a steady long-term defence effort would be more cost effective and economical than fluctuating allocations on account of periodic economic and security crises.

Structures for Defence Planning

Most of the defence planning machinery and planning methodology were developed in the decade 1964-74:

- In order to integrate defence planning with the overall economic planning effort, defence and economic development plans were made co-terminus.
- The Committee for Defence Planning (CDP) was established under the Cabinet Secretary.
- The Joint Intelligence Committee (JIC) was constituted in the Cabinet Secretariat to provide external and internal threat assessments.
- Planning Units were also established in the Department of Defence Production and Defence Research and Development Organisation (DRDO).
- A Planning and Coordination Cell was created in the MoD to coordinate and compile various plans into a comprehensive 'defence plan' for cabinet approval. However, the civilian bureaucrats in the MoD lacked the necessary expertise to arbitrate jointmanship between the services and only succeeded in

appending together the different requirements of individual services without the requisite analysis.

- In the Services Headquarters, Perspective Planning Directorates were established in the late 1970s.
- In 1986, the Directorate General of Defence Planning Staff (DG DPS), comprising officers from the three Services, DRDO, MoD and the Ministry of External Affairs was constituted to coordinate and harmonise defence planning under the Chiefs of Staff Committee (COSC).

Weaknesses

While efforts have been made to improve defence planning and suitable structural changes have been instituted within the MoD, implementation of the process continues to be tardy.

Guidance. The Cabinet Committee on Security (CCS), chaired by the Prime Minister, meets as often as necessary to review emerging situations that can have an adverse impact on national security so as to issue suitable policy directives. However, the National Security Council (NSC), that is also chaired by the Prime Minister, whose charter involves the evolution of an integrated NSS and the provision of guidance for long-term defence planning, seldom meets.

Plans. Five-year defence plans are rarely accorded formal government approval. In fact, the 10th Defence Plan (2002-07) and the 11th Defence Plan (2007-12) were not approved at all and drifted along on an ad hoc basis.

Funding. Annual defence budgets, in which funds are committed only for one year at a time, add an element of uncertainty to the planning process. Furthermore, unutilised funds continue to lapse back to the Ministry of Finance (MoF) at the end of the financial year.

Coordination. The absence of an empowered Chief of Defence Staff (CDS) is a glaring anomaly. The COSC works on the basis of consensus and is unable to agree on inter-service priorities for force structuring and modernisation as every service wants a larger share of the pie. The Headquarters of the various services make their own assumptions of the optimal military strategy that should be applied to future wars and plan their force structures accordingly. Consequently, the Long-term Integrated Perspective Plan (LTIPP) is integrative merely on paper while in reality, it remains a compilation of single-service plans.

Defence Acquisition. Despite the much-trumpeted reform in procurement process, the acquisition of new weapons and equipment by the armed forces is still mired in bureaucratic red tape.

Defence Research and Development (R&D). There is a dichotomy between the time-consuming quest for technological self-reliance and the desire of the services to import arms and equipment based on immediate operational exigencies. The disconnect in the interface between R&D, production agencies and users remains unresolved. Thus, 'make' or 'buy' decisions are still contentious and DRDO projects continue to be delayed with consequent cost overruns.

Recent Efforts at Reform

The only time a serious security review was undertaken in the recent past was after the Kargil Conflict of 1999 when the Kargil Review Committee (KRC) headed by the late K. Subrahmanyam – the doyen of Indian strategic thinkers – was appointed. The committee was asked to "review the events leading up to the Pakistani aggression in the Kargil District of Ladakh in Jammu & Kashmir; and, to recommend such measures as are considered necessary to safeguard national security against such armed intrusions". Besides K. Subrahmanyam, who was appointed chairman, the Committee comprised three members: Lieutenant General K.K. Hazari (retd), B.G. Verghese and Satish Chandra, Secretary, NSC Secretariat, who was also designated as member-secretary.

Although it had been given a very narrow and limited charter, the KRC looked holistically at the threats and challenges and examined the prevalent loopholes in the management of national security. The committee was of the view that "the political, bureaucratic, military and intelligence establishments appear to have developed a vested interest in the status quo". Consequently, the committee made far-reaching recommendations regarding the development of India's nuclear deterrence, management of national security, intelligence reforms, border management, defence budget, use of air power, counter-insurgency operations, integrated manpower policy, defence R&D and media relations. The committee's report was tabled in Parliament on February 23, 2000.

The Cabinet Committee on Security then appointed a Group of Ministers (GoM) to study the KRC report and recommend measures for implementation. The GoM was headed by then Deputy Prime Minister and Home Minister L.K. Advani and comprised Defence Minister George Fernandes, External Affairs Minister Jaswant Singh, Finance Minister Yashwant Sinha and National Security Adviser Brajesh Mishra. In turn, the GoM set up four task forces on intelligence reforms, internal security, border management and defence management to undertake in-depth analyses of various facets of national security management. These were headed, respectively, by former Jammu and Kashmir Governor G.C. Saxena, former Defence and Home Secretary and Principal Secretary to the Prime Minister N.N. Vohra, former Home Secretary Madhav Godbole and former Union Minister Arun Singh, who was then an advisor to the Ministry of External Affairs on security matters and who had himself headed the Committee on Defence Expenditure in 1983.

The GoM recommended sweeping reforms to the existing national security management system. The CCS accepted all its recommendations, except for one regarding the implementation of the CDS post which still hasn't taken place. Among others, the CCS approved implementation of the following key measures:

- Decision on approving the post of CDS was shelved pending wider consultations subject to achieving a consensus. The tasks of the CDS would include single-point military advice to the government, inter-services prioritisation of defence plans and improvement in jointmanship among the three services. A CDS is yet to be appointed – ostensibly because political consensus has been hard to achieve and there are differences among the three services regarding whether or not a CDS is necessary. The new National Democratic Alliance (NDA) government has once again stated that it will strive to achieve political consensus on the appointment of a CDS.
- Headquarters Integrated Defence Staff (IDS) was established with representation from all the services.
- Two tri-service commands, the Andaman and Nicobar Command and the Strategic Forces Command, were established.
- The tri-service Defence Intelligence Agency (DIA) was established under the COSC for strategic threat assessments.
- Speedy decision-making, enhanced transparency and accountability were sought to be brought into defence acquisitions. Approval of the Defence Procurement Procedure (DPP) 2002 was formally announced. (The DPP has been amended several times since then. DPP 2016 was issued in May 2016.)
- The Defence Acquisition Council (DAC) and the Defence Technology Board, both headed by the Defence Minister, were constituted.
- Implementation of the decisions of the DAC was assigned to the Defence Procurement Board (DPB).
- The National Technical Research Organisation (NTRO) was set up for gathering electronic and other technical intelligence.

- The CCS also issued a directive that each of India's land borders with different countries will be managed by a single agency like the Border Security Force. The concept of "one border, one force" was adopted.
- The CCS nominated the Central Reserve Police Force (CRPF) as India's primary force for counter-insurgency operations. (This experiment has not yet fully succeeded as the CRPF is yet to settle down in its new role as a counter-insurgency force.)
- The establishment of a National Defence University (NDU) was approved. However, the NDU has not yet taken shape. The draft bill that is to be introduced in parliament has been released for public comment in August 2016.

Decision-making is gradually becoming more streamlined. The new Defence Planning Guidelines that have been laid down are based on three inter-linked stages in the planning process:

- The 15-year LTIPP, is to be drawn up by the Headquarters IDS in consultation with the Services Headquarters and approved by the DAC.
- Five-year defence plans for the services (current 12th plan, 2012-17), including the five-year Services Capital Acquisition Plan (SCAP), is to be drawn up by Headquarters IDS in consultation with the Services Headquarters and approved by the DAC.
- The Annual Acquisition Plan (AAP), is to be drawn up by Headquarters IDS and approved by the DPB. Budgetary allocations for the ensuing financial year (ending March 31) will be made on the basis of the AAP.

A major realisation that has emerged is that any defence plan must be prepared on the basis of a 15-year perspective plan. The first five years of the plan should be very firm (Definitive Plan), the next five years may be relatively less firm but should be clear in terms of direction and progression (Indicative Plan), and the last five years should be tentative (Vision Plan). A reasonably firm allocation of financial resources for the first five years and an indicative allocation for the subsequent periods are prerequisites.

Perspective planning is gradually being extended to incorporate a tri-service approach. It is now being undertaken in Headquarters IDS, where military, technical and R&D experts take an integrated view of future threats and challenges based on a forecast of the future battlefield milieu, evaluation of strategic options and analysis of potential technological and industrial capabilities. Issues like intelligence, surveillance and reconnaissance, air defence, electronic warfare and amphibious operations, which are common to all the services, are now receiving requisite attention. However, unless a CDS is appointed to guide integrated operational planning, jointmanship will not be possible and perspective planning will continue to be mostly single-service oriented in its conceptual framework.

Naresh Chandra Task Force

Despite the new measures approved for implementation by the CCS on May 11, 2001, many lacunae remain in the management of national security. In order to review the progress of the implementation of the proposals approved by the CCS in 2001 and take stock of the new developments over the last 10 years – such as the threats emanating from the sea, à la the Mumbai terror strikes, and the rapid deterioration of the regional security environment due to the growing spread of radical extremism and creeping Talibanisation – the government appointed a Task Force on National Security in mid-June 2011.

The task force was led by former Cabinet Secretary and Ambassador to the US Naresh Chandra, and comprised 13 other members. The members included former High Commissioner to Pakistan G. Parthasarathy, Air Chief Marshal S. Krishnaswamy (retd), Admiral Arun Prakash (retd), Lt Gen. V.R. Raghavan (retd), former Chief of the Department of Atomic Energy Anil Kakodkar, former Secretary Research and Analysis Wing (R&AW) K.C. Verma, and former Union Home Secretary V.K. Duggal, among others. The task force was given six months to submit its report. The committee submitted its report on May 23, 2012. The report was circulated to the various ministries and departments of the Government of India for their comments and suggestions. Simultaneously, the government had appointed another Task Force chaired by Ravindra Gupta, former secretary in the government, to analyse the requirements of defence modernisation and self-reliance. This task force is also understood to have submitted its report, but the details are not yet known.

The report of the Naresh Chandra Committee on defence reforms in India focused attention on the hollowness of the national security decision-making process and the urgent need for change. Over a period of one year, the Naresh Chandra Committee engaged in wide-ranging consultations with various governmental bodies, but it does not appear to have consulted strategic studies think tanks and independent experts with specialised domain knowledge. Though the report of the Naresh Chandra Committee has not been made public, the recommendations purportedly made by the committee have been appearing sporadically in the press.

The recommendations made by the Naresh Chandra Committee, that are available in the public domain, appear to be incremental rather than revolutionary. As per news reports, the committee has urged the government to ensure adequate military preparedness to deal with a militarily assertive China. By far the most salient recommendation of the committee is to appoint a permanent Chairman of the present COSC, that is, another four-star post in addition to the army, navy and air force chiefs of staff. This falls short of the inescapable operational requirement of appointing a CDS and simultaneously creating integrated theatre commands for joint warfare in future conflicts. While a permanent Chairman of the COSC will certainly be able to better coordinate, the modernisation plans of the three services and improve the management of tri-service institutions as opposed to a rotating chairman, he will have no role to play in integrating operational plans for joint warfare. The solution lies in the establishment of several tri-service integrated theatre commands with Commanders-in-Chief (Cs-in-C) who report to the CDS while the chiefs of staff of the three services are primarily planners responsible for recruiting, raising and equipping of new units, acquisition of weapons and equipment, specialised training and maintenance.

Other recommendations of the committee include the creation of three new tri-service commands to better manage future challenges and vulnerabilities: Special Operations Command, Aerospace Command and Cyber Command. The committee has also recommended the establishment of a Bureau of Politico-Military Affairs to deliberate on security issues having foreign policy implications. Recommendations have also been made regarding the setting up of an Advanced Projects Agency – on the lines of the Defence Advanced Research Projects Agency (DARPA) – under the Scientific Advisor to the Defence Minister to oversee defence R&D, the posting of additional armed forces officers to the MoD and the Ministry of External Affairs and civilian Indian Administrative Service (IAS) officers to the Services Headquarters for better integration and coordination. The committee has recommended increasing the amount of Foreign Direct Investment (FDI) in defence joint ventures from 26 to 49 per cent which has been implemented. The committee's recommendations are exceptional and, if implemented, will go a long way towards overcoming present shortcomings.

Since then, the Dhirendra Singh (former home secretary) Committee on Defence Procurement, 2015, and the Shekatker (Lt Gen, former corps commander) Committee to Enhance Combat Capability and Rebalance Defence Expenditure, 2016, have been appointed to look into reform of specific issues pertaining to the management of national security.

Planning for National Security Must be Institutionalised

A lot still needs to be done to institutionalise the defence planning process and improve the management of national security in India. The first and foremost requirement is for the government to formulate a comprehensive NSS, inclusive of internal security, so that all the stakeholders are aware of what is expected of them. The NSS should be formulated after carrying out an inter-departmental, inter-agency, multi-disciplinary strategic defence review. Such a review must take the public into confidence as opposed to being conducted behind closed doors. As is the case with most other democracies, the NSS should be signed by the Prime Minister, who is the head of government, and must be tabled in parliament and released as a public document. Only then will various stakeholders be compelled to take ownership of the strategy and work unitedly to achieve its aims and objectives.

The 12th Defence Plan that ended on March 31, 2017, was not formally approved by the government and did not receive committed financial backing. The government has also not approved the LTIPP 2007-22 formulated by the Headquarters IDS. Without these essential approvals, defence procurement is being undertaken through ad hoc annual procurement plans, rather than carefully prioritised long-term plans that are designed to systematically enhance India's combat potential. Such ad-hoc measures will adversely impact India's ability to sustain conflict over the anticipated duration of future wars. These are serious lacunae that need to be addressed as effective defence planning cannot be undertaken in a policy void.

Reforms Approved by the Government

Early in 2016 the MoD constituted a Committee of Experts with Lt Gen D.B. Shekatkar (Retd) as the Chairperson, to recommend measures for enhancing combat capabilities and rebalancing defence expenditure so as to improve the "teeth to tail ratio" of the armed forces. Of the recommendations made by the Committee, 99 were sent to the armed forces for making an implementation plan. In August 2017, the MoD approved 65 of these recommendations pertaining to the Indian Army.

The reforms to be implemented include the re-deployment and restructuring of approximately 57,000 posts of officers, JCOs and Other Ranks and civilians. The major reforms to be implemented include the following[1]:

- Optimisation of Signals establishments to include Radio Monitoring

Companies, Corps Air Support Signal Regiments, Air Formation Signal Regiments, Composite Signal Regiments and merger of Corps Operating and Engineering Signal Regiments.
- Restructuring of repair echelons in the army to include Base Workshops, Advance Base Workshops and Static/Station Workshops in the field army.
- Redeployment of Ordnance echelons to include Vehicle Depots, Ordnance Depots and Central Ordnance Depots apart from streamlining inventory control mechanisms.
- Better utilisation of Supply and Transport echelons and Animal Transport units.
- Closure of Military Farms and army postal establishments in peace locations.
- Enhancement in standards for recruitment of clerical staff and drivers in the Army.
- Improving the efficiency of the National Cadet Corps.

While these reforms, to be implemented by December 31, 2019, are undoubtedly welcome, they do not include changes in the national security decision making process. Nor do they enhance defence planning or contribute towards streamlining the defence procurement procedure. There is much that remains to be done by way of defence reforms. Some macro-level recommendations in this regard are made below.

Recommendations

The government must commit itself to supporting long-term defence plans, or else defence modernisation will continue to lag and the present quantitative military gap with the People's Liberation Army (PLA) of China will become a qualitative gap as well in 10 to 15 years. This can only be avoided by making the dormant NSC a pro-active policy formulation body for long-term national security planning. (The CCS deals with current and near-term threats and challenges and reacts to emergent situations.)

The defence procurement decision making process needs to be sped up. The army still does not possess towed and self-propelled 155 mm howitzers for the plains/mountains and urgently needs to acquire this equipment for counter-insurgency and counter-terrorism operations. The navy has also been waiting awhile for submarines and the construction of the indigenous air defence ship is lagging behind schedule as well. The plans of the air force to acquire 126 Multi-Mission, Medium-Range Combat Aircrafts (MMRCA) in order to maintain its edge over the regional air

Figure 1: Priority Measures Necessary

- Formulate a comprehensive NSS, after undertaking a strategic defence review.
- Appoint a CDS to head the function of defence planning and provide single-point military advice to the CCS.
- Approve LTIPP 2007-22, and the ongoing Defence Plan (2017-22), with committed financial backing.
- Enhance defence budget to 3.0 per cent of the GDP for defence modernisation and upgrade the military strategy against China to deterrence.
- Hasten long-pending defence procurement plans, such as C4I2SR, artillery modernisation, acquisition of modern fighter aircraft and aircraft carriers and submarines, must be hastened.
- Urgently attend to the modernisation plans of the central paramilitary and police forces also need urgent attention.
- Redress the anomalies created by the Fifth, Sixth and Seventh Pay Commissions that have led to a civil-military divide including the ex-servicemen's legitimate demand for OROP.
- Construct a National War Memorial-cum-Military museum in New Delhi to honour the memory of all those soldiers, sailors and airmen who have made the supreme sacrifice in the service of India.

forces also got stuck in the procurement quagmire, and resulted in the acquisition of a mere 36 Rafale fighters, which is staggeringly low compared to the requirement projected. Currently, all three services need a large number of light helicopters and not enough is being done to fulfil this requirement. Furthermore, India's nuclear forces require the Agni-IV and V missiles and nuclear powered submarines with suitable ballistic missiles to acquire genuine deterrence capabilities. The armed forces do not have a truly integrated Command, Control, Communications, Computers, Intelligence, Information, Surveillance and Reconnaissance (C4I2SR) system suitable for modern network-centric warfare. Such a system would optimise their individual capabilities tremendously and the government needs to look into planning and implementing it post haste.

The long-pending high-priority weapons and equipment acquisitions will require extensive budgetary support. With the defence budget languishing at 1.62 per cent of India's gross domestic product (GDP) – compared with China's 3.0 per cent and Pakistan's 3.5 per cent plus US military aid – it will not be possible for the armed forces to undertake any meaningful modernisation in the foreseeable future. Leave aside genuine military modernisation that will substantially enhance combat capabilities, the funds available on the capital account at present are inadequate to suffice even for the replacement of obsolete weapons systems and equipment that are still in service well beyond their useful life cycles, e.g., the MiG-21. The Central Armed Police Forces (CAPFs) also need to be modernised as they are facing increasingly potent threats while being equipped with obsolete weapons.

The government must also immediately appoint a CDS or at least a permanent Chairman of the COSC who can provide single-point advice to the CCS on military matters and India's nuclear deterrence. This should be followed by the establishment of tri-service integrated theatre commands that can synergise the capabilities and the combat potential of the individual services. It is time to set up tri-service based Aerospace, Cyber and Special Forces commands to meet emerging challenges in these fields and to better manage all available resources. A tri-service Logistics and Maintenance Command is also long overdue. Any further delay in these key structural reforms in higher defence management, on the grounds of the lack of political consensus and the inability of the armed forces to agree on the issue, will be extremely detrimental to India's interests in light of the dangerous developments taking place in India's neighbourhood. International experience shows that such reform has to be imposed in a top down manner and can never work if the government keeps waiting for it to come about from the bottom up.

The softer issues that do not impinge immediately on planning and preparation for meeting national security challenges must never be ignored as these can have adverse repercussions on the morale of the officers and men in uniform in the long term. The numerous anomalies created by the implementation of the Fifth, Sixth and Seventh Pay Commission reports must be speedily resolved. In fact, the slow and laborious handling of this issue has led to a dangerous "them versus us" civil-military divide, and the government must make it a priority to bridge this gap quickly.

Ex-servicemen feel they have received a raw deal and have been surrendering their medals and holding fasts to get justice for their legitimate demand of One Rank, One Pension (OROP). The anomalies pointed out in the implementation of OROP must be resolved as soon as possible. While a Department of Ex-servicemen's Welfare was created in the MoD in keeping with the Common Minimum Programme of the United Progressive Alliance (UPA), until recently, there wasn't a single ex-serviceman in it. Such measures do not generate confidence in the civilian leadership, among serving soldiers and retired veterans. Also, rather unbelievably, India is still without a National War Memorial.

Major Committees Appointed since 1983

The following committees and statutory bodies have dealt with the various defence planning, decision-making, defence procurement and defence reforms issues highlighted here:

- The Arun Singh Committee on Defence Expenditure (CDE), 1983.
- The K C Pant Committee on the NSC, 1989-90.
- The Abdul Kalam Committee on Self-reliance in Weapons Acquisition, 1992.
- The KRC Report, 2000.
- The GoM-appointed task forces on Higher Defence Management, Border Management, Internal Security and Intelligence, 2000-01.
- The GoM chaired by Deputy Prime Minister and Home Minister L.K. Advani, 2001-02.
- The P. Rama Rao Committee on restructuring the DRDO.
- The Vinod Misra Defence Expenditure Review Committee, 2008-09.
- The Naresh Chandra Committee, 2011-12.
- The Ravindra Gupta Committee on Defence Modernisation and Self-reliance, 2011-12.
- The Dhirendra Singh Committee on Defence Procurement, 2015.
- The Shekatker Committee to Enhance Combat Capability and Rebalance Defence Expenditure, 2016.
- The 10th Finance Commission headed by Vijay Kelkar.
- The Standing Committee(s) on Defence in Parliament.
- The Comptroller and Auditor General (CAG).

Concluding Observations

The Indian Army and its sister services have held the nation together through the long history of post-independence conflicts with its neighbours and prolonged deployment in conflict zones for internal security. Dark clouds can once again be seen on the horizon, but the efforts being made to weather the gathering storm are inadequate. The government must immediately initiate steps to build the capacities that are necessary for defeating future threats and challenges. It must take the opposition parties into confidence as a bipartisan approach should be adopted when dealing with major national security issues. In fact, there is a requirement to establish a permanent National Security Commission – mandated by an act of parliament – to oversee the development of military and non-military capacities for national security.

A fluid strategic environment, rapid advances in defence technology, the need for judicious allocation of scarce budgetary resources, long lead times required for creating futuristic forces and the requirement of synergising plans for defence and development make long-term defence planning a demanding exercise. The lack of a cohesive NSS and defence policy has resulted in inadequate political direction regarding politico-military objectives and military strategy. Consequently, defence planning in India has until recently, been marked by ad hoc decision-making to tide over immediate national security challenges, as a result of which long-term planning has been continually neglected. This is now gradually being corrected and new measures have been instituted to improve long-term planning.

Systemic weaknesses and structural shortcomings in India's national security decision-making system have led to sub-optimal synergisation of available combat resources, meagre as they are. The government must accord the highest priority to the implementation of the recommendations of the Naresh Chandra Committee so that the country's armed forces are well prepared to meet future threats and challenges and are in a position to contribute positively to security in South Asia and the Indian Ocean region alongside India's strategic partners.

The aim of this book is to take stock of long-pending defence reforms, analyse the decision-making structures, identify the shortcomings affecting the management of national security and make suitable recommendations to substantially upgrade capabilities and streamline procedures. Each of the succeeding chapters deals with one facet requiring analysis and recommendations for change. The structures and processes for national security decision making and management are complex and intricately interlinked. Quite naturally, it has not been possible to cover each one in detail in a single volume. Based on the feedback received, a companion volume could be considered.

NOTES

1. Press Information Bureau press release "Ministry of Defence approves first phase of reforms in The Armed Forces" dated August 30, 2017.

SECTION I

REFORMS IN OTHER MILITARIES

2

Reforms Initiated by Major Military Powers

Rajneesh Singh

Introduction

The US, UK and India are all democratic governments that share many similarities in their organisational structure as well as systems and processes of governance. Yet there are some key differences in functioning between the three as well. These similarities and differences also extend to the structure of the higher defence organisation (HDO) and the functioning of the higher defence management (HDM) of the three countries. This is because the three countries face vastly different security challenges that need to be dealt with in specific ways. Furthermore, there are differences in the manner in which the challenges are perceived and tackled by the respective governments, and there are also differences in the availability of resources with the three countries that can be used to effectively tackle their respective challenges. Therefore, some analysts consider it incongruous to study British and US reforms to draw lessons for the Indian HDO; however, it is not so. This is because at the fundamental level, all three countries have democratic forms of government and their HDOs are similarly manned by elected representatives, civil bureaucracy and military officers, albeit with different job functions. The HDOs in the three countries are also assigned similar management responsibilities and their elected representatives have comparable directional and oversight functions. India can, therefore, benefit greatly from the study of defence reforms in the US and UK.

The HDOs in the US and UK have come a long way since the time when the services played a dominant role in policy formulation as opposed to the bureaucracy that had a more restrained role. The elected representatives of the two countries took a conscious decision and implemented path-breaking reforms based on the inputs from some civil servants and military officers.[1] The enhancement of operational efficiency and administrative effectiveness of the defence establishments of the two countries are the results of these reforms. India, on the other hand, has a defence establishment which is an archaic continuation of Ismay's model, conceptualised over six decades earlier.[2] There have been multiple attempts to reform the Indian HDO – particularly in the wake of Kargil – but they have fallen short of transforming the establishment so as to effectively combat 21st century security challenges. The Indian defence establishment continues to be besieged with problems, many of which are attributable to its HDO architecture and its management practices.[3]

The defence establishments of the US and UK have demonstrated a relatively high level of operational effectiveness and administrative efficiency, both in war and in peace, attributable in large measure to their implementation of defence reforms. India can benefit greatly from a study of these reforms and more specifically from the rationale and methodology underlying their implementation in these countries. Some of the measures that interest India include:

- The creation of a centralised decision and policy making authority at the highest level of the HDO,
- The integration of civil and military staff to conduct strategic-level staff work, and the measures taken to share authority and responsibility between the three pillars of the HDO, namely, the elected representatives, civil bureaucracy and military officers.
- The decision to have a single source of military advice is a measure that has greatly improved the functioning of HDOs in the US and UK and needs to be deliberated in the Indian context.

This chapter aims to study and analyse the defence reforms undertaken by the US and UK to bring out lessons for India. The study would be restricted to the following three issues:

- Structural reforms related to the architecture of the HDO.
- Relationship between the principle constituents of the HDO, namely the elected representatives, civil bureaucrats and military officers.
- Process of defence reforms per se.

Structural Reforms

Integration of Civil and Military Officers

The US and the British reforms have ensured that their civil and service officers work together in various branches and departments of their respective HDOs. This enables the appointment of the "best person for the job". The practice also encourages synergy by enabling the integration of the opinions and recommendations of 'generalist' bureaucrats with those of 'specialist' service officers, at all levels of the HDO, before concrete proposals are drafted for decision by elected representatives. The British and US systems thus ensure that their elected representatives are provided with holistic counsel, which includes inputs from all the units concerned. This practice also enables quicker decision-making, since the views of the civil and service bureaucracies are integrated at all levels of the HDO, unlike the Indian system. In India, multiple points of views from the three Service Headquarters and the other departments and branches of the Ministry of Defence (MoD), are provided to the Defence Minister after limited reconciling in the office of the defence secretary. This leads to miscommunication and inefficiency and needs to be reformed for synergised functioning.

Centralisation versus Decentralisation

In the UK, subsequent to the defence reforms, the Secretary of Defence has been made responsible for policy formulation, decision making and oversight functions. These functions are undertaken with the assistance of the permanent undersecretary and the Chief of Defence Staff (CDS), who function from the "head office". The "head office" oversees the functioning of the services, joint headquarters, procurement agency and so on. One of the objectives of the Levene Committee, constituted by the British Government in 2010, was to study whether the British defence establishment had become over centralised, leading to inefficiency.[4] The study concluded that the direction in which the British reforms were moving, that is, towards even greater centralisation of authority in the higher echelons of the HDO, was perhaps more effective in countering the security challenges of the 21st century. The case with the US is similar.

In India, the final authority of the defence establishment lies with the Defence Minister who functions from the MoD along with his principal defence advisor, the defence secretary. The Defence Minister's principal military advisors – the three service chiefs – function at a level lower than the MoD, with a tenuous connection of management practices between the two organisations. This arrangement has resulted in the imprecise and unclear delegation of authority and accountability, making the Indian HDO less effective and less efficient. The delays in vital procurements, expression of public dissatisfaction by the services on many policy decisions, such as the pay commission reports and other similar issues, are cases in point.

In India, there is a prevalent fear that greater unification of the services under one military officer will possibly diminish the control of the elected representatives over the services. It is perhaps felt, if the services speak in one voice, it would become difficult to uncover divergent views which are so essential for decision-making by the elected representatives. These fears are slightly unfounded and India would benefit from the design of the HDO architecture. Even though the HDO framework centralises the authority at the highest levels, its management practices provide enough opportunities for decision-makers to receive inputs, including divergent ones, from all concerned quarters.

Creation of New Appointments and Redesigning of HDO

The appointment of the Secretary of Defence in the US was instituted in 1947 and the appointment of the chairman of the Joint Chiefs of Staff (JCS) a little later. In the UK, the appointment of the CDS also came much later, when reforms were initiated after World War II. In both the countries, the system became effective and efficient not when the said appointments were instituted, but when the institution of the appointments was accompanied by holistic structural reforms, as well as reforms in systems and processes. Appointments by themselves did not bring the desired efficiency.

In India while there are varying levels of consensus regarding the appointment of an independent permanent chairman of the Chiefs of Staff Committee (COSC) or even a CDS, there is almost no discussion regarding the structural reforms that should accompany the appointment. If the US and the British experiences are anything to go by, India would certainly benefit from the implementation of holistic reforms which would involve instituting the appointment of a single point military advisor to the government, provided such appointments are accompanied by structural reforms and reforms in management practices. Appointments are important, but accompanying reforms in structures and systems and processes are equally important.[5]

Enhancement of the Jointness in Services

Recent wars and conflict situations have proved beyond doubt that the most effective way of dealing with military security challenges is by conducting joint operations. Services traditionally like to maintain status quo and are predisposed to resist changes that may impinge on their turf. The services in all countries try to consolidate their respective domains and even attempt to secure additional responsibilities for themselves. This goes against the basic tenet of jointness which relies on synergising the capabilities of individual services through joint efforts and the employment of the most effective means available within the three services, regardless of all other considerations. The US and UK have enhanced the joint war-fighting capabilities of their armed forces through reforms at two levels. At the highest level of the HDO, these countries have institutionalised the appointment of a single-point military advisor to the government in the form of the permanent chairman of the JCS and the CDS, and have given these appointments a "defence" outlook and not restricted the appointment in the "straitjacket" of single service. At the level of the services, the countries have created joint organisations, that are equipped and manned by personnel from all the services. The billets in the joint organisations are tenanted by selected officers from all the services and the commanders of the joint organisations have the power to select, discipline and affect their subordinates' career progression. These measures have made the joint organisations very effective operationally.

In India, the debate for enhancing the jointness of the armed forces has been mired in and side-tracked by the suspicion surrounding the appointment of a single-point military advisor, as well as the attempts made by the three services to safeguard their respective turfs. This is no different from the attitude displayed by the services and other interest groups in either the US or the UK. The two countries, unlike India, did however manage to overcome opposition from all quarters for the greater good of the defence establishment. It is in India's national interest to institute measures to enhance the jointness of the armed forces, sooner rather than later.

Relationship between the Principal Constituents of the HDO

The relationship between the three principal constituents of the HDO – the elected representatives, the bureaucracy and the military – is contingent on many factors including the situation within the country. It follows a different trajectory during a war/conflict situation and a different one during peace time. The relationship that the Prime Minister and the Defence Minister share with the military chief should be based on mutual trust and confidence, and there needs to be a sense of honesty which is essential to ensure that there is no ambiguity in understanding political directives. The British experience suggests that during wars national interests are best served when the Prime Minister and the chiefs have direct interaction, without any intermediaries – not even the Defence Minister. The Defence Minister usually embodies an anomalous position during wars. He serves the interests of the establishment better by acting as a facilitator and by encouraging direct interaction between the Prime Minister and the chiefs. His responsibility also extends towards ensuring that political requirements and military planning are coordinated and that realism prevails.

Peace time situations have multiple dynamics, and prudence demands that decisions be taken after due deliberation. The government may have to walk a tightrope between its various competing agendas of governance, (including those of the social sector), and ensuring the security of the country. Even within the security establishment, various interest groups are constantly trying to pursue their personal agendas. All this stipulates that the government will have to take difficult decisions after due deliberation and take into consideration the varying views and sensibilities of all interest groups without vitiating the atmosphere. The final responsibility of the security of the country is the government's, and as the elected representatives, they must have the final say in all decisions.

The military and the civil bureaucracy share a very delicate relationship in India. Even though protocol issues between the various appointments have been defined by the government, there is a need for greater clarity in the working relationship between them. The lack of clarity has led to undercurrents of hostility with respect to the appointments, and this is incredibly unhealthy for the system. There is a need to bring equilibrium between the civil bureaucracy and the service officers in the defence establishment. The Indian administrative system, which is a legacy of the British model, can learn much from the way that the British have been able to ensure equilibrium between their civil bureaucracy and the military. Defence reforms in the UK have led to the institution of the appointments of the CDS and the Permanent Undersecretary. These two appointments have been provided with equal status. The appointments have been made jointly responsible for some of the tasks and for others one of the appointments takes the lead based on the specific expertise required. The allocation of roles and responsibilities is dependent on the core competence of the two services, the civil bureaucracy and the military. In the British model, the CDS and the Permanent Undersecretary work from the same office. They share joint responsibility for the assignments and the staff below them reports to them equally. The two appointments, thus, have similar access to the staff below them, as well as the minister above them. Another factor that has helped create a sense of equilibrium between the two interest groups is the high level of integration of the civil bureaucrats and the service officers, in many of the branches of the HDO. It is perhaps because of these two reasons that the rift between them is not as pronounced as it used to be and that the issue of equilibrium has been tentatively resolved.

The Reform Process

In the US and UK, like in India, the reform process was initially resisted by the various interest groups involved, including the elected representatives, who were unwilling to delegate many of the powers of policy and decision-making to the executives and to enhance the jointness of the services. The military reverses, however, that the US suffered in the 1970s and the 1980s provided the necessary impetus to initiate and follow up with the reforms. The US and UK have both followed the evolutionary reform process wherein changes dictated by circumstances have been implemented in a gradual manner. There have, however, been occasions in the UK when measures have been taken to impose the will of some elected representatives without building consensus, and this had caused great stress in the system.[6]

In the US and UK, some of the interest groups, enjoyed a position of eminence prior to reforms, and the lessons of war required them to give up their entrenched position. In India, the position of the elected representatives is not a subject of debate; however, there is a need to identify and maintain equilibrium in the relationship between the bureaucracy and the services. This would essentially require the integration of service officers with the bureaucracy for staff work before the decisions are made by the elected representatives. This would negatively impact the sole preserve of the civil bureaucracy's right of access to the ministers. The chiefs – because of the legacy of the 1962 Indo-China War – continue to enjoy a great deal of functional independence in operational matters, and some administrative issues as well. In India, therefore, it is the bureaucracy and the chiefs, whose authority and influence needs to be reduced, and it is they who must concur with and initiate reforms. This is not easy, and it is here that India can learn from the US and British experience. The determination of the government and the selection of the Defence Minister, therefore, becomes vital.

In the US, in the 1970s and 1980s, the military suffered some very embarrassing reverses, and the Congress, convinced that military reforms were the need of the hour, went ahead and passed the Goldwater Nichols Act. This, despite the fact that the executive faction, the military and the Pentagon were divided over the legislation. There was strong bipartisan support for the legislation in the Congress and the President sided with the Congress. As a result, the bill was passed with overwhelming support in the Congress.[7] In the UK, too, the reforms that could muster the support of the elected representatives were implemented with minimum delays, while the others dragged on for years. In India, convincing the elected representatives would be a good starting point because if they are not convinced, the most that one can expect is a compromise and weak reform measures. The role of the Defence Minister in initiating and implementing reforms thus becomes crucial. The minister selected should have the qualities of a reformer, such as a capacity for management, political skill and the requisite acumen to convince both his cabinet colleagues and opposition members.

The British Levene Committee offers a different idea to assist in the selection of members of reform committees. The Levene Committee was headed by a distinguished businessman with stints in the government and the banking sector, while six other members had similarly illustrious careers in the civil service. Extending the choice of members to include experts from the industry instead of restricting that choice to known defence analysts is also an idea worth considering. This will enable the government to benefit from the best practices available in private and government organisations.

The implementation of the recommendations of reform committees needs to be pursued against all opposition. Interest groups have been known to engage in undercutting, behind-the-back dealings, wrangling, etc. The Levene Committee had recommended that the committee itself should be reconvened on an annual basis for three years to report its progress to the minister who would then report it to the Parliament. This would enable the committee – which is familiar with the nuances of the recommendations – to monitor the progress of the report. Furthermore, the involvement of the parliament provides legitimacy and a sense of urgency to the process. All these methods of reform implementation can serve as important lessons for India.

Conclusion

The Indian HDO is a legacy of the British model. In 1947, India and the UK had a similar security architecture and management system. However, that was the point where they diverged. A realisation had already begun to set in among the military thinkers and analysts in the UK regarding the need to reform their system. This was a result of the lessons learnt during World War II. Military thinkers in the US went through a similar analytical process and came to the same conclusion. As a result, both the US and the UK were able to progressively reform their respective HDOs and by the mid-1980s both their organisations and systems had more or less acquired the form in which they exist today. It would be erroneous to state that the current system is ideal system for even today, reforms are a process in continuation, but a start has nevertheless been made.

The Indian HDO, on the other hand, continues to function in much the same way as it always has since 1947. Although there have been some organisational changes – especially after the Kargil War – the fundamental nature of the 'inherited' system continues till date. In order to counteract the obsolescence, Indian defence reforms will have to be implemented at two levels; the highest level of the HDO will have to be reformed to be able to provide strategic direction to the defence establishment, undertake policy formulation and provide oversight to various defence programmes. The reforms will also have to be undertaken at the level of the services in order to ensure that they conduct operations jointly – since that is the most effective way of fighting modern wars. The US and British models have stood the test of time, in war and in peace, and they offer many lessons for the ills plaguing the Indian HDO.

NOTES

1. The UK follows the 'chief of defence staff (CDS) model' for its defence management. The HDO of UK has changed significantly from the days when the system did not have a Ministry of Defence (MoD) or a Minister for Defence. The services enjoyed far greater autonomy in policy making and policy formulation and services related management functions to the extent that single Service Chiefs could dictate government and NATO policies. The role of the bureaucracy was subdued in comparison. Today, the UK conducts its governance of defence through an integrated civil and military organisation where collective and individual functions and accountabilities as also system of oversight are well defined. See Rajneesh Singh, *British Reforms to Its Higher Defence Organization: Lessons for India*, Institute for Defence Studies and Analyses, New Delhi, 2014, p. 7. In the US the lessons of World War II motivated the establishment to have a serious relook at the HDO and HDM practices. The result was the National Security Act (NSA) and its subsequent amendments and the landmark Goldwater Nichols Act (GNA) of 1986. Many strategists credit US military successes to the reforms undertaken since 1947 besides other factors, viz., the technological advancements and the downfall of the Soviet Union. The US, because of the reforms to the military, has been able to co-ordinate the functioning of all its services to a very large extent. See Rajneesh Singh, *United States Reforms to Its*

Higher Defence Organization: Lessons for India, Institute for Defence Studies and Analyses, New Delhi, 2014, p.8.

2. Ismay's model was formulated on certain fundamental principles of civil military relations, i.e., supremacy of the elected representatives over the military, coordination amongst the services to enhance jointness and minimalistic bureaucratic control. The model also ensured direct interaction between the political executive and the defence services. The model provided for three tiers of committees, viz., Defence Committee of Cabinet, Defence Minister's Committee and Chiefs of Staff Committee with a number of sub-committees. Over the years some of the committees established by Ismay were either suspended or they lost their significance. Admiral Arun Prakash opines that Ismay's defence management model was meant to "evolve and change as per the needs" of the country. The Indian HDM, however, has remained in a "time-warp since independence, and has thus become outdated and dysfunctional". See Arun Prakash, "Defence Reforms: Contemporary Debates and Issues", in Anit Mukherjee (ed.), *A Call for Change: Higher Defence Management in India*, Institute for Defence Studies and Analyses, New Delhi, 2012.
3. Over the years, many attempts have been made to reform India's security establishment. The attempts at reforms got impetus after the Kargil War. Many of the recommendations proposed in the Group of Ministers (GoM) report of 2001 have been implemented, yet quite a few important recommendations have been overlooked by the government. The 'cosmetic integration' of Service Headquarters with the MoD, the absence of CDS and real or perceived belief of the services of their continued isolation from the core security structures and decision-making processes are some of the issues which the military personnel stress to highlight the instability in the civil military equilibrium of the Indian HDO.
4. The Government of the UK launched the Strategic Defence and Security Review (SDSR) in October 2010. The key objective of the SDSR was to determine "the Armed Forces which the UK will need over the next decade and beyond to meet the most likely future threats". A committee was constituted under the chairmanship of Lord Levene to study the HDO of the UK and recommend measures to make it operationally more effective and administratively efficient. The committee entrusted with the task came out with the report: *Defence Reform: An Independent Report into the Structure and Management of the MoD.*
5. In India, there is some consensus on instituting the appointment of single-point military advisor to the government. The appointment should be accompanied by structural reforms which should integrate the three Service Headquarters, headed by their respective Chiefs, with the MoD to form three of its departments. The structural reforms should be accompanied by cross postings of civil and military officers in the various branches of the MoD, based on professional competencies of the two services. The suggested structural reforms would mandate the government to formally articulate the rules for interaction between the civil bureaucracy and the military officers, including between the heads of the two services.
6. Duncan Sandys, Defence Minister in late 1950s and 1960s in the UK, was not very popular with the Chiefs mainly for the manner in which he pursued with the reforms and his style of functioning. He was "able to dominate the defence

establishment. He achieved this as a result of the full support he received from the Prime Minister and the Chancellor of the Exchequer". The minister relied on the close group of advisers and paid scarce regard to the Chiefs. He tried to change too many things too fast. This was not to the liking of the Chiefs who were not keen to give up their entrenched positions. The Prime Minister was also aware of the stresses in the system as a result of the reforms being pursued by Duncan Sandys, and this cost him his ministerial position in the cabinet reshuffle. See Bill Jackson and Dwin Bramall, *The Chiefs*, Brassey's, London, 1992; Michael Dockrill, *British Defence since 1945*, Basil Blackwell, Oxford, 1998, pp.5-6.

7. On May 07, 1986, the Senate approved its version of the reorganisation bill by a vote of 95 to 0. On August 05, 1986, the House approved its version by a vote of 406 to 4. In the entire Congress, only four members did not support the reforms under consideration. With the Congress united in support of defence reorganisation, the joint conference to resolve inter-committee issues went quickly and smoothly. The conference met formally on August 13 and September 11, 1986. While over 100 amendments were considered, there were only three substantive areas that required resolution and were easily resolved. Senator Goldwater characterised the conference as the most cordial and cooperative in his memory. The conference report was published on September 12, 1986, and this substantial piece of legislation sailed through the Senate and the House of Representatives on September 16 and 17, respectively. By October 01, 1986, the Goldwater Nichols Act was law. See Douglas C Lovelace, Jr., "The DoD Reorganization Act of 1986: Improving the Department Through Centralization and Integration", in Douglas T. Stuart (ed.), *Organizing For National Security*, US Army War College, Carlisle Barracks, 2000, p. 78.

3

Military Might: New Age Defence Reforms in China

Monika Chansoria

The wind underlying the momentum of Chinese military power and the politics that control it is taking a gradual, yet very definitive direction. In what can be termed perhaps, the largest military reforms to be executed over many decades of China's recorded history of military modernisation, three new military branches were created on December 31, 2015. The Chinese President Xi Jinping, who is also the chairman of the most powerful military body in China – the Central Military Commission (CMC) – founded and conferred military flags to the three newly constituted wings, namely: – the General Command of the People's Liberation Army's Army (PLAA), the Rocket Force and the Strategic Support Force (SSF). At the same function, Xi also named the respective commanders and political commissars for all three branches. The reforms have specifically been directed at military leadership and command systems. This approach continues in line with the last published Chinese Defence White Paper (May 2015) that directly addressed the imbalance of influence between the Services, and called on the PLA to abandon "the traditional mentality that land outweighs sea".[1]

The four traditional "general departments" that formerly served as both the headquarters of the PLAA and as the joint staff for the entire military, stand dismantled and have been replaced by 15 new functional CMC departments. Simultaneously, the seven military regions (MRs, 军区)

have ceased to exist and have paved way for five theatre commands (战区) instead. More importantly, according to the CMC's guidelines, it is now in-charge of the overall administration of the PLA, People's Armed Police, militia, and the reserves. While the freshly constituted joint war zone commands focus on combat preparedness, the services continue to remain in-charge of overall development.

Now reportedly, a sweeping transformation of China's military is afoot, and this will have tremendous implications for its strategy and operations. Xi's vigorous efforts to realise his dream of a strong country with a strong military, are finally taking shape. Xi is credited with laying stress on four main points: adjusting China's military leadership and command system; optimising structure and function; reforming policies and systems; and promoting deeper civil-military integration.[2] Xi became the chairman of China's CMC and the general secretary of the Chinese Communist Party (CCP) in November 2012. Thereafter he became the President of the People's Republic of China (PRC) in March 2013. The subsequent reforms that have been implemented since, have strengthened Xi Jinping's role within the CMC under what is being labelled a "CMC chairman responsibility system".[3] The "CMC chairmanship responsibility system"[4] is distinct from the so-called CMC vice chairman responsibility system that was allegedly practised under Jiang Zemin and Hu Jintao, wherein many routine duties were handled by the CMC vice chairmen.[5] Under the reformed system, "all significant issues in national defense and army building [are] planned and decided by the CMC chairman", and "once the decision has been made, the chairman conducts 'concentrated unified leadership' and 'efficient command' of the entire military".[6]

While popularising his image among the Chinese masses, Xi is nevertheless, making an astute and deliberate attempt to strengthen his grip on power, especially by placing effective checks on the powerful elite. The most profound manifestation of this can be seen in the act of reducing the membership of the most powerful political decision-making body of the CCP – the Politburo Standing Committee which has been cut from nine to seven members. Another noteworthy fact, is that no member is exclusively responsible for domestic security as of now, and it remains Xi Jinping's fief.[7] Moreover, the PLA demonstrates its open allegiance to Xi Jinping through state-run and controlled newspapers carrying full-page expressions of absolute loyalty by military commanders across regions[8] in an attempt to quell any form of rift between the Party and the PLA.

The Cult Called Xi Jinping

Owing to his political capital, his association with the PLA, and his status as a witness of military diplomacy up close, Xi's control over the PLA is far greater than both Hu Jintao and Jiang Zemin's ever was. The latter leaders struggled to consolidate their authority during their respective tenures. Unlike his predecessor, Hu Jintao, Xi Jinping is putting out clear signals regarding who calls the shots in China. Hu had been challenged by the then Politburo Standing Committee member Zhou Yongkang (who was in-charge of the entire law-enforcement apparatus, including the police, secret police and judiciary). Incidentally, Zhou Yongkang is presently being tried for corruption charges and his investigation and trial grabbed international headlines as Zhou is among the highest-ranking officials to have been subjected to this kind of a trial. Such an act has been unheard of in China ever since the Party took over in 1949.

The anti-corruption campaign is indeed the most potent source of Xi's power over the Chinese military. Furthermore, Xi Jinping has spared no political elite when it comes to charges of corruption, and in doing so he has effectively neutralised any and all potential political rivalry that could have threatened his power and control in any way. According to Nan Li at the Naval War College, through his anti-corruption campaign, Xi has "shown ability to impose his will on the PLA"[9] – a skill that his immediate predecessor, Hu Jintao, lacked utterly and that Jiang Zemin wielded inconsistently.[10] Hu Jintao had a more hands-off approach, often delegating the day-to-day running of the PLA to his two CMC vice chairmen, which differs enormously from Xi's hands-on leadership style. During Hu's time as chairman, no major military reforms took place. If Xi pushes for structural changes to the CMC and personnel shake-ups that break with the Jiang Zemin-era norms, it would indeed add credibility to the narrative that he prioritizes the expansion of his own power base over improving the effectiveness of the PLA.[11] Xi Jinping has offered enough evidence of his personal determination and grit with his ruthless anti-corruption campaign in the military. Contrarily, he has also exercised remarkable caution in his personnel management of the PLA's top brass, thus far. The Politics and Law Commission, the Commission for Discipline Inspection or the Audit Office (all under direct CMC supervision) have come out as the clear winners of this overhaul. Since the 15 units newly created under the CMC include the Discipline Inspection Commission, the Politics and Legal Affairs Commission and the Audit Office, the new setup will aid Xi in his efforts to fight corruption at higher levels of the PLA while reinforcing his grip over the military.[12]

A reflection of Xi's determination to further strengthen his control over the PLA could be seen when he drew a direct line between the era of Mao Zedong and the present at a major meeting in Gutian in November 2014. At the commemoration of the 85th anniversary of the Gutian Congress held in 1929, during which Mao first affirmed the famous dictum "... *political power grows out of the barrel of a gun*", Xi convened 420 of his most senior officers to meet in this small town situated in the south-eastern Fujian Province.[13] The 1929 Gutian Congress was held on November 1 in the Shanghang County. It was the ninth meeting of the CCP since its founding in 1921, and the first following the Nanchang Uprising in August 1927 that marked the founding of the Red Army. Most of the attendees of the 1929 Congress were soldiers, and Mao Zedong chaired the meeting as the Comintern-appointed political commissar.[14] The lasting legacy of the Gutian meeting was Mao's criticism of what he called "the purely military viewpoint". Mao criticised a number of wayward views in the military beginning with the belief that "military affairs and politics were opposed to each other", even going so far as to say that "military affairs [had] a leading position over politics".[15] The second was the incorrect view that the task of the Red Army "is merely to fight", instead of serving as "an armed body for carrying out the political tasks of the revolution" as well as "doing propaganda among the masses, organising the masses, arming them, helping them establish revolutionary political power and setting up political organisations".[16] Perceptibly, the Gutian Conference became the seminal moment where the principle of the CCP's control of the military was enshrined as a core party doctrine, and "set the tone for the army's political work during the revolutionary era" and beyond.[17]

As per successive reports filed by Xinhua, all the members of the CMC showed up at the 2014 Gutian Conference including Fan Changlong (member of the Political Bureau of the Central Committee of the CCP, and vice chairman of the CMC, CCP), Xu Qiliang (member of the Political Bureau of the Central Committee of the CCP, and vice chairman of the CMC, CCP), and Zhang Yang (member of the CMC of the CCP and director of the General Political Department, PLA). Besides, other members of the CMC of the CCP who attended the conference were Chang Wanquan, Fang Fenghui, Zhao Keshi, Zhang Youxia, Wu Shengli, Ma Xiaotian and Wei Fenghe.[18] Additional non-military attendees included politburo member Wang Huning and the CCP General Office Director Li Zhanshu.[19] The rest of the crowd was drawn from "relevant leaders of the four general headquarters, the major leaders and political department directors of the large units, leaders of CMC General Office, political commissars of quasi-MRs and army-level units, the relevant comrades of the general headquarters and large units' offices, representatives of the grassroots and heroic models, and the relevant leaders of Ministry of Public Security".[20]

Chairman Mao's statement on the Party's absolute control over the military continues to hold ground in present-day China with the PLA's political work system being the principal means through which the CCP 'controls the gun'. Professional militaries, world over, primarily serve to ensure the survival of the state. China's PLA, has been an exceedingly politicised 'Party's army' ever since its inception. Perhaps, the most vital mission for the PLA is guaranteeing the regime's enduring survival, above everything else. China's state-controlled media is known to berate the very idea of 'apolitical militaries'. The communiqué released at the sixth plenum of the 18th CCP Central Committee urged the Party to "... closely unite around the Central Committee with Xi Jinping as the 'core'". The Party's senior leadership – extending from the provinces, regions and provincial-level cities – have already begun referring to Xi as their 'core leader' and displaying open allegiance, a trend that was even followed by the Party Secretary of Tibet, Chen Quanguo when he announced resolute safeguarding of "... the absolute authority of the party centre under Comrade Xi Jinping as general secretary ... Staunchly safeguard, support and be faithful to General Secretary Xi Jinping, the core". When Xi Jinping visited the newly established CMC Joint Battle Command Centre (军委联指总指挥 on April 20, 2016, he was decorated with the new title of 'Commander-in-Chief' (总司令) – fuelling speculations about Xi now being on par with the revolutionary General Zhu De who had held this title until 1954.

The military reforms convey an unambiguous message by Xi Jinping: that the Party, through the CMC, remains firmly in control. In fact, Xi has further tightened his grip over the PLA by assuming a more direct role as the head of the new Joint Operations Command Centre, which puts him in charge of the operational command of the PLA's military operations and plans. This new role holds tremendous political significance. The tiers of political work in the PLA are interlocking, and reinforcing systems that provide the Party with the ability to infiltrate the military hierarchy, through the political commissars, the Party committee system, and the Party discipline inspection system. By constituting the Discipline Inspection Commission specifically for the PLA, and making it answerable directly to the CMC, Xi has stiffened the noose around China's military elite – thereby ensuring that the Party's political control over the gun continues unabated, and the loyalty of the gun remains first to the Party and then to the state.

China's defence spending is the second largest in the world following the US, and it accounts for about 41 per cent of total military spending in Asia, including Oceania. It chalked up an 11 per cent increase from 2014 to 2015, much larger than the region's average increase that has been slightly less than 3 per cent. Furthermore, China had also informed the current session of the National People's Congress that its defence spending for 2016 would further rise by about 7 to 8 per cent from 2015. According to an estimate, China's defence spending in real terms is 1.4 times the publicly announced figure.[21] China aims to complete military reforms and develop an armed forces capable of informationised warfare by 2020, according to the recently published 13th five-year Military Development Plan (2016-2020) issued by the CMC. By 2020, the PLA will have finished the mechanisation of all its forces and progressed towards incorporating information and computer technology. The priorities include strategic restructuring of different services, development of weaponry and logistics, information technology (IT) facilities, combat training and international military cooperation. More resources will be directed to projects that enhance combat readiness.[22] Most of these reforms are likely to begin yielding results by 2020. What is most critical here is the timing. The year 2021 marks the 100th anniversary of the founding of the CCP and 2049 marks the 100th anniversary of the PRC as a nation state. The realisation of these twin bicentennial goals remains the nucleus of Xi Jinping's "China Dream", most significantly including the vital goal of national rejuvenation (read reunification).

Geographic Consolidation and Theatre Commands

The growth and reform of China's military in terms of strength and scope is noteworthy. Referred to by Xi Jinping as a "breakthrough", the overhaul primarily points towards a shift away from an outright army-centric system towards a joint command, with by and large, equal representation from the three services. Most joint staff–type functions have been moved to the CMC, while a separate PLAA headquarters has been created, which is comparable to the headquarters of the PLA Navy, Air Force, and Rocket Force (formerly known as the Second Artillery Force).[23] With the disbanding of the four erstwhile General Headquarters, and their subsequent reorganisation into 15 units, it is evident that the former General Staff Department (GSD), General Political Department and the General Logistics Department, remain the prime losers. All the 15 new units have been placed under the direct control of the CMC, thus ensuring even tighter political control. For that matter, the reshuffling of generals

Figure 1: Chinese Theatre Commands[24]

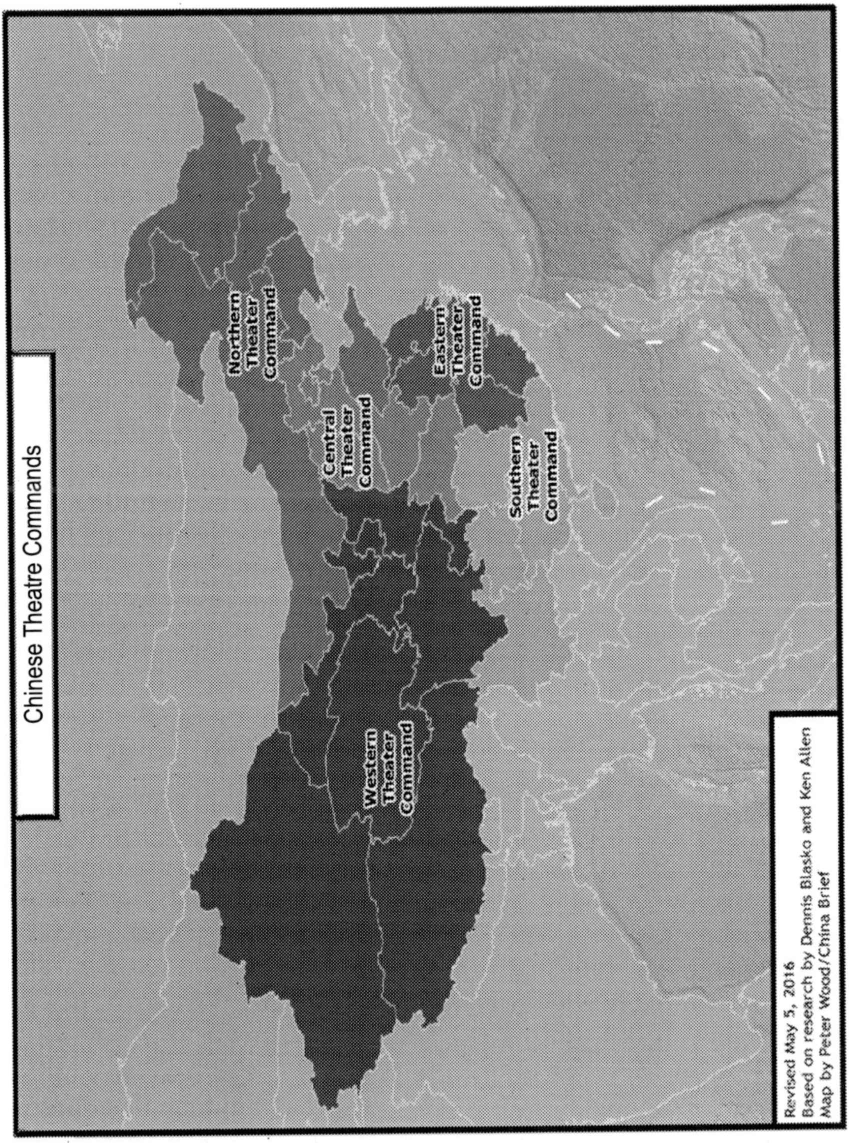

was also carried out at the same level of hierarchy. For instance, four of the seven former MR Commanders became theatre command leaders.

A major milestone in the reforms can be seen in the elimination of the MRs that have now been replaced with theatre commands (see Figure 1). On February 1, 2016, Xi announced that the MRs had been replaced by five new theatre commands (战区). Listed in protocol order these are: the Eastern, Southern, Western, Northern, and Central theatres, headquartered in Nanjing, Guangzhou, Chengdu, Shenyang and Beijing.[25] The theatres are aligned against land and (where applicable), maritime security challenges in their respective geographic areas. For instance, the Eastern Theatre Command covers the Taiwan Strait and East China Sea, while the Southern Theatre Command covers the South China Sea.[26] As was the case with the MRs, the theatres have subordinate units drawn from individual services. The purpose of reorganising the MRs into theatre commands is to improve the PLA's ability to prepare for and execute modern, high-intensity joint military operations in the future. Aside from the enlarged geographic areas of responsibility, a key difference between the new theatre commands and old MR commands, is that the former is explicitly designed to be joint headquarters similar to the geographic combatant command headquarters of the US military.[27] Theatre commands now directly focus on the specific strategic directions determined by potential external threats. Operational authority has moved on to a two-tiered system in which decisions will be made by the CMC and carried out by the theatre commanders.[28] Instead of two MRs dealing with a hypothetical India conflict, there is now one. Instead of three MRs bordering Russia, there are now only two, and one shares an approximately 30-mile border. The Sino-Vietnamese border region appears unchanged by this restructuring, with two theatre commands replacing two MRs.[29] Under the new system, transition from peacetime to wartime command will be easier. Under the former system, the MR commander was not necessarily the wartime theatre commander. This individual would likely be appointed by the CMC and sanctioned to set up a theatre that might span multiple MRs. Under the new system, the theatre commander is also the joint forces commander.[30] The reformed theatre commander and command structure, allows the PLA to truly implement the active defence strategy as a pre-emptive posture over and above facilitating potential relocation to a wartime command post.[31]

Western Theatre Command and Its Ramifications for India's Security

China's political and military leadership has often been discussed and forecasts indicate that future conflicts might become localised along China's peripheries. In this context, the act of downsizing the PLA by 300,000 personnel signalled the initiation of wide-ranging reforms and restructuring. Although troop reduction was projected at 'promoting peace', downsizing essentially forms a part of plans to streamline and strengthen the PLA and fashion it into a hi-tech, lethal, 'informationised' force capable of upgrading personnel with the right skills. This is being implemented through acquisition, development and familiarisation with advanced hi-tech armaments; intensification of training under new conditions to "fight and win local wars under hi-tech informationised and complex electromagnetic conditions"; and raising the cyberwarfare capability of all PLA formations.[32] Before ushering in the 2016 defence reforms and consolidating MRs to theatre commands, the erstwhile Lanzhou and Chengdu MRs (primarily meant for military operations against India) were retained as independent Theatre Joint Commands while preserving their operational orientation and their application of sustained offensive pressure and posturing towards India. Today, the new Western Command comprises more than half of China's land area, 22 per cent of its population and more than one-third of Chinese land-based military.[33] By incorporating the Qinghai region in the Western Theatre Command, the rapid induction and deployment of high-altitude trained troops into Tibet and across Ladakh will be far more feasible, by virtue of enhanced and coordinated joint planning. What is also noteworthy is the appointment of General Zhao Zongqi as the commander of the Western Command. Zhao, who until recently was the Jinan MR commander, has served for over two decades in Tibet. First as the deputy chief of staff (1984-99) and then as the chief of staff (1999-2004) of the Tibet Military District. He holds a good military and political grip over the precarious Tibetan issue.

As a continuation of the military reforms, India's land borders with China now fall under the purview of one single Western Command. On the contrary, from the Indian side, the Ladakh region falls under the 14 Corps of the Northern Command of the Indian Army, while Arunachal Pradesh falls under the Eastern Command and is divided into two parts: The Tawang area controlled by the 4 Corps; and the Rest of Arunachal Pradesh (RALP) which comes under 3 Corps. Although the Indian Army's *Dual Task Formations* have been mandated to operate from the Eastern to

Western sector, and from the Western to Eastern sector, depending upon the operational requirements, there still needs to be increased synergy that can be applied to the working and coordination of these formations. The lack of lateral mobility, i.e., the rapid switching over of forces within the Arunachal theatre – say for instance, from the Tawang sector to the RALP – continues to remain a serious challenge from an Indian military standpoint. Currently, the predominant way of enhancing mobility is by airlifting the forces operating in the Eastern and Western theatre within acceptable time frames. This need for airborne services arises due to the large distances involved and the inadequacy of surface transportation, both rail and road. However, the magnitude of equipping the forces and ensuring their efficient mobility in shorter durations with lesser warning periods – by rail (which is time consuming) or by air – has its own share of limitations. Additionally, switching over troops as part of the inter-theatre mobility strategy is also likely to face issues – particularly those of acclimatisation – which remains a prerequisite for operating in terrains beyond heights of over 9,000 feet.

While the actual number of Chinese PLA troops currently present in Pakistan-occupied-Kashmir (PoK) has been a constant subject of debate, what can no longer be doubted, or debated, is that China has firmly perched itself in PoK alongside the 772 km long Line of Control running between India and Pakistan.[34] With the reported stationing of a unit of PLA soldiers near the Khunjerab Pass and Chinese military officials frequenting the Field Command Office of Gilgit, (which happens to be Pakistan's military headquarter in the region), Chinese intentions of pervasively establishing its military edge in India's northern sector cannot be negated, or ignored, anymore.[35] The first joint patrolling exercise undertaken by Chinese and Pakistani troops along the PoK border in July 2016 was propped up and publicised considerably by Beijing and Islamabad. Although Chinese troops are known to have conducted patrols in the area since 2014, joint patrols by China's PLA and Pakistan's border police force along the stretch connecting PoK and Xinjiang outwardly remains the first of its kind. It has been long known that by means of sponsoring and investing in numerous "infrastructure development projects" inside Gilgit-Baltistan, the Chinese Construction Corps – a highly organised paramilitary force – has successfully managed to establish its permanent presence in the region. With the joint patrols by the frontier defence regiment of the PLA, the presence and potential future deployment of the regular Chinese Army inside PoK remains a foregone conclusion. Against this backdrop, the new Western Theatre Command of China has now been spread across the region to meet with India's Western, Northern and Eastern Commands. In any future conflict between India and China, be it limited or otherwise, the application and coordination of operations between the Chinese PLA's single Western theatre command and the three separate commands of the Indian Army, are what will shape the odds in a warlike situation. Such methodological differences in military approach will have grave ramifications primarily over the synergy-related aspects of war and the conduct of operations.

Revamped Organisational Structure

Upgrading the departments and staff of the General Command of the Army appears essential for downsizing and ensuring greater interoperability for joint operations – particularly post the unification of the land forces with other services. Xi Jinping has repeatedly stressed the fact that the PLAA should optimise its power structure and troop formation amidst transformations from regional defence to full-spectrum combat.

This needs to be read in the context of Xi's announcement in September 2015, wherein he stated that China would cut its troops by 300,000, with non-combatant agencies and their personnel constituting the core of these cuts. The continued attention being given to "Big Ground Army, Big Military Region System Mindset" (大陆军、大军区体制下的思维定势) is understandable given the virtual omnipresence of Ground Force officers throughout the previous PLA structure.[36] The unveiling of these organisational reforms, including subordinating the Ground Force to army service headquarters, raises the stature and role of the strategic missile force. In order to achieve enhanced jointness, it is essential for the ground force to become a real service. Historically, the PLA's ground service component has lacked a headquarters and has instead dominated the entire military by controlling all four of the PLA's general departments (which doubled as its de facto headquarters). Under the new system, however, the army will now possess its own headquarters – referred to as the PLAA Leading Organ – and it will also be on par with the PLA's naval, air and newly formed strategic missile service. The main goal appears to be the reduction of army domination and the improvement of the PLA's jointness.[37] The larger aim seems to be the placement of the services on more even footing in the traditionally army-dominated PLA and the enabling of the military to more effectively harness space, cyberspace and electronic warfare capabilities. A question that still remains unanswered, however, is whether the ground force personnel will continue to dominate most of the top positions in the PLA despite the reforms, or will this change over the next several years, as a result of future retirements and promotions under the reforms? For example, will a PLA Navy, PLA Air Force or PLA Rocket Force officer serve in a position such as commander of one of the new theatre commands or director of the new Joint Staff Department under the CMC?[38]

By establishing an upgraded missile force (PLA Rocket Force), the Chairman of the CMC has ensured a return of the Second Artillery Corps to its core function, that of providing strategic pre-eminence to China's nuclear and missile arsenal. This is mainly because, for long, the Second Artillery Corps have been functioning as a military branch and have now been elevated in stature from an independent branch (兵种) to a full-fledged service (军种). The Rocket Force will continue to serve as the core strategic deterrence power, by means of reinforcing medium- and long-range precision strike capabilities, technological advancements and enhanced command and control. Although China's Ministry of National Defence has underlined the fact that instituting the Rocket Force does not mean a major change in China's overall nuclear policy, the continued ambiguity that Beijing maintains in the application of its No-First-Use nuclear policy does not rule out the possibility of coercive military options completely. Aside from deterrence, the Rocket Force is expected to focus more on nuclear counter-attack capabilities, intensifying the construction of medium- and long-range precision strike power, and reinforcing strategic checks and balances. In China's revamped robust approach, proponents of coercive nuclear and limited war-fighting strategies could well find encouragement.

An independent SSF (战略保障部队) (aimed at integrating space, cyber and electronic warfare capabilities), has been put in force to take charge of a wide range of support functions, including intelligence, technical reconnaissance, surveillance, electronic warfare and logistics. What remains ambiguous is the organisation and functioning of the SSF. Furthermore, the creation of the SSF may further dilute the influence of the army, whilst ensuring information dominance and improving flexibility and responsiveness that enhances the PLA's ability to fight multi-domain conflicts.[39] The SSF's capabilities in the cyber and space domains, if used, could be extremely escalatory. For all these factors, the SSF appears to be directly (and appropriately) subordinate to the CMC rather than a theatre command or service. However, it appears likely that units within the theatres will be under operational control of the theatre commander.[40]

Figure 2: Revised PLA Structure after Implementation of Defence Reforms[41]

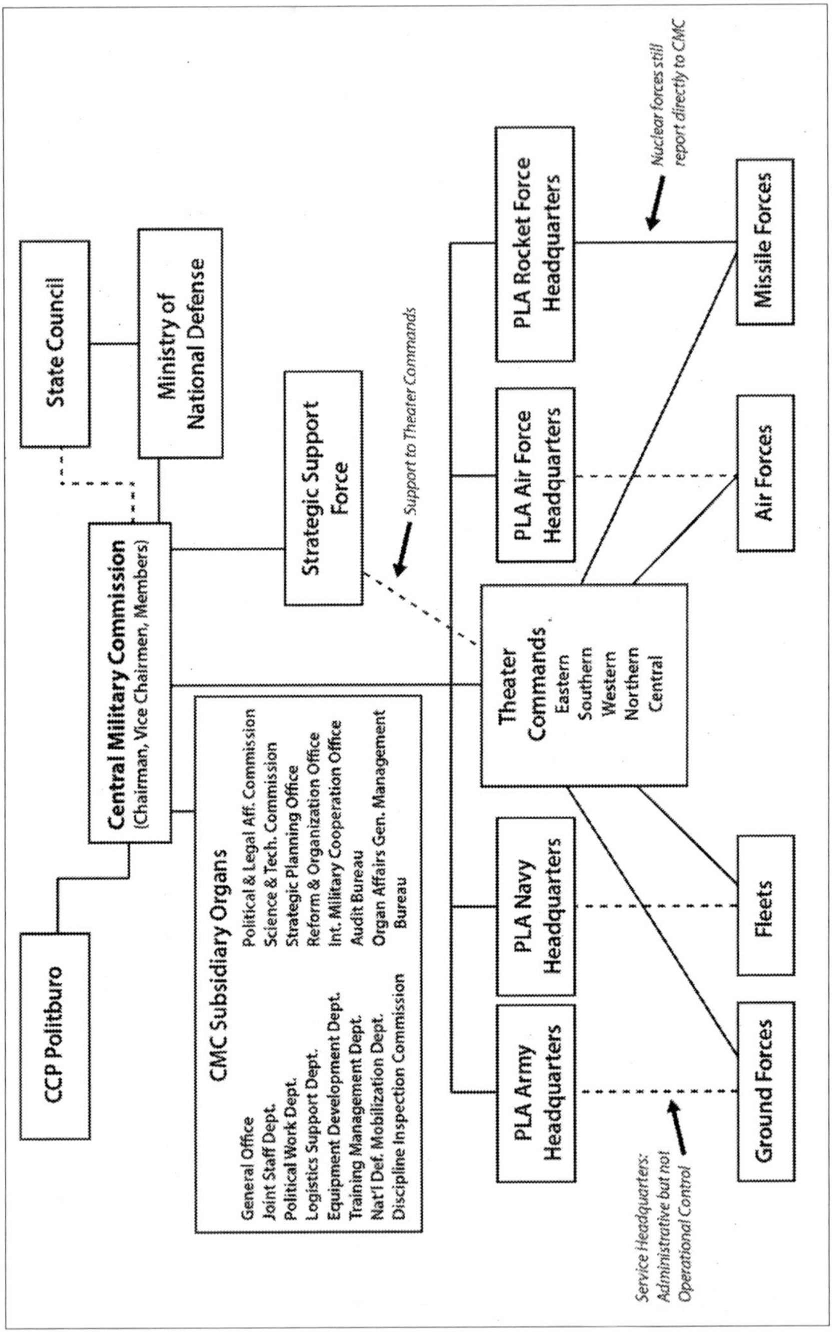

Focusing on Combat Jointness

The reforms that are being currently implemented envisage the establishment of a joint operational command structure by 2020 (see Figure 2). By eradicating the conventional structure wherein the army played a leading role, under the new organisational framework the operations of the army, navy, air force and strategic rocket force would be controlled in a unified way from a centralised headquarters, in order to ensure that the PLA can be turned into a nimble and capable military force. Part of the restructuring is aimed at enhancing the PLA's readiness and strengthening its deterrence and warfighting capabilities. These changes have been recognised as significant steps that could resolve some longstanding problems in the area of "jointness" that have been caused by the PLA's previous organisational structure. It is a well-known fact that there have been three major problems that have primarily inhibited the PLA's transformation to joint operations for two decades. First, the PLA views "jointmanship" in unique and flexible terms which allows for independent interpretation and undermines synergy of effort. Second, there is resistance, perhaps even confusion, regarding what "joint operations" mean and why they should be conducted in the first place. Finally, the command and control of the PLA under the erstwhile MR system and an army-dominated General Staff perpetuates combined arms operations, at best augmented by parallel air, navy, and missile forces operations, rather than facilitating joint integration.[42] Yang Zhiqi, former director of the earlier GSD, Military Affairs Department, had urged the PLA to accelerate the switch from a combined arms command system to a joint operations command system way back in 2000. The joint operations command system is an essential link that could aid in the implementation of joint operations. Yang argued that a joint command system could not be established at the last minute during a crisis, but needed to be put in place and tested during peacetime first. Yang observed, that while the PLA had made substantial progress towards achieving greater joint coordination between services during operational level training, once the exercise began, all the services tended to fight in different ways which jeopardised the whole process. Yang attributed this deficiency to a fundamental lack of an "authoritative" joint command.[43]

Keeping the above-mentioned backdrop in mind, the creation of a separate PLAA headquarters and the transfer of the joint staff functions, previously performed by the general departments to the CMC, would eliminate the inherent institutional bias caused by having a single organisation responsible for both PLAA specific and joint functions.[44] In

December 2000, the Nanjing MR published an article that stressed the importance of forming a joint operations command system.[45] The article identified several problems that centred on command and control and specifically criticised "factionalism" (parochialism) between the services. The article argued for the need to establish truly separate units under Joint Operations Groups (JOGs), in order to eliminate command and control interference by the units' parent services. The article stressed that the services should only provide combat support and coordination to units assigned to a JOG.[46] The recent creation of theatre commands, aimed at replacing collected single service organisations that happened to be located in the same place, implies that the PLA is capable of conducting joint operations at the theatre level.[47] With each theatre command establishing a joint command post, the PLA Air Force, Navy and Rocket Force would come under the command of the theatre commander, at least for a limited/ small-scale conflict/contingency.

Combat jointness, in particular, is a continuing goal that requires tremendous attention and reform. Currently, joint operations, i.e., the ability of the Army, Air Force, Navy and Rocket Forces to work together in coordinated campaigns – remain a key bottleneck for the PLA. Most long-distance operations are conducted by a single service. In one such operation, the PLA Air Force Spokesperson Senior Colonel Shen Jinke (申进科) noted that Chinese aircraft overflew the Bashi Channel and the Miyako Strait.[48] The former is a strategically vital waterway between the northern Philippines' island Luzon and the south of Taiwan; while the latter – also known as the Kerama Gap – is a waterway between the Miyako Island and the Okinawa Island.[49] In April 2016, Commander Liu Yuejun (刘粤军) and Commissar Zheng Weiping (郑卫平) of the Eastern Theatre published an editorial on the reform, noting that joint operational command was essential for effective command.[50] Opposing the prevalent resistance to the reorganisation, much of the editorial focused on obeying the Party's commands and the strategic benefits of such disruptive, but necessary reforms.[51] In the backdrop of all these changes, more exercises can be expected all through 2017 in order to refine joint operations and address the remaining bottlenecks in communication. However, even in such a scenario, what needs to be borne in mind is that if joint operations between the service branches were really put into practice and theatre command leaders continued to be army generals (as is currently the case), the Ground Forces Army leaders would gain authority by having command and control over air force and navy units in their theatre of operations.[52] According to Nan Li, apportioning leadership, command systems and force structures more evenly among the services in order to support integrated joint operations was emblematic of the intent to increase emphasis on developing the ability to engage in high-intensity combat in both the "Near Seas" (Yellow, East, and South China Seas; the current top priority) and, gradually, the Far Seas (the waters well beyond).[53]

The recent changes to the organisational structure of the PLA shall most likely have a positive bearing in improving its capabilities to conduct military operations. But until fundamental and visible changes to the PLA's organisational structure, culture, and functioning are actively put in place, the challenges to the organisation will continue to loom large. The PLA certainly faces a number of structural and technological hurdles, the most prominent one being the current downsizing that is taking place. The Chinese military is slated to get trimmed down to 2 million service members from its current figure of 2.3 million by the end of 2017. Additionally, for the coming few years at least, the ground forces shall continue to dominate the PLA, and this will be its single biggest challenge in so far as truly realising jointness is concerned. For the reorganisation of PLA to achieve true jointness, these parameters need to be met and addressed for sure.

Old Bottlenecks Galore

Despite all the major disbandment and shuffles, one of the key remaining obstacles is the continued army dominance of PLA's command organisations. The dominance by the Ground Forces seemingly continues with all the commanders and four of the five political commissars of the ostensibly joint theatre commands being PLAA officers.[54] The PLA is highly centralised with low levels of horizontal integration. Most personnel spend their entire careers within a single chain of command and most units have infrequent contact with units outside their chain of command. Thus, there is a fundamental incompatibility between the nature of the PLA's doctrine and its organisational structure.[55] By this count, it appears that the recent structural changes are designed to *increase* the centralisation of the PLA, instead of decreasing it. Abolishing the general departments and moving their functions to the CMC will tend to have the effect of increasing central control over these functions. The PLA has adopted a "CMC chairmanship responsibility system", under which "all significant issues in national defence and army building" will be "planned and decided by the CMC chairman". This is a stark contrast from previous protocol wherein senior officers at the CMC, general departments and MRs were allowed to make some of these decisions on their own.[56] The effects of this move are aimed at increasing centralised control at the upper levels of the PLA, and are likely to permeate down to the lower levels, culminating in an organisation that is even more centralised than it was before.[57] To exploit ephemeral opportunities tactically in today's wars, an agile and decentralised military set-up with lower levels of standardisation and a higher degree of horizontal integration has become an essential prerequisite. The ongoing overhaul and reorganisation of the PLA structure does attempt to meet these objectives to an extent, however currently, the process still seems to be a tall order.

Conclusion

Leading editorials and opinion pieces in mainstream Chinese state-controlled media have highlighted the fact that military reforms have been implemented in the wake of the 'constantly changing international situation'. They claim that this changing situation is what underlies the actions of the Chinese Army that is trying to secure the nation's interests. The PLA, apparently, is said to be adjusting to keep up with the pace of China's rise. Interestingly, experts and analysts in China are arguing that the mission of China's armed forces stretches beyond the nation's maritime and land territories. This clearly brings out the dichotomy in China's interpretation and application of power, both militarily and politically. As much as China harps on its intent to pursue "peaceful rise/development", that it reinforces with the incessant claim that Beijing shall "never seek hegemony" the constant attempts to create a fresh status quo in almost all its existing territorial disputes in the East China Sea, South China Sea and those in the Himalayan borderlands suggest otherwise. The message that Xi Jinping has conveyed by virtue of these reforms is clear: the Party is firmly in control with the help of the CMC, and has, in fact, further tightened its grip over the PLA. According to a guideline released by the CMC, a new structure will be established in which the CMC will take charge of the overall administration of the PLA, the People's Armed Police, the militia and the reserve forces.

All these developments are taking place at an opportune time for Xi Jinping, primarily since it has enabled him to pick his cohort during the 2017 19th Party Congress, in which a new standing committee – the nucleus of China's decision-making power apparatus – was constituted. Beginning 2018 onwards, Xi Jinping's hold over the political and military affairs of the state shall consolidate. In the backdrop of China's political leadership's future and Xi Jinping's future relations with the PLA, the looming still question remains: Will Xi further consolidate his power and seek to retain control for yet another term post-2022, or would he have to pave way for an anointed successor during the 2022 Congress? While the title of "core" leader puts Xi on par with Mao Zedong and Deng Xiaoping, the litmus test for Xi would lie in ensuring China's economic stability, even through the midst of the economic muddle, given that China's economic growth rate is becoming progressively undefined. Economic steadiness has often been interpreted as an essential prerequisite to preserve the communist regime's continuing reign in China. A dwindling economic chart could cause far-reaching social strife – a scenario that any Chinese leader, 'core' or otherwise, would be loath to grapple with. In order to meet this challenge, which could well threaten the regime's survival, the PLA would be expected to serve as the ultimate guarantor, albeit one that has not fought a major combat war since 1979.

NOTES

1. As per a release by the Chinese Ministry of National Defense, May 29, 2015; also, see Ye Hongzhi, "To Promote the Reform of the Military to Have New Thinking", *PLA Daily*, December 1, 2016.
2. Andrew S. Erickson, "Sweeping Change in China's Military: Xi's PLA Restructuring", *The Wall Street Journal*, September 2, 2015.
3. For more details see, "China releases guideline on military reform," *Xinhua* news release, January 1, 2016; also, see, Masayuki Masuda, "China: Quest for a Great-Power Role," *East Asian Strategic Review* 2017, National Institute for Defense Studies, Japan.
4. Ibid.
5. Sun Chiaye [孫嘉業], "Who Is Responsible on the Central Military Commission?" [中央軍委誰負責?], *Ming Pao* [明報], January 29, 2015, cited in James Mulvenon, "The Yuan Stops Here: Xi Jinping and the 'CMC Chairman Responsibility System'", *China Leadership Monitor,* No. 47, Summer 2015, at www.hoover.org/sites/default/files/research/docs/clm47jm.pdf.
6. James Mulvenon, No. 3.
7. For more details, see "The Power of Xi Jinping", *The Economist*, September 20, 2014.
8. Ibid.
9. Cheng Li, Promoting "Young Guards": The Recent High Turnover in the PLA Leadership (Part II: Expansion and Escalation) *China Leadership Monitor*, no. 49, March 1, 2016, The Brookings Institution; and see, Andrew S. Erickson, "Sweeping Change in China's Military: Xi's PLA Restructuring." *The Wall Street Journal,* September 2, 2015
10. As cited in Andrew S. Erickson, No. 2.
11. Dirk H. Schmidt, "No Radical Break with the Past in China's Military Reform Programme", blog post, Mercator Institute for China Studies, Berlin, October 7, 2016.
12. Ibid.

13. James C. Mulvenon, "Hotel Gutian: We Haven't Had that Spirit Here since 1929", *China Leadership Monitor*, No. 46, Hoover Institution, Winter 2015.
14. Ibid.
15. Mao Zedong, "On Correcting Mistaken Ideas in the Party", in *Collected Works of Mao Zedong*, Vol.1, December 1929, at https://www.marxists.org/reference/archive/mao/selected-works/volume-1/mswv1_5.htm
16. Ibid., cited in James C. Mulvenon, No. 10.
17. "Xi Urges Serious Reflection on Xu Caihou's Case", *China Daily*, November 1, 2014, cited in James Mulvenon, No. 3.
18. Cao Zhi and Li Xuanliang, "All-PLA Political Work Conference Concludes at Gutian; Fan Changlong, Xu Qiliang attend and address the conference", Xinhua, November 2, 2014.
19. Cao Zhi and Li Xuanliang, "(Military) All-Army Political Work Conference held in Gutian", Xinhua, November 1, 2014.
20. Ibid., cited in James C. Mulvenon, No. 10.
21. "China's Sweeping Military Reform", Opinion, *The Japan Times*, March 8, 2016.
22. According to a Xinhua release, May 2016.
23. Roger Cliff, "Chinese Military Reforms: A Pessimistic Take", *Joint Forces Quarterly*, No. 83, Fourth Quarter 2016.
24. Kenneth Allen et al., "The PLA's New Organizational Structure: What is Known, Unknown and Speculation (Part 1)", *China Brief*, 16 (3), February 4, 2016.
25. "China's Military Regrouped into Five PLA Theater Commands", Xinhua, February 1, 2016, at http://news.xinhuanet.com/english/2016-02/01/c_135065429.htm.
26. "Experts: The Five PLA Theater Commands Have Clear Goals, With the Southeast Coastal Front Being the Key Link of Future Military Operations" [专家：五大战区目标清晰 东南沿海 **是作**战重点], *Global Times* [环球时报], February 2, 2016, at http://mil.huanqiu.com/observation/2016-02/8489177.html.
27. Ibid., pp. 53-54.
28. "Zhongyang junwei guanyu shenhua guofang he jundui gaige de yijian" (The Central Military Commission's Opinions on Deepening National Defense and Military Reforms), Xinhua, January 1, 2016.
29. Michael S. Chase and Jeffrey Engstrom, "China's Military Reforms: An Optimistic Take", *Joint Forces Quarterly*, No. 83, Fourth Quarter 2016.
30. "Spokesperson: PLA's Theatre Command Adjustment and Establishment Accomplished", *China Military Online*, February 2, 2016.
31. Michael S. Chase and Jeffrey Engstrom, No. 25.
32. For more details, see Jayadeva Ranade, "What China's Military Plans Mean for India", *Rediff.com*, October 27, 2015.
33. Ibid.
34. Monika Chansoria, "China Not Neutral on Kashmir, Anymore", *The Sunday Guardian*, August 13, 2016.
35. Ibid.
36. "In a Fortnight: China Hails Progress toward Military Reforms, Improved Jointness", *China Brief*, 16 (18), December 5, 2016.
37. Michael S. Chase and Jeffrey Engstrom, No. 25.

38. Ibid.
39. Ibid.
40. Phillip C. Saunders and Joel Wuthnow, "China's Goldwater-Nichols? Assessing PLA Organizational Reforms", *Strategic Forum*, No. 294, April 2016.
41. As cited in Phillip C. Saunders and Joel Wuthnow, "China's Goldwater-Nichols? Assessing PLA Organizational Reforms", *Strategic Forum*, No. 294, April 2016, p. 3.
42. Susan M. Puska, "Rough but Ready Force Projection: An Assessment of Recent PLA Training", in Andrew Scobell and Larry M. Wortzel (eds.), *China's Growing Military Power: Perspectives on Security, Ballistic Missiles, and Conventional Capabilities*, US Army War College, Carlisle, September 2002, pp. 229-30.
43. Views expressed by Yang Zhiqi, *Jiefang Jun Bao*, October 31, 2000, cited in Susan M. Puska, No. 37.
44. Roger Cliff, No. 20, p. 54.
45. Nanjing Military Region Renmin Qianmin, December 29, 2000, cited in Susan M. Puska, n. 37.
46. Ibid.
47. Roger Cliff, No. 20, p. 54.
48. As per a China Central TV report aired December 1, 2016.
49. For more details, see Peter Wood, "Chinese Military Aviation in the East China Sea", *China Brief*, 16 (16), October 26, 2016.
50. Liu Yuejun and Zheng Weiping, "Resolutely Carry Forward the Historical Task of Laying the Foundation for the Development of the Theatre: Studying and Implementing the Instructions of President Xi Jinping at the Founding Conference of the Theatre", *Seeking Truth*, April 1, 2016.
51. *China Brief*, No. 28.
52. Dirk H. Schmidt, No. 8.
53. Nan Li, cited in Andrew S. Erickson, No. 2.
54. Roger Cliff, No. 20, p. 54.
55. Ibid., p. 55.
56. Ibid., p. 56.
57. However, this does not change the number of organisational layers between them and the commander of China's armed forces (President and CMC Chairman Xi Jinping). For more details, see Roger Cliff, No. 20, p. 56.

SECTION II

STRUCTURAL REFORMS

4

Higher Defence Organisation: Independence to the Mid-1990s

R. Chandrashekhar

During the British Raj, particularly post the settlement of the Curzon-Kitchener stand-off in the early 1900s, the Commander-in-Chief (C-in-C), India, was the Supreme Commander of the British Indian Army. He was an extraordinary member of the Viceroy's Executive Council and the de facto Defence Minister with a status second only to the viceroy himself.

An interim government was appointed in India on September 2, 1946, and Sardar Baldev Singh was made the Defence Minister. The C-in-C now ceased to be a member of the Viceroy's Executive Council but remained the executive head of the three Defence Services and advisor to the Defence Minister. A committee was set up under the chairmanship of the Defence Minister and it was constituted by the C-in-C, the defence secretary and the financial advisor. A proposal was also forwarded regarding the setting up of a Cabinet Committee on Defence under the interim government, however since the Muslim League did not accept the concept of 'joint responsibility' of the cabinet, it could not be implemented.

Post-independence Mechanisms

The post of C-in-C was abolished on August 15, 1947, and briefly replaced by the position of Supreme Commander of India and Pakistan. However, this position was also abolished soon after in November 1948. Each of the three Armed Forces were placed under separate C-in-Cs who possessed complete operational command over their respective forces. The role of the erstwhile C-in-C was merged with the office of the Governor-General of India, and when India became a republic on January 26, 1950, the powers were eventually vested in the office of the President.

The then Department of Defence and War Department were merged to form the Ministry of Defence (MoD) that in due course of time, was enlarged to perform further higher functions of defence management such as threat assessment, force levels, budgeting, defence production, etc. All these activities, had, up until that time been carried out at Whitehall, the Service Headquarters in the UK. The role of the MoD, and the Defence Secretary who heads it, was succinctly summed up by H.M. Patel, its earliest incumbent, who stated that:

> "While the Government was convinced of the undoubted importance of allowing the three services to developing its own way in matters which are distinctly its own, it was no less convinced that the necessary separation should not be pushed too far, for matters in which common organisation was possible could obviously be dealt with efficiency and economy if so organised, and what is more important would in the process assist in building up a feeling of the essential oneness of the defence organisation."[1]

A Defence Cabinet Committee (DCC) was formed on September 30, 1947, and it was chaired by the Prime Minister (who was also the External Affairs Minister at the time). The committee was constituted the Deputy Prime Minister (also the Home Minister), Finance Minister and the Defence Minister. The Cs-in-C of the three Armed Forces also attended the DCC meetings so that they could provide on-the-spot clarifications. Likewise, the Defence Secretary and the Financial Advisor (Defence) were also required to attend so that they could provide clarifications on administrative and financial aspects.

Ismay's Proposals

At the behest of the Government of India, Governor General Lord Mountbatten asked his then Chief of Staff, Lord Hastings Lionel Ismay, to evolve a system of higher defence management that would be most suited to the requirements of a newly independent India. Given that the period post-partition was a period of considerable turmoil, Lord Ismay put forth a set of practical and pragmatic proposals for a system that was committee based and included all the stakeholders involved.

Aside from the DCC there were also the Economics Cabinet Committee and the Foreign Affairs Cabinet Committee. For smoother functioning of the former, Lord Ismay recommended a set of subordinate structures which would not only support the Cabinet Committee on Defence but also provide a robust graded structure for coordinated decision-making at various levels.

An earlier iteration of such a Defence Minister's Committee – with the Defence Minister as chairman, and the C-in-C, Defence Secretary and Financial Advisor as members – had been set up during the interim government's leadership in 1946. This Committee, that was reconstituted to include the Cs-in-C of all three Services, examined the papers and proposals that were required to be submitted to the DCC and took decisions on matters that concerned all three or at least two of the three Services but did not require decision-making at the level of the DCC.

In 1948 separate committees were formed under the chairmanship of the defence secretary for each of the three services. The committees had the concerned Service Chiefs, Financial Advisors and Joint Secretaries as members. These committees were responsible for considering administrative and policy matters concerning the respective service they were attached to. Eventually these committees became the Defence Minister's Committees for the Army, Navy and Air Force.

The next step in Lord Ismay's proposals comprised of setting up a Chiefs of Staff Committee (COSC), consisting of the three Service Chiefs. Since the Chiefs were professional advisors to the government it was their responsibility to prepare military plans and render advice on all operational matters and military matters in general. The mantle of chairmanship of the COSC was given to the Chief who had been serving for the longest period on the Committee.

Under Lord Ismay's proposals, the COSC was to be supported by a series of other committees that were supposed to address the details of the coordination between the Services themselves, as also between the Services and the MoD. The proposal also recommended the inclusion of civil servants as members of the committee in order to avoid further detailed scrutiny of matters considered by the Committees at the MoD.

Some other 'inter-Services' committees that were also set up were the Joint Planning Committee, Joint Training Committee, Joint Intelligence Committee (JIC), Inter-Services Equipment Policy Committee and the Medical Services Advisory Committee. Additionally, there were also the Principal Personnel Officers Committee (PPOC) and the Principal Supply Officers Committee (PSOC), both of which were composed slightly differently. These committees included the Principal Staff Officers (PSOs) of the three Services Headquarters, as well as representatives of the MoD and the Ministry of Finance (Defence). This arrangement was made to ensure that if a proposal was unanimously accepted by either of these committees, it would not have to go through further examination in the Ministry, thereby cutting down on procedural and administrative delays. Despite such benevolent intentions, however, these committees did not prove very effective.

In 1965, the JIC was removed from the ambit of the Military Wing. The MoD had even considered winding up the PPOC and PSOC sometime during 1976, but the Services Headquarters had strongly objected against such a move. The committees continued but their contributions remained marginal at best.

The 'Military Wing' of the Cabinet Secretariat

A separate 'Military Wing' was set up in the Cabinet Secretariat in October 1947 and it was headed by a Deputy Secretary (Military). This appointment was to be headed by a Services officer of the rank of Brigadier and the post was to be held in rotation by the three Services. The Cabinet Secretary held administrative control over the Military Wing. Secretariat support for the COSC and the inter-Services committees was to be provided by the Military Wing, that could thereby provide a 'window' of formal access between the COSC and the higher decision-making levels. (The Wing was subsequently placed under the control of the MoD in 1989 and eventually subsumed under the Headquarters Integrated Defence Staff [IDS].)

The Services 'Distanced'

Lord Ismay's proposals had included a provision ensuring that Service Chiefs had 'direct access' to the DCC "if necessary through the Defence Minister's Committee."[2] The then Defence Secretary H.M. Patel, however, objected to this recommendation, since all the three Service Cs-in-C at the time were British officers. His objections were accepted by the Defence Minister's Committee on December 20,1947, and since then, the Service Chiefs have only been able to access the DCC through the Defence Minister.

Services Headquarters become 'Attached Offices'

This 'distancing' of the Service Chiefs from the apex level of political leadership was followed by another tectonic change which was the issuance of the "Organisation, Functions, Powers and Procedure of Defence Headquarters, 1952". Much to everyone's, dismay, this was put into effect without any interface with the then military leadership. The new 'Procedure' resulted in the Services Headquarters being excluded from the departmental structure of the Mod thenceforth and functioning solely as 'Attached Offices' to the Department of Defence. A concerning aspect of this rather disconcerting decision was the manner in which it was approved and imposed. On May 27,1952, the Defence Secretary H.M. Patel informed the Chairman of the COSC General K.M. Cariappa of the proposal to designate the Services Headquarters as Attached Offices and sought his response within 20 days. After hectic consultations with the other two Cs-in-C, General Cariappa wrote back to the Defence Secretary on June 13, 1952, stating that the Services Chiefs had strong reservations regarding the intended changes and that the issue needed to be discussed in further detail. However, these considerations were dismissed, no discussion took place and requests from General Cariappa's office seeking an early scheduling of a discussion were ignored until, on July 7, when the Cabinet Secretariat notified the General of the government's decision to approve the proposal.

The major implications of accepting this proposal were that the MoD acquired the authority to make policy decisions on all defence matters. This authority further strengthened their hold over virtually all the aspects of the administration and functioning of the Services Headquarters, and through the HQs, over the Defence Services. The responsibilities of the Services Headquarters – which were functioning as 'Attached Offices' – were restricted to 'executing' and overseeing the implementation of policies laid down by the government aside from serving as "the repository of technical information and [advising] the Government on technical aspects of [the] questions dealt with by them."[3]

'Cs-in-C' to 'Chiefs of Staff'

The title 'Commander-in-Chief' carried with it the heritage of a position of exceptional authority. After independence, all three Service Chiefs assumed the title 'Commander-in-Chief' of their respective Services. The Constitution of India which came into force on January 26, 1950, however, stipulated the President of India would be the C-in-C of the Armed Forces of India. After this declaration, there was indeed a 'clash of nomenclature' that required a resolution. In 1955, the appointments of the three Service Chiefs were re-designated as the 'Chief of the Army Staff' (General), the 'Chief of the Naval Staff' (Vice-Admiral) and the 'Chief of the Air Staff' (Air Marshal). The Chief of the Air Staff was raised to the rank of Air Chief Marshal in 1965 and the Chief of the Naval Staff rose to the rank of Admiral in 1968.

The following announcement was made in parliament by the then Prime Minister Jawaharlal Nehru further elucidating the reasons underlying this re-designation:

> "It would be better if in future the designation of the Commander-in-Chief should be dropped and they should be called the Chiefs of Staff... It is proposed that the Heads of the Services in future be called Chief of Army Staff, Chief of the Naval Staff and Chief of the Air Staff, and in the course of a few days, orders to this effect will be issued. In some countries, they do not have these Commanders-in-Chief in this manner, in fact in most countries they have some kind of Defence Councils...No doubt it may be desirable for us also to form these Councils...We are going into this matter and hope gradually to develop these Councils."[4]

The issue before the Chiefs of Staff that emerged post this declaration was whether they were to continue as the operational commanders of their respective forces or whether they were to function as Chiefs of Staff and consequently delegate operational responsibility to commanders. They chose the latter hierarchy, and established separate 'juridical entities' under the Army, Navy and Air Force Acts.

Allocation of Business Rules and Transaction of Business Rules

In 1961, the President of India Dr Rajendra Prasad (also the C-in-C of the Armed Forces of India) issued the Allocation of Business Rules and the Transaction of Business Rules over his own Signature. The Allocation of Business Rules, 1961, allots and distributes the business of the government among its different departments, and these departments are then assigned to a minister chosen by the President under the advice of the Prime Minister. The Transaction of Business Rules, 1961, seeks to define the authority, responsibility and obligations of each department in the matter of transacting the business allotted to it. The rules state that the business allotted to a department will be disposed of by, or under the direction of, the Minister-in-charge and they further specify the cases or classes of cases to be submitted to the President, the Prime Minister, the Cabinet or its Committees for prior approval, as well as the circumstances under which the department primarily concerned with the business under disposal needs to consult the other departments concerned and secure their concurrence before taking the final decision. According to these rules, the responsibility for the defence of India is placed with the Defence Secretary and there is no mention in these rules of the charter and role of the Service Headquarters or their Chiefs.

The Menon-Thimayya Face-off

In 1959, the then Chief of Army Staff, General Thimayya, conducted two war games – one each in the Western and Eastern theatres that he personally supervised. The conclusion derived from these war games was that the Chinese could launch a major incursion across any part of the border at any point in time. They could also create a situation with the likelihood of a major operation unless threatened by strong retaliatory action by India. The war games also proved that the available troop and equipment levels were inadequate to contain Chinese aggression. Based on the assessments of both the exercises, the Army Headquarters drew up a comprehensive proposal for increasing force levels, enhancing equipment and effecting a revised deployment plan that was forwarded to the MoD for approval. Although the then Defence Minister, Krishna Menon, accepted the need for modernisation, he saw no immediate requirement necessitating the growth of the Army at the rate Thimayya recommended as essential.

While a professional difference of this nature cannot be faulted ipso facto, subsequent developments queered the pitch. In the course of a chance social meeting at a time when the Defence Minister was not in Delhi, General Thimayya drew the Prime Minister's attention to the need for raising additional forces and improving the state of equipment and communications, also mentioning the reservations of the Defence Minister. On his part, Prime Minister Nehru asked General Thimayya to first talk to Defence Minister Menon stressing that bypassing a Minister may not be in order.

Upon his return, Menon had a meeting with the Prime Minister, and when appraised of General Thimayya's meeting with Nehru, fumed that the Army Chief had mentioned the matter in his absence and he further reinforced the fact that General Thimayya had no business meeting the Prime Minister without his specific approval, terming it as disloyalty and impropriety. General Thimayya submitted his resignation, but before the letter reached him, Prime Minister Nehru called and persuaded the Chief to withdraw the resignation, conceding that Menon was indeed a "difficult man" to work with. The Chief, on his part, agreed that the Defence Minister's problems were about his methods of "man-management". However, when the issue came up in Parliament eventually, the Prime Minister's statement emphasised the fact that "under our practice, the civil authority is, and must remain supreme". He also referred to the army's "fine mettle" and "excellent morale" but added that the Chief should not have acted in haste in the manner he did. The primary responsibility for the stand-off thereby came to rest on the Chief's shoulders. Several analysts feel that had the Chief resigned, it would perhaps have forced the government to reconsider the seriousness of the situation and reassess the threat from China. From a higher defence management perspective, this episode demonstrates perfectly the objections H.M. Patel raised regarding the Chiefs having direct access to the DCC. The Chiefs were now firmly under the control of the Defence Minister with no direct access to the Prime Minister (and thereby to the union cabinet), irrespective of the gravity of the issue.

'Concordance' under Y.B. Chavan

Following the military debacle of 1962, Krishna Menon was removed from the cabinet and replaced by a somewhat reluctant Y.B. Chavan who was then the Chief Minister of Maharashtra. Chavan had a reputation of being an able administrator and he sought to weld the three Service Chiefs and the Defence Secretary into a team. He implemented the practice of beginning the day with a meeting attended by the Service Chiefs, the Defence Secretary, and when required, the Cabinet Secretary and Director Intelligence Bureau, as well. These "'morning meetings' were held not only to sort out problems but also to forge good working relationships."[5]

Chavan soon realised that a serious problem that had plagued the tenure of his predecessor, was that of junior Army Officers being allowed direct access, even if informal, to the Defence Minister. Chavan insisted that the new Army Chief maintain firm command of the Army Headquarters and ensure that his Principal Staff Officers knew that while the Defence Minister was accessible to them, all proposals emanating from the Army Headquarters needed the approval of the Chief of Army Staff. Some of his other 'correctives' were the restoration of (then) Air Marshal P.C. Lal and the closure of an ongoing case against (then) Major General Sam Manekshaw. Both these officers went on to become Chiefs of their respective Services.

The Sundarji Era

In his book *From Poona to Prime Minister's Office: A Cabinet Secretary Looks Back*, the then Cabinet Secretary B.G. Deshmukh provides a glimpse into the dynamics of higher defence management during the late 1980s, especially under General K. Sundarji's tenure as the Chief of Army Staff. During a discussion on Ex Brass Tacks held at the Ops Room, General Sundarji explained that "Pakistan was moving its armour from South in Sindh and concentrating it in the north against our Punjab border and that the Army's assessment was that this was not only a tactical move but also a strategic one to threaten the Punjab". The Cabinet Secretary then asked why Pakistan should make itself vulnerable in Sindh when we had a significant presence there. There was only one major bridge over the main river and in case we bombed it, Pakistan's heavy armour would get stuck there and maybe it was removing its armour to avoid this possibility. Since we had a very strong deployment in Punjab and far superior to Pakistan's we need not worry unnecessarily about its movement of heavy armour.[6]

B.G. Deshmukh adds that he was later told that his remarks were not taken very well as they went against the Army's view and he was also informed that the Army did not appreciate a civilian – even if he was a cabinet secretary – voicing such a different opinion. If one were to analyse this on a higher defence management template, the issue that emerges is that the assessment of the Services, even on operational matters is not above being directly challenged or questioned.

This aspect came can be re-emphasised in another episode mentioned by Deshmukh pertaining to the Indian Peace Keeping Force (IPKF). He states that "Rajiv Gandhi consulted Gen Sundarji, who, 'in his flamboyant style' stated that 'If the LTTE does not agree and wants to take on the Indian Army, we will finish them within a week or ten days'."[7] As cabinet secretary, he set up a committee to regularly review the situation in light of the substantial IPKF presence in Sri Lanka. He adds that during the meetings, differences arose between the Research and Analysis Wing (R&AW), the Intelligence Bureau (IB) and the MoD. Gen Sundarji was personally embarrassed as the IPKF could not control and subdue the LTTE as he had promised. The Army then blamed both IB and RAW for not briefing it properly about the weaponry possessed by the LTTE or its morale and staying power. In reply, the IB and RAW said the Army itself was responsible because of its overconfidence and underestimation of the enemy, that is, LTTE.[8]

A major problem arises here with respect to the empirical and factual data on which the military bases its assessments and conclusions. If the assessments are based on 'inputs' for which it is dependent on other agencies, the military's claim to be the prime formulator of decisions in the strategic realm is weakened as they are making these decisions on the basis of interpreted information. A need emerges therefore, for a coordinated and inclusive decision-making apparatus.

The Rodrigues Interview (1992)

Another 'landmark' episode that caused a trust deficit and impacted the relative balance within the higher defence management structures was the fallout that occurred at an interview granted by the Chief of Army Staff General S.F. Rodrigues to Ramindar Singh, senior editor of the Lucknow daily *The Pioneer*. The interview was conducted on March 4, 1992, and published in two parts on March 11 and 12, 1992. General Rodrigues had agreed to the request on condition that the script for the interview be sent for perusal prior to its publication, to which the interviewer had given a 'gentleman's promise'. Ramindar Singh also sought permission to tape-record the interview which, too, was graciously and trustingly accorded. The interview was, however, published without having been sent back for a perusal, as was previously agreed. It contained references to some politicians as 'bandicoots', and also carried a rather controversial statement in the context of civil-military relations, that (for the armed forces) "good governance is also our concern."[9] The General had obviously spoken freely and trustingly, treating the correspondent informally. The episode reached its denouement with the then Defence Minister Sharad Pawar making a statement at the floor of Parliament which mentions, inter alia,

> I have discussed the matter with the General and find that while certain impression has been created, he made it abundantly clear to me that he stands fully committed to follow Government's policy and directions in regard to each of the various issues referred in his interview. I am satisfied with the General's explanation. However, I feel that such interviews by serving officer are best avoided. I wish he had resisted the temptation.[10]

Analysts have opined that the Chief should perhaps have been provided a window to 'save face and grace'.

Admiral Bhagwat's Dismissal

A similar 'lack of grace' or withholding of respect on the part of the political class is also evident in their handling of another episode, also involving a Service Chief. Civil-military relations in post-independence India touched a low-point with the dismissal of the then Chief of Naval Staff, Admiral Vishnu Bhagwat. The Admiral was dismissed after he took an uncompromising stance and refused to abide by the government's directions regarding the appointment of a Deputy Chief of Naval Staff, contrary to his recommendations. From the civil-military perspective, here too, there was no visible attempt on the part of the government to persuade the Chief of Naval Staff and address his concerns.

To support his stance, Admiral Bhagwat relied on an affidavit submitted by the government in its response to a writ petition filed by

Lieutenant General R.S. Kadyan, challenging the appointment of Lieutenant General H.R.S. Kalkat as General Officer Commanding-in-Chief (GOC-in-C) Eastern Command. In the affidavit, the government had elaborated the procedure followed for the selection of army commanders. Admiral Bhagwat read the averments in that affidavit to mean that a decision contrary to his recommendation was defective and hence 'un-implementable'. There were undoubtedly other causative factors behind the dismissal of the Chief of Naval Staff. However, for the purposes of developing a broad understanding of the highs and lows in civil-military relations, it is essential that a robust system be in place that provides reasoned explanations for specific government decisions as opposed to unquestioned commands.

Recognition of the Need for 'Reform'

Estimates Committee of Parliament, 1958

The fact that the higher defence organisation structure has intrinsic flaws was realised as early as 1958 by the Estimates Committee of Parliament, headed by Balwantrai Mehta. The report submitted by this Committee on the "'Organisation of the Ministry of Defence and Services Headquarters" found that "the existing system was inefficient, not [made] for economy or speedy decision making, ridden by considerable duplication with various segments functioning in a compartmentalised manner instead of moving jointly towards achieving common objectives." The Committee also observed that there was a drastic imbalance in the distribution of responsibility and authority between the Services' Headquarters and the MoD. The report suggested a comprehensive review of the existing powers and recommended the delegation of more power to the Services' Headquarters. To this end, it proposed the establishment of a 'Council' system as was the practice in the UK. Such a system would require the amalgamation of the finance and accounts systems to bring about economy and efficiency. The committee further suggested that the Railway Financial Administration System be studied for adoption to the Defence Organisation as a whole.

Administrative Reforms Commission, 1967

The Administrative Reforms Commission, 1967 addressed, for the first time, two cardinal issues that the Services have constantly maintained are imperatives for the establishment of an efficient military structure. These issues are – the need for an Integrated Ministry of Defence and the appointment of a Chief of Defence Staff (CDS). The Commission had two Committees for Defence matters, each headed each by two eminent personalities, Nawab Ali Yavar Jung and Shri S.N. Misra. Both Committees considered the integration of the Ministry of Defence and the Services Headquarters essential, but had different perceptions regarding on the appointment of the CDS.

Ali Yavar Jung echoed the core stance of the military on the need for an Integrated Defence Ministry and stated that "the subordination of the Military to the civil power should be interpreted in the political and not in the bureaucratic sense."[11] S.N. Misra also endorsed this viewpoint in his own recommendation, where he stated that "The principle of civilian control over the Defence machinery should be interpreted to mean not bureaucratic of civil service control but essentially ultimate political control by the Parliament and the Cabinet."[12] With respect to the duplication of functions at the level of the MoD and the Service Headquarters, Ali Yavar Jung stated that "there is the factor to consider seriously of duplication of work which constitute a waste, both financial and in terms of talent and time. Such duplication occurs mostly in the name of coordination and supervision; it contributes little except delay."[13]

On the appointment of the CDS, however, he felt that the Services:

> should retain their separate identities but all operational matters need to be coordinated and operations eventually integrated. This alone would ensure a single line of ultimate professional responsibility; without it the Services would not be able, all of a sudden, to bring about the effective unified command which is required in war. We believe there is a need for a Chief of Defence staff who would be the coordinator and the executive at the top echelon of all the three operational commands. The structure in peacetime should conform to the requirements of war.[14]

However, Sharda Mukherji, widow of Air Marshal Subroto Mukherji, who was also a member of the committee strongly dissented on the issue of appointing a CDS. The then Air and Naval Chiefs also expressed their dissent regarding the same before the committee. The time for a 'consensus' amongst the Services had not yet come.

CDS Scuttled?

Lieutenant General Depinder Singh provides an episode regarding the appointment of the CDS in his book *Field Marshal Sam Manekshaw: Soldiering with Dignity*. He states:

> On a date prior to 26th January 1972 the Prime Minister had ordered that the Army Chief be promoted to the rank of Field Marshal and appointed Chief of Defence Staff, and that the appointment be made on the morning of Republic Day 1972. For some unfathomable reason, that was not done thereupon the Prime Minister directed that the announcement be made on the 28th January 1972 as the Chief (the Field Marshal) and the other two Chiefs were being awarded the Padma Vibhushan that afternoon. This too fell through and nothing more was heard by us. Over the years, the bureaucracy has evolved a perfect system to stall, what, to them, is an unwholesome direction. A very simple expedient is resorted to: a point concerning one service will be referred to the other two services and their views sought. If one or more services send a negative reply, the project is consigned to the dustbin as being 'unacceptable to the other two services'. I have no doubt that this proposal too met this fate as though the Navy was agreeable to Sam's promotion; the Air Force was vehemently against it, citing, as a very unconvincing reason, that this would amount to belittling the Air Force's achievements.[15]

Appointing Directorate General Defence Planning Staff (DG DPS)

It was much later, however, that the 'first steps' towards formal integration were taken through the establishment of an inter-Services organisation, called the DG DPS. This organisation, was mandated to provide support to the COSC, and it comprised of representatives from the three Services, the Ministry of External Affairs and the Defence Research and Development Organisation. It addressed the following major issues:

(a) Threat analysis and formulation of threat assessments
(b) Evolution of Military aims
(c) Formulation of the concept of combined operations
(d) Conception and recommendations (to COSC) regarding balanced force levels to achieve military aims
(e) Joint training and joint logistic management
(f) Coordination of perspective plans for 15-20 years period
(g) Maintaining close interaction with research and development (R&D), Defence Production, Industry and Finance

Committee on Defence Expenditure (CDE)

The erstwhile Raksha Rajya Mantri Arun Singh was, appointed in 1990, by the then Prime Minister V.P. Singh as chairman of the Committee on Defence Expenditure to analyse and advise the government on issues of India's Nuclear Doctrine and its related No First Use Policy. (The former

Chief of Army Staff General K. Sundarji and K. Subrahmanyam were the other members of the committee.) The report of the CDE is not available in the public domain. Its principal recommendations, however, as culled from various articles, media reports and discussions, seem to have been for the integration of the MoD with the Services Headquarters. The committee seems to have recommended the nomination of the Defence Secretary as the principal administrative advisor to the Defence Minister. His functions and responsibilities would include – coordinating perspective plans, budgets, overall policies for administration, accounting, parliamentary matters, interfacing with other ministries and departments of the government and matters relating to various states. The Committee apparently recommended the establishment of 'Services Boards' for the management of individual Services to improve efficiency in all functional and administrative matters. It was also recommended that the respective Chiefs of Staff be made responsible for all revenue expenditure in respective Services to improve flexibility and ensure speedy decision-making. Insofar as the CDS is concerned, apparently the CDE did not recommend the appointment, but it is believed to have recommended the setting up of a Joint Chiefs of Staff (JCS) to be headed by an Army Commander rank officer with a stipulation that the JCS was not to compromise or diminish in any way the right of the three Service Chiefs to access the Defence Minister. There were other recommendations the CDE is said to have made which often find mention, such as the closing down of some Ordnance Factories and low-technology defence production units, the harnessing of private sector capacities in order to obtain the goods being produced; the integration of civil and military finance officers across the MoD; and the enhancement of the participation of scientists, private industry, etc.

The National Security Council (NSC) and National Security Advisor (NSA)

The NSC of India was established by the Atal Bihari Vajpayee government on November 19, 1998, with Brajesh Mishra being appointed the first NSA. Aside from the NSA and the Deputy NSA, the ministers of Defence, External Affairs, Home and Finance and the Deputy Chairman of the Planning Commission, are all members of the NSC. It is only the Strategic Policy Group, – which is the first level of the three-tier structure of the NSC, chaired by the Cabinet Secretary – that undertakes a "Strategic Defence Review" and has the three Services Chiefs as its members. Hence, while the responsibility of the armed forces to ensure the security of the nation remains prime, their formal contribution in the formulation of strategic concepts that frame those decisions now has become subordinate to that of the NSA.

Conclusion

The period from Independence till 1998 can be said to be one during which the 'administrative distance' between the national political leadership and that of the military leadership widened, a divide that was also infused with an impermeable non-osmotic layer of separation. It took a catastrophe of the magnitude of the Kargil War to shake off the archaic bureaucratic insolence.

NOTES

1. Kale Memorial Lecture on "The Defence of India". Delivered at the Gokhale Institute of Politics and Economics Pune (1963).
2. 'Historical Review' – Ministry of Defence Report on the Management of Defence
3. As mentioned in the terms of the *Manual on Office Procedure.*
4. Proceedings of the Lok Sabha 25 May 1955.
5. "Debacle to Revival: YB Chavan as Defence Minister 1962-1965" by RD Pradhan (Rupa).
6. B.G. Deshmukh, *A Cabinet Secretary Looks Back*, Harper Collins, New Delhi, 2004.
7. A Cabinet Secretary Looks Back" by BG Deshmukh (Harper Collins).
8. Ibid.
9. The Pioneer 12th March 1992.
10. Lok Sabha Proceedings 17th March 1992.
11. 'Historical Review' – Ministry of Defence Report on the Management of Defence.
12. Ibid.
13. Ibid.
14. Ibid.
15. 'Field Marshal Sam Manekshaw: Soldiering with Dignity' by Lt Gen Depinder Singh (Natraj Publishers).

5

Defence Reforms: The Vajpayee Years

Anit Mukherjee

Prime Minister Atal Behari Vajpayee's coalition government was at the helm of affairs from 1998 to 2004 and significantly shaped India's defence policies. Some of this was by design, such as the nuclear tests in 1998 which allowed India to come out of the secrecy closet and led to its subsequent accommodation within the existing nuclear order, signified by the 2005 US-India Nuclear deal. Even before the tests, the government also appointed the K.C. Pant Committee to recommend a national security management system for India. These steps eventually led to the creation of the National Security Council (NSC), Strategic Policy Group (SPG) and the National Security Advisory Board (NSAB). In all these activities (from nuclear testing to creating national security structures), Brajesh Mishra, the principal secretary to the Prime Minister, played a key role.[1] However the most significant development was the 1999 Kargil War, which was forced on India and revealed many weaknesses. The public outcry at that time led the government to create the Kargil Review Committee (KRC) and the subsequent Group of Ministers (GoM) Committee. These led to one of the most significant attempts at restructuring the Indian military.

With the benefit of hindsight, this chapter re-examines the defence reforms that were initiated during the Vajpayee regime. In doing so it focuses on the big ideas, their implementation, sources of resistance and the debates therein. To be clear, this chapter does not simply list out what measures were implemented – as this has been done elsewhere – but re-examines the reform committees based on what we know now.[2] It begins by describing the composition, functioning, recommendations and salient debates of the two reform committees. Then, it analyses the reform measures that were accepted and the ones which weren't. The next section gives an overall assessment of defence reforms during this period. It concludes with some observations about the contemporary relevance of the debates surrounding defence reforms.

The Kargil Review Committee (KRC)

The KRC was appointed on July 29, 1999 and consisted of four members. It was led by K. Subrahmanyam, a prominent member of the strategic community, former Vice Chief of the Army Lieutenant General K.K. Hazari, B.G. Verghese, a distinguished columnist; and Satish Chandra, then chairman of the Joint Intelligence Committee (JIC), India's apex intelligence analysis body. Within a short span of six months, the committee interviewed numerous serving and former officials including Presidents, Prime Ministers, Defence Ministers, civilian bureaucrats, intelligence agencies and military officers, and submitted its report to the government. After some hesitation, the government tabled the report in the parliament in February 2000. One of the most significant decisions was to publish for public consumption the KRC report, with some redactions. This was an unprecedented step, and copies of the report were quickly snapped up. This revealed that contrary to the complaints of India's strategic community, there was (and remains) a considerable amount of interest in matters pertaining to India's defence and national security. It also allowed for the subsequent debate on defence reforms in India, as without its publication analysts would have continued debating in the dark!

The KRC was not an investigative committee and did not set about to assign blame or identify individual lapses – an aspect for which it received some criticism. However, it did undertake a large number of oral interviews combined with site visits, and public testimonies. The committee also accessed a number of files including classified documents and military situation reports (sitreps). Some of these were already in the custody of the NSC Secretariat (NSCS), which was leaned upon extensively by the KRC while preparing its report.

There were many recommendations made by the KRC regarding different aspects of national security. However, on the matter of defence reforms – the focus of this book – the KRC gave a scathing indictment of India's national security structures when it argued that:

> An objective assessment of the last 52 years will show that the country is lucky to have scraped through various national security threats

> without too much damage, except in 1962. The country can no longer afford such ad hoc functioning. The Committee therefore recommends that the entire gamut of national security management and apex decision-making and the structure and interface between the Ministry of Defence and the Armed Forces headquarters be comprehensively studied and reorganised.[3]

In making this judgment, the KRC pointed out certain features of India's higher defence management that are still relevant today. Table 1, below, reproduces these observations and explains their contemporary relevance.[4] As can be seen, the most fundamental problems afflicting higher defence management that had been raised by the KRC, have still not been addressed and therefore, there are continuing tensions between the civilian-dominated Ministry of Defence and the Service Headquarters. Furthermore, since the respective service chiefs are reluctant to give up any of their powers, India's unique system of "dual-hatted" chiefs continues.[5] The KRC also commented on the prevalence of "command culture" within the military which prevents political leadership from obtaining a more broad-based view from other subordinates or junior officers. Additionally, jointness remains problematic as civilians have not forcefully insisted upon it.[6] All these problems can be traced back to the reluctance of both civilian and military bureaucracies to change the status quo. Civilian bureaucrats justify the existing structure as upholding the supremacy of the civil and maintaining democratic control over the military. On the other hand, the military has quickly implemented measures that create additional organisations and posts but is reluctant to give up any of their powers. As a result, there is very little incentive to bring about substantial changes.

The main argument made by the KRC was that "there has been very little change over the last 52 years" in India's "security management system". They therefore recommended that the entire apparatus of national security management "be comprehensively studied and reorganised".[7] To the credit of the Vajpayee government, this was promptly done and a GoM was set up for this purpose. However, the approach taken by the Task Force of Defence – the one most relevant for this book – differed from the KRC's expectations and caused further complications later.

The Group of Ministers (GoM) Committee Report

In April 2000, the Vajpayee government constituted a GOM consisting of Home Minister L.K. Advani, Defence Minister George Fernandes, External Affairs Minister Jaswant Singh and Finance Minister Yashwant Sinha "to

Table 1: Observations Made by the KRC on Higher Defence Management and Their Contemporary Relevance

KRC Observations	Issues under Discussion
India is perhaps the only major democracy where the Armed Forces Headquarters are outside the apex governmental structure... The status quo is often mistakenly defended as embodying civilian ascendency over the armed forces, which is not a real issue. In fact, locating the Services' Headquarters in the Government will further enhance civilian control.	*Lack of Integration between the Ministry of Defence and the Service Headquarters and the functioning of the latter as "Attached Offices"*: Problematic working relations between the two continue as the military complains about the "Allocation of Business" Rules.
The Chiefs of Staff have assumed the role of operational commanders ... rather than that of Chiefs of Staff to the Prime Minister and Defence Minister. They simultaneously discharge the roles of operational commanders and national security planners/managers, especially in relation to future equipment and force postures.	*The Chiefs of Staff having a dual-hatted role as operational commanders and staff officers:* Service chiefs continue to wear both the operational and staff hats. As a result, they are overworked and unable to pay attention to either.
Army Headquarters has developed a command rather than staff culture. Higher decisions on equipment, force levels and strategy are not collegiate but command-oriented. The Prime Minister and the Defence Minister do not have the benefit of the views and expertise of the Army Commanders and their equivalents in the Navy and Air Force.	*Problem of Command Culture Continues:* An issue that has been long debated, the problems accruing from a command culture, where the chief dominates other senior officers, have long been recognised.
Most opposition to change comes from inadequate knowledge of the national security decision-making process elsewhere in the world and a reluctance to change the status quo and move away from considerations of parochial interest.	*Vested interests in both the civilian bureaucracy and the military resisting change to protect parochial interests:* The opposition to change is widely acknowledged and prevents any substantive restructuring of India's higher defence management.

review the national security system in its entirety and in particular, to consider the recommendations of the KRC".[8] The GoM in turn constituted four task forces, each headed by a chairperson, namely:

(a) Task Force on Intelligence Apparatus headed by G.C. Saxena
(b) Task Force on Internal Security headed by N.N. Vohra
(c) Task Force on Border Management headed by Dr Madhav Godbole
(d) Task Force on Management of Defence headed by Arun Singh

These task forces adopted differing methodologies, including a mix of site visits and interviews, according to their mandates. They then presented their reports to the GoM. Similar to the KRC, the combined reports of the Task Forces were released in the public domain, with some security deletions. The GoM dealt with many issues, including intelligence, border management and internal security reforms. However, the most relevant Task Force, for the purposes of this book was the Task Force on the Management of Defence.

The Task Force on the Management of Defence

The Task Force on Defence consisted of a total of 13 members, viz., Arun Singh (Chairman), Vice Admiral P.S. Das (retd.), Lt. Gen. S.S. Mehta, Air Marshal T.J. Master, Vice Admiral Arun Prakash, Narendra Singh Sisodia, Dhirendra Singh, S.K. Misra, Dr A.S. Bains, Gyan Prakash, Vice Admiral Madanjit Singh and V.S. Jafa. They shared one thing in common: all of them were either working or had experience in the military, Defence Ministry or Finance Ministry (Gyan Prakash). On the positive side, this meant that they had the requisite personal experience and insights that emerge from working in a bureaucracy. On the flip side, however, this also meant that they came to represent their own institutional interests, whether service based or departmental (Indian Administrative Service [IAS], Finance Ministry, Defence Ministry, etc.). This problem was aggravated perhaps by the absence of a genuine outsider – an academic or a researcher. Such an 'outsider' could have, at least in theory, brought greater analytical rigour to this group which instead relied largely on personal experience and opinions. Despite this, to its credit, the Task Force ended up making a number of wide-ranging recommendations. Due to limitations of space, one cannot discuss all these recommendations, so the following paragraphs highlight the three most salient debates.

First, and perhaps the single most important recommendation made by the Task Force, was for the creation of a Chief of Defence Staff (CDS). The primary justification for this was that the "COSC [Chiefs of Staff Committee] has not been effective in fulfilling its mandate".[9] This was a very strong claim but it was made without any supporting evidence. As a result, when certain constituencies expressed their opposition to this post there was no factual data explaining why the COSC had been ineffective. Opposition to the CDS came from many quarters including the Indian Air Force, civilian bureaucrats and IAS officers to name a few. Even then Prime Minister Vajpayee was set to overrule their objections and was poised to appoint a CDS. However, at the last moment, the Congress party expressed its firm opposition and persuaded the government to delay implementing this measure arguing that it needed the approval of all political parties. Since then the official position of the Ministry of Defence on this issue is that it is awaiting the "consensus of all political parties".[10] According to a member of the Task Force, not appointing a CDS "ripped the heart out of the GOM recommendations".[11] This issue continues to be relevant to this day as many argue for and against a CDS-type post (currently referred to as Permanent Chairman, COSC).

The second recommendation was regarding the integration of service headquarters with the government. This recommendation was originally made by the KRC however, there was a difference between what the Task Force understood to be the issue and what the KRC recommended.[12] The Task Force argued that there is an "erroneous perception that the Armed Forces Headquarters do not participate in policy formulation and are outside the apex Governmental structure".[13] It therefore recommended re-designating the service headquarters and delegating administrative and financial powers from the Ministry to the military. Both these measures were implemented however this did not fundamentally address the problematic working relations between the Defence Ministry and military. As a result the issue of integration of service headquarters with the Ministry of Defence continues to resonate to this day.

The third recommendation made by the Task Force was the creation of a Joint Command, called the Andaman and Nicobar Joint Command (ANC). This step was taken with the expectation that it would lead to more geographically delineated joint commands in the future. However, as we now know, such a move has been resisted by all three services who are content with the existing "coordination approach" to jointness. As a result, not only has the ANC failed to realise its potential but the idea of joint commands has been effectively buried.[14]

Despite these criticisms, the Arun Singh Task Force must be commended for ushering in a number of changes. Creating the Integrated Defence Staff (IDS), establishing the Defence Intelligence Agency (DIA) and pushing through the idea of an Indian National Defence University (INDU), among other measures, has certainly improved aspects of India's defence policy.

Assessing Defence Reforms in the Vajpayee Era

How then should we assess defence reforms under the Vajpayee government? Firstly, we must understand and appreciate the stellar role played by Brajesh Mishra, Jaswant Singh, Arun Singh and

K. Subrahmanyam in pushing through different ideas despite bureaucratic inertia and resistance. All of them in their own particular way pushed forward ideas to reform national security and defence structures. In doing so they partnered with reformist military officers like Admiral Sushil Kumar, Admiral Arun Prakash, Lt. Gen. S.S. Mehta and many others. This brings into spotlight the critical role played by advisers in pushing through reforms. Indeed, once Arun Singh left his position as an adviser in the Defence Ministry, much of the momentum for reforms was lost. This was also because the subsequent Defence Minister George Fernandes was not very invested in the idea of defence reforms. Therefore, the power and potential influence of 'outside' advisers should be acknowledged – especially in the Indian system which is dominated by civilian bureaucrats and politicians with very little experience of working with national security issues.

Secondly, much progress was made by the Vajpayee government and a number of far-reaching reforms were introduced. While Prime Minister Vajpayee has been rightly criticised for demurring at the last moment in appointing a CDS one can be charitable and assume that had he been re-elected in 2004, he might have followed through with the appointment. The initial impetus for reforms was therefore made by the Vajpayee government; however, its successor, the Congress-led United Progressive Alliance (UPA) government, completely lost the plot on the matter of defence reforms.[15] This highlights the importance of political leadership in ushering in defence reforms.

Finally, the study of defence reforms during this era indicates that one should not leave the implementation of various initiatives to the bureaucracies – whether civilian or military. As students of organisational behaviour well know, bureaucracies readily accept and implement measures that enhance their powers while 'shirking' or delaying in implementing those that they consider inconvenient. This is a real danger for reformist officials and their ideas. For example, the Indian military readily accepted the creation of an IDS, DIA, INDU, etc., as these created additional posts; however, they effectively scuttled the idea for a joint command by undermining the ANC. One could similarly argue that civilian bureaucrats have undermined the idea of the military's participation in decision-making by undermining the IDS.[16] There is a need, therefore, to create an implementation cell to see through the implementation of various defence reforms.

From Vajpayee to Modi: Another Opportunity?

The KRC and GoM reports are important milestones in any discussion on defence reforms in India. One must now also add the Naresh Chandra Committee and the Shekatkar Committee whose reports are publicly unavailable and the fate of its recommendations uncertain. To his credit, early in his tenure Prime Minister Narendra Modi had publicly spoken about the need for defence reforms and has argued that it will be "an area of priority" for him.[17] Similar sentiments were expressed by former Defence Minister Manohar Parrikar. However, while there has been progress in procurement processes, no major reforms in higher defence management have occurred thus far. What can the Modi government do to galvanise the debate surrounding defence reforms and thereby complete Vajpayee's unfinished task?

First, it is important to get a complete understanding of the strengths and weaknesses of India's defence structures. The only way to do so is to release more of the committee reports into the public domain. Hence, the reports of the Committee on Defence Expenditure (CDE), the Naresh Chandra Committee and the Shekatkar Committee reports should be released, with redactions if necessary. Additionally, the Appendices of the KRC – which are lying on dusty shelves in the NSCS – should also be made publicly available. While redactions can be made on information still considered sensitive, denying access to the entire document is counterproductive. These measures will allow for a more informed public debate. Ideally, of course, that debate should be held in Parliament; however, India's politicians have not yet shown themselves capable of this task. Indeed, the absence of a parliamentary discussion on the KRC or the GoM was the lament of K. Subrahmanyam.[18]

Second, and perhaps more importantly, the government should overrule opposition from status quo minded bureaucrats (whether civilian or military) and impose some form of defence reforms. In public policy, no decision is final and one can re-visit the efficacy of defence reforms periodically. By not acting on defence reforms, however, the government risks continuing with the weaknesses in India's national security. That is not what Prime Minister Vajpayee would have wanted.

NOTES

1. S.D. Pradhan, "Contribution of Brijesh Mishra in Strategic Affairs and Security Reforms", *Strategic Analysis*, 37 (2), 2013, pp. 161-170.
2. For more on the internal debates and recommendations made by the two reform

committees, see Anit Mukherjee, "Failing to Deliver: The Post Crises Defence Reforms in India, 1998-2010", *IDSA Occasional Paper no. 18,* March 2011.

3. Kargil Review Committee, *From Surprise to Reckoning: The Kargil Review Committee Report,* Sage Publications, New Delhi, 1999, p. 259.
4. This table reproduces text from Kargil Review Committee, *From Surprise to Reckoning,* pp. 258-259.
5. Prakash Katoch, "Integrated Theater Command", *Indian Defence Review,* 28 (3), July-Sept 2013, also see Anit Mukherjee, "Facing Future Challenges: Defence Reforms in India", *RUSI Journal* 156(5), October 2011.
6. Anit Mukherjee, "Fighting Separately: Jointness and Civil-Military Relations in India", *The Journal of Strategic Studies,* 40:1-2, 2017, pp. 6-34,
7. Kargil Review Committee, *From Surprise to Reckoning,* p. 259.
8. *Reforming the National Security System: Report of the Group of Ministers on National Security,* Government of India, New Delhi, 2001, p.1.
9. Ibid., p.100.
10. Standing Committee on Defence, *Thirty Sixth Report: Status of Implementation of Unified Command for Armed Forces* (New Delhi: Lok Sabha Secretariat, February 2009), p. 5, and reply to unstarred question no. 846 on 'Chief of Defence Staff,' Lok Sabha Questions, 24 July 2015.
11. Arun Prakash, "India's Higher Defence Organisation: Implications for National Security and Jointness", *Journal of Defence Studies,* 1(1), August 2007, p. 24.
12. This is discussed in greater detail in Anit Mukherjee, No. 2, pp. 20-22.
13. *Reforming the National Security System,* No. 7, p. 99.
14. For more about problems in ANC, see Anit Mukherjee, "The Unsinkable Aircraft Carrier: The Andaman and Nicobar Command", in Anit Mukherjee and C. Raja Mohan (eds.), *India's Naval Strategy and Asian Security,* Routledge, London, 2015, pp. 86–105.
15. For an assessment of defence reforms and policies under the UPA government, see Sandeep Unnithan, "Worst Defence Minister Ever", *India Today,* March 07, 2014; Anit Mukherjee, "Cleaning the Augean Stables", *Seminar,* No. 658, June 2014, pp. 41-44.
16. Frank O' Donnell and Harsh V. Pant, "The Evolution in India's National Security Apparatus: Persisting Structural Deficiencies", in Harsh V. Pant (ed.), *Handbook of Indian Defence Policy: Themes, Structures and Doctrines,* Routledge, New Delhi, 2016, p. 331.
17. "PM Chairs Combined Commanders Conference on board INS Vikramaditya at Sea", Press Information Bureau, Prime Minister's Office, Government of India, December 15, 2015.
18. "Report of the Kargil Review Committee: An Appraisal", *CLAWS Journal,* Summer 2009, pp. 17-18.

6

Defence Planning: A Review

Narender Kumar

"It is not destruction that is war's ultimate aim, but peace. Peace should be the ruling idea of policy, and victory the only means towards its achievement."[1]

– J.F.C. Fuller

Introduction

As a rising regional power, India requires a structured long-term defence planning (LTDP) process that can guarantee its safety against unpredictable and uncertain security environments. The planning process for the same is dependent upon multiple factors, such as evolving security situations, political decision-making processes, national security culture, civil-military interface and the structure of defence forces. Defence forces aspire to always remain at a technological and strategic advantage that facilitates them to deal with a full-spectrum conflict in the near future. They are also encouraged to maintain a constant state of readiness to deal with local wars at all times. All of the above notwithstanding, the phenomenon of defence planning is, fundamentally stretched between organisational intent and actual practice.[2]

In an environment where the threat arises from state and non-state actors and the mode of warfare ranges from conventional to hybrid, the overall security situation is full of strategic unpredictability. Furthermore, this unpredictability is intensified by the fact that China is rising economically and militarily at a phenomenal pace and Pakistan is acquiring unprecedented hybrid capabilities. Given the unstable geostrategic environment and the need for defence preparedness, ambiguity in defence planning should be replaced by an institutionalised planning process. It is high time that India structures its military forces for the uncertain challenges of the future. "A strategy needs to be defined that explains how the maintenance and possible use of armed force can help reduce strategic risks, by making them less likely, less potentially destructive, or both."[3] The LTDP is not about a budget or a technical procedure, it is a process that needs to be debated by political leadership, policymakers, defence planners and services. Against the above backdrop, all strategic defence planning must, therefore, take the long-term view.[4]

What is Defence Planning?

It is imperative to understand and differentiate between 'national security planning' and 'defence planning'. National security refers to the responsibility of a nation to protect the values, principles, citizens, institutions, freedom and integrity of a state against external and internal threats. National security planning stems directly from an overarching national security strategy: "National security strategy is the art and science of employing the nation's political, economic and military power to achieve stated national security objectives in peace and war."[5] The primary responsibility of securing the nation remains with all the organs of the state including the Parliament. This securing of sovereign interests is effected through a variety of tools that constitute national power, such as political, diplomatic, economic and military power. A concise definition of national security, therefore, would be: "Safeguarding the sovereignty, territorial integrity, citizenry and socioeconomic functionality of a nation from an aggressor intent on undermining a particular valued aspect of a nation through violent or unjust means."[6] To add to this definition, some of the most appropriate objectives of national security are defined by the New Zealand Government's *National Security System Handbook,*[7] that states, "the objective of national security is ensuring public safety", "preserving sovereignty and territorial integrity", "sustaining economic prosperity", "maintaining democratic institutions and national values", "protecting the natural environment", "strengthening international order to promote security" and "protecting freedom of movement".[8] Defence planning is one of the most important tools that can be employed by the government for the sake of ensuring national security.

Defence planning is largely about developing capabilities and options for mid and long term [periods].[9] It is a process that deals with uncertain future security challenges that may unfold due to unpredictable external and internal security challenges that hamper the stability of a country. In India, the debate surrounding capacity building is often dominated by short term views regarding the current security situation as well as the economics/politics of implementing military modernisation in a resource constrained economy. The argument put forth most often is, "if India is unlikely to fight a conventional war in the near future, then why spend so much on defence at the cost of other social development schemes?" This mind-set exists primarily due to a lack of strategic culture and an inadequate knowledge of national security issues. But the fact of the matter remains that while capability building takes time, the intent of one's adversaries can change rapidly.

In order to truly understand what defence planning means for the Indian context it would be fruitful to examine the statements made by military leadership regarding the same. The former Chief of the Army Staff, General V.P. Malik has said that "Defence planning is the process of determining the national security objectives of a nation and formulation of policies and strategies that will govern the allocation of funds and acquisitions, use and disposition of resources to achieve objectives."[10] Former Chief of Naval Staff Admiral V.S. Shekhawat has defined the defence planning process as a subset of overall national-level planning in the political, economic and social spheres.[11] While these statements look at the problem from a holistic lens, it is necessary to state the fact that the defence planning process is not merely a budgetary exercise, as is being advocated by some analysts. While it is true that until and unless resources are made available plans cannot fructify, there is much more than mere budget allocation that goes behind the formulation of the defence planning process. In order to develop a holistic approach to LTDP, the process should go through several stages such as political guidance, environmental assessment, analysis of the mission for the armed forces, existing capability assessment, determination of future requirement of capabilities, options for capability development, critical security concerns and timelines for development of capabilities. The process necessitates contemplating the potential nature of the operating environment in the distant future and developing a plan for attaining success. The most appropriate definition of a long-term defence plan is the nation's desire to uphold and promote its values and interests,[12] coupled with a vision to secure vital national interests and a plan to develop capabilities through a planned budget. While there is no universally accepted time period associated with long-term defence planning, it generally involves exploring 10 to 30 years, or more, in the future.[13]

Objectives and Models of the Defence Planning Process

Before examining India's defence planning process, it is imperative to analyse the various models of defence planning that are currently in place across the world. These models serve the most powerful armies, even the ones that have no immediate threat from external and internal adversaries. Many different analytical approaches have been applied to LTDP over the years. Each of these general approaches originates from a specific perspective on the problem. There is no universally accepted method for LTDP. The North Atlantic Treaty Organization's (NATO) *Handbook on Long-Term Defence Planning* broadly categorises various defence planning models that are based on three different parameters. Historically proven facts, technological optimisation and scenario based planning form the basis of the planning process of the defence plan. In fact, many of the long-term planning methods employed for the defence sector have been adapted from the commercial sector. Dejan Stojkovic and Bjørn Robert Dahl[14] have described the defence planning process as encompassing – top-down Planning, Resource-constrained Planning, Technological Optimism, Risk Avoidance, Incremental Planning, Historical Extension, Capability-based Planning, Scenario-based Planning and Threat-based Planning.

The former President of the US, Harry S. Truman said, "Strategy, programmes and budget are all aspects of the same basic decisions."[15] The objective of defence planning, therefore, is to deliver a strategy of defence by building requisite capabilities. The LTDP process is aimed at investigating potential operating environments and developing a force structure that can adapt to counter the evolving threats that might arise in the future. Defence planning must cater for the maintenance of modern defence forces as well as the infrastructure required to apply military power. It should also invest in developing the indigenous defence industry and maximising capabilities, in order to fulfil the nation's security requirements in a full-spectrum conflict. All things considered, it is a complex process that requires synergy among inter-ministerial and inter-governmental agencies. It is a structured process that requires long-term perspective. The process of defence planning can be categorised as under:

Development of National Security Strategies and Policies

Defence planning is a highly political process that is determined by national political leadership on the basis of threat perceptions and security challenges that might arise in the near and distant future. Political leadership lays down national security objectives, strategy and broad strategic goals.

Strategic Defence Review

A strategic defence review is essential for efficiently determining security risks, threats, available resources and constraints. It is only on the basis of accurate threat simulation that policies, priorities of defence plans, and infrastructure development can be facilitated.

Development of Long-term Defence Plans

The development of a long-term defence plan includes – assessment of existing capabilities, determination of military capabilities and options for the future, force structure plans, infrastructure development and timelines for building capabilities. The defence plan is also aimed at developing a course of action that determines how to effectively use different military capabilities in order to achieve declared goals.[16] It also prioritizes developing the capabilities of all organs of military power that are controlled by the state. The long-term defence plan should optimise existing organisational structures and establish a link between planning and budgetary support. The LTDP, in a nutshell, is the meeting point between the vision of political leadership and the development of military capabilities.

Budgetary Support Based on Priority of Development of Capabilities

The process of defence planning is put into action once resource allocation takes place. The starting point for converting vision into action is budgetary support. The entire exercise is futile if it is not given financial support.

Development of Military Capabilities

Defence planning is primarily an act of defence resource management that aims to create military capabilities in order to fight the nation's current and future wars. It necessitates strategic and systematic planning and provides nation states with the tools required for the completion of national defence objectives as well as the transformation of available resources into a comprehensive set of military capabilities needed to ensure security in the future. Defence planning should also include force planning that consists of delineating targets for force structure, systems, infrastructure, weapons systems, development of research and development (R&D), niche technologies (indigenous and imported), command and control as well as the time frame required to achieve these goals.

Pragmatic and Flexible Planning Parameters a Pre-condition for the Implementation of Long-term Defence Plan

The global security environment is becoming increasingly dynamic and unpredictable. Increased collusion between state and non-state actors as well as hybrid warfare possess the potential to destabilise strong nations in a matter of months and days. To cater for such asymmetric threats, a long-term defence plan needs to be flexible and practical so that it can serve as a guide for developing and implementing short term plans and programmes. A long-term defence plan should also necessitate regular evaluation of the progress of short-midterm plans, and allow for adjustments when necessary.[17]

The defence planning objectives and process described above are broad guidelines that should be followed. They are not preconditions, nor are they binding. In practice, LTDP is more commonly conducted by employing a combination of these planning approaches.[18] Aside from the above factors, three essential components of the defence planning process that need to be noted are:

(a) The defence planning process is a function of the apex political body of the nation. Inter-ministerial and inter-departmental inputs are vital for the implementation of plans as well as the smooth functioning of the planning process. Inputs from the various ministries associated including – Foreign Affairs, Home, Finance, Defence, Communication, Railways, Road and Transport and Science and Technology – are essential for the implementation of strategic defence reviews, environmental assessment, resource allocation, infrastructure development, manpower accretion and the overall development of military capabilities.

(b) Military diplomacy plays an important role in the formulation of defence plans. While there is no universal definition of defence/military diplomacy, in broad terms, it can be defined as using uniformed diplomats and the act of diplomacy as leverage to achieve common understanding, interoperability, capability building and to develop trust between militaries. It forms an essential component of capability building, military strategy formulation, doctrine creation, force structuring and military modernisation. It also assists by providing critical inputs in the defence planning process.

(c) Strategic partnerships have emerged as an important factor in defence planning and capacity building. Considering the cost involved in R&D and defence infrastructure, it is not possible for any nation to build holistic capabilities by itself. The core objectives of alliances and partnerships are collective defence, crisis management and cooperative security.[19] Military power can be leveraged through alliances to protect vital national interests. For example, Indian military diplomacy formed an alliance with the Soviet Union post the 1965 War and leveraged it effectively during the 1971 Indo-Pak War. The strategic partnership with the Soviet Union later assisted India in building comprehensive military capabilities.

Defence Planning Process in India

The defence planning process of India, is rooted in the defence organisation evolved by Lord Ismay, (chief of staff of Lord Mountbatten), and it was expected to meet the security requirements of the newly independent country. Lord Ismay had created a system that would ensure a smooth transition from the erstwhile colonial power to an independent nation that could deal with immediate security threats. Ismay recommended three committees: the Cabinet Committee on Security (CCS) (chaired by the Prime Minister), the Defence Minister's Committee (chaired by the Defence Minister) and a Chiefs of Staff Committee (COSC), (this committee would function as an overseer maintaining central coordination between each of the individual forces that were administered and operated by their respective Commanders in Chief). The COSC was established to serve as a link between various cogs in the hierarchy. It was supposed to facilitate coordination between the services on the one hand, and between the services and the Ministry of Defence (MoD) on the other. The aim was, above all, to provide quick decision-making with minimum delays caused by red tape.[20] The idea was to create a system wherein defence planning could be undertaken in a structured manner during the formative years of nation building until India was in a position to evolve its own system.

However, Nehru trashed the very idea of a "strategic plan for a Government directive on defence policy"[21] proposed by the then Army Chief, General Lockhart. He refused the plan by declaring that India had no enemies extrinsically and that the police was good enough to deal with the law and order situation intrinsically. Unfortunately, he was proved wrong in the subsequent years and India, who had championed the notion of non-violence as a tool for global harmony and peace, was forced to fight four conventional wars after independence, all within a span of 25 years. Contrary to the Gandhian philosophy of non-violence and the Nehruvian model of maintaining harmony, the preservation of the unity and integrity of the nation required an identification of potential threats and the capability to defend the nation and maintain sovereignty. At an earlier date, Chanakya, a master strategist, had identified military capabilities as a critical factor for nation building (at the time the role of the police and the military overlapped, and there was no distinction between the functioning of the two organisations). The first realisation regarding the need for a strong security structure came after the 1962 War with China, when Nehru admitted in the Rajya Sabha, that "If we had foresight, known exactly what would happen, we would have done something else... what India has learnt from the Chinese invasion is that in the world of today there is no place for weak nations. We have been living in an unreal world of our own creation."[22] However, in spite of five wars and protracted internal conflicts in the North East and Jammu & Kashmir, the higher defence organisation and defence planning process saw little change. Instead of evolving an efficient system, successive formulations of the defence architecture continued adding layers to the original defence planning structure that made it cumbersome, lethargic and dysfunctional. Instead of being integrated with the MoD, the three services continue to remain attached offices to the MoD and have little say as far as policy decisions are concerned.

Post-Chinese aggression in 1962, the government introduced the Defence Planning Cell within the MoD, that undertook the task of formulating the defence five-year plan. The first five-year plan was prepared for the period between 1964-69. However, the plan "was not based on long term requirements nor [did] it have the assurance of resources to support it".[23] Such an arrangement was bound to fail and was later dumped in favour of another Committee for Defence Planning (CDP). The problem with such committees is the lack of accountability and responsibility required for ensuring the allocation of resources and the implementation of five year plans. In 1986, the Directorate General of Defence Planning Staff (DGDPS) was established under the COSC. The inefficiency in the entire system of defence planning was exposed during the Kargil War and the then Chief of Army Staff Gen. V.P. Malik was forced to say that, "We shall fight with whatever we have."[24] The fact of the matter is that armies do not go to war in the hope of winning, they go to war with a plan, after developing the capabilities required to win. In 2001, the DGDPS was merged with the Integrated Defence Staff (IDS) and a separate branch of Perspective Planning & Force Development was created in the IDS to formulate Long-term Integrated Perspective Plan (LTIPP). There were two objectives behind the creation of the LTIPP, one was to have 15 years' perspective plans for force development and the second was to have five-year plans for immediate requirements. In the absence of a national security strategy or national security objectives, the Raksha Mantri's operational directive is formulated to provide broad policy guidelines for capability building and operational readiness.

The defence planning process should flow from the higher defence organisation's vision. The apex body of the higher defence organisation is the CCS. The Prime Minister is the chairman and the ministers of Home Affairs, Foreign Affairs, Defence and Finance are its members. The National Security Advisor (NSA), chairman COSC, service chiefs and cabinet secretary (as well as other secretaries) also attend the meetings as and when required. The second most important committee is the National Security Council (NSC). Like the CCS, It is headed by the Prime Minister and comprises of the ministers of Defence, External Affairs, Home Affairs and Finance as members. The NSA and the deputy NSA are also members of the NSC (Earlier, the Deputy Chairman of the Planning Commission also used to be a member, but the Planning Commission stands dissolved now). Furthermore, other members from associated organisations may be invited to attend its monthly meetings, as and when required. Aside from issues of national security, the NSC also deals with internal and external security threats to India. The NSC Secretariat (NSCS) provides the NSC and the Prime Minister's Office (PMO) with inputs regarding potential courses of action; however, the advice or proposals made by the NSCS are not binding. The major difference between the two is that the CCS is a decision-making body that deals with current security issues, major decisions related to security, budgeting, approval of raising of a new Strike Corps/acquisition of major weapon systems; whereas the NSC is more concerned with the long-term planning process. It also acts as a facilitating body that assists the PMO and the apex political leadership of the country in the decision-making process. The NSA, the Strategic Policy Group (SPG), the National Security Advisory Board (NSAB) and the NSCS together constitute the NSC. Yet, in spite of such an elaborate system of committees and advisory bodies, the defence planning process is mostly left to the Services Headquarters.

The Services Headquarters work out their LTDP independently and forward the same to the IDS that is responsible for the preparation of the LTIPP. The plans are formulated on the basis of service-specific threat perceptions. In the absence of the Chief of Defence Staff (CDS)/permanent chairman COSC, there is hardly any inter-service prioritisation of plans. (It inevitably becomes a turf war where the three Services push their individual agendas as opposed to ensuring collective capability building.) The plans are then forwarded to the MoD that presumably vets the plans without the necessary professional inputs and domain knowledge. The LTIPP is endorsed by the RM after a brief presentation by the respective Headquarters. However, given bureaucratic obfuscation, infighting within the services, and the lack of follow through, these plans are denied dedicated resource allocation and lack the PMO's approval.

There is a need to recognise that infrastructure development is vital for the application of military capabilities and it needs to be included in the LTIPP. The development of infrastructure is an important component of capability building and requires the active participation of inter-ministerial and inter-governmental agencies. An important case in point, is the neglect of infrastructure development along the Northern Border, despite the 1962 debacle. Infrastructure development is very much a part of the defence planning process and it cannot be neglected.

Shortcomings in the Defence Planning Process

In India, there is a conspicuous absence of a structured defence planning process and the entire system appears to be in a state of flux. There are major organisational voids, functional inefficiencies and procedural gaps. India has still not evolved a functional system for defence planning. While highlighting the importance of clear objectives and directions to the armed forces, Gen. J.F.C. Fuller has said that, "The heart of the problem is not to be sought in types of weapons, but in the aim which governs their use."[25] The application of military force should be governed by a national strategy and mission statement. Ironically, both are missing in India. There is a need to examine and analyse what planning mechanism is the most suitable for the Indian context. Analysts should concentrate on weighing the benefits and risks of various planning approaches. Whether India needs to adopt a defence planning approach that is top-down or bottom-up, resource-constrained or risk avoidance, capability based or threat based, scenario based or on the basis of technological optimisation can only be determined after an extensive survey of current conditions. Existing shortcomings in the defence planning process are as follows:

(a) There are far too many advisory committees (whose advice is not binding for the PMO/CCS/NSC). The MoD is responsible for capability building and the implementation of defence plans but it is not held accountable for its failure in providing the requisite resources. The dual tasks of capability building and the implementation of defence plans are inevitably left to the Services Headquarters, and no other agencies aside from the MoD are held accountable for failures in capability building. Aside from the NSAB, the several other committees that could potentially be held accountable – including the NSC and the SPG – do not even meet or review the internal and external security situation as per mandated periodicity. The meetings of most of the important advisory bodies take place only during crises. They seldom meet during peace time to review or take stock of the implementation of defence plans. As a result, some of these committees merely exist for the sake of existence as archaic remnants of past crises and no longer serve any functional purpose.

(b) Inadequacies in the defence planning process emanate from the absence of clear cut national security objectives and the lack of a national security strategy. The NSC and the NSA have been in existence since 1998, along with a host of committees, but national security objectives and strategies are yet to be formulated. In the absence of these two basic documents for national security, planning remains directionless. The country's security apparatus currently hinges on ad-hoc measures and before implementing strategic reforms, there is a need to address the basic question of 'defence planning for what?'

(c) Currently, there is a tremendous amount of debate regarding whether national security objectives and an overarching strategy should be defined based on a strategic defence review, or whether the strategic defence review should follow after the government has enunciated objectives and strategies. In the absence of well-defined national security objectives, there is a need to carry out a strategic defence review that will form the basis of the policy statements of the government. Once the national security objectives and strategy are defined, thereafter strategic defence review is a periodic process that can be conducted as and when required. Any nation that is plagued by internal and external security threats cannot side-line the importance of this document that would define whether a nation is prepared to deal with security challenges or falls short of the required threshold. At the moment, there is no institutionalised system by which the political leadership is apprised of the threat and capability mismatch. Earlier, the services chiefs use to directly apprise the

Prime Minister through a demi-official letter which now stands suspended.

(d) Another problem that emerges, is that defence plans are not linked to dedicated resources. A case in point is the 12th Defence Plan, 2012-17, which is about to terminate but has not received formal government approval yet. In such a fluid state defence plans remain restricted to paper and rarely get transformed on ground. The gestation period for introducing a weapons system in India is anywhere between five years to 15 years and yet the budget allocation is restricted to one year with no roll-on provisions and/or linkages with five-year defence plans. The LTIPP is for 15 years and services plans are for 5 years, but budget allocation is based on an annual budget that isn't linked to either of these plans.

(e) The PMO, NSC and NSCS have no professional military advisors in their organisations. This causes a major problem as they lack the specific professional expertise required for suitable decision making regarding the country's defence architecture. Institutional linkages between the political leadership and the military are supposed to be provided by the CDS, but for some unknown reason the political leadership has handicapped itself particularly with respect to the issue of establishing a seamless defence planning process. It would not be incorrect to state, that India's national security decision-making process so far, has been archaic. "The military high command stands divorced from national security decision making and the structure of the newly created NSC reflects this deficiency."[26]

(f) One of the main functions of the IDS is to streamline the defence planning process, but in the absence of a CDS or permanent chairman COSC, the IDS only compiles the Long Term Integrated Perspective Planning (LTIPP) and without prioritising collaborative inter-services' needs, forwards the entire service-related Long Term Perspective Plan (LTPP) of each service to the MoD. The MoD has burdened itself with the housekeeping functions of the armed forces, which are best left to them, and it has not been conditioned or trained to think through long-term international and national security issues.[27] Neither does the MoD have qualified professionals on its staff to perform such specialist tasks nor is there any intrinsic military advice available. The plans that are eventually approved by the MoD, are not passed on the basis of professional merit/vetted by an institutional system but are instead arbitrarily approved on the basis of personal equations with individual service headquarters."

(g) After a brief discussion, the LTIPP is endorsed by the RM and is neither discussed by the NSC nor approved by the apex decision-making body. As a result, it remains a stand-alone document that is non-binding. There is no compulsion for the MoD to implement the plan, or for the Finance Ministry to allocate its resources.

(h) There is a tremendous amount of ambiguity regarding the model of the defence planning process. There is a need to adopt a model that can meet the specific requirements of the Indian context. This decision needs to be taken by the political leadership in consultation with the Integrated Defence Headquarters (Services Headquarters) and the Finance Ministry.

(i) Defence Public Sector Undertakings (PSUs) and Defence Research and Development Organisation (DRDO) programmes are unable to meet the timelines of capability development as per the LTIPP or five-year defence plans. This has led to non-implementation of plans for acquisition of certain critical weapons and equipment.

Way Ahead

Given India's complex security environment and massive expenditure on national defence, the planning mechanism needs to be strengthened by the articulation of national security objectives[28] and a streamlining of the defence planning process. This most important function of national security cannot be sustained with such a fragmented approach. Cosmetic and incremental changes will not serve any functional purpose until India shuns obsolete, fatigued ideas and organisations. The planning process needs an extensive review and transformation. Some of the recommended measures are as follows:

(a) India needs its own Goldwater-Nichols Act to undertake defence reforms and to streamline the defence planning process. The act should make it binding for the President and Prime Minister to deliver national security objectives and a national security strategy. Furthermore, the apex level of political administration should also review roles and missions at least once every three years, as is mandated by the Goldwater-Nichols Act. As mentioned earlier, in the Indian context, national security is only debated when there is a crisis, and there is no fixed agenda or periodicity for NSC/CCS meetings. Until or unless these basic issues are streamlined, the question will remain, defence planning for what? To add gravitas to the process of defence planning, the Prime Minister should personally sign and approve the LTIPP and five-year defence plans and the PMO should periodically review the implementation of plans and approve the strategic defence review.

(b) The defence planning process in India is a paradox, and the system is so complex that no plan can see the light of day within the given timeframe. There is a need to go back to the basics, reformulate the model motivating the planning process, and cut short the stages of the defence planning process. Clear political guidance is required in order to determine which of the above mentioned nine models would suit India best. While defining a model is not part of the defence planning process, it is nevertheless essential for the Indian context, since no model currently exists. Considering the complexities of the Indian security dilemma, the options that emerge are as follows:
   (i) Resource Constrained Planning
   Or
   (ii) Threat-cum-capability-based Planning

(c) The MoD is responsible for communicating policy guidelines that have been laid down by political leadership, but it is neither accountable nor responsible for ensuring capability building or implementing defence plans. It acts as an intermediary layer between the political leadership and the Services Headquarters. Similarly, the IDS was created to integrate services with the MoD, but it has become another layer between the government and the Service Headquarters and is rarely able to integrate the two effectively. If any successful modernisation is to take place, the integration of the MoD and Services Headquarters is a necessity. Not only is the relationship a necessity but the relationship must also be one of equals as opposed to the master-servant hierarchy that currently exists. Complete integration is vital, with defence professionals serving as part of the MoD for providing specialised advice, and ensuring the efficient implementation and review of the defence planning process.

(d) Integrated Planning at the level of Services Headquarters is a must, and the authority to prioritise tasks and requirements, should be with the CDS or Chairman COSC. This will remove the current anomaly of the IDS being unable to overrule the Services Headquarters.

(e) The budget plays a vital role in the defence planning process. Once missions and capabilities are defined and defence plans are approved, what matters is the allocation of the budget. There are various models that can be applied, but a military that is continuously engaged in national security duties due to internal and external threats needs a budget support that caters for short- and long-term capability building. The model given in Figure 1 is a globally accepted norm.

Figure 1: Continuous Budget Support to Prevent Mismatch in Assigned Mission and Capabilities

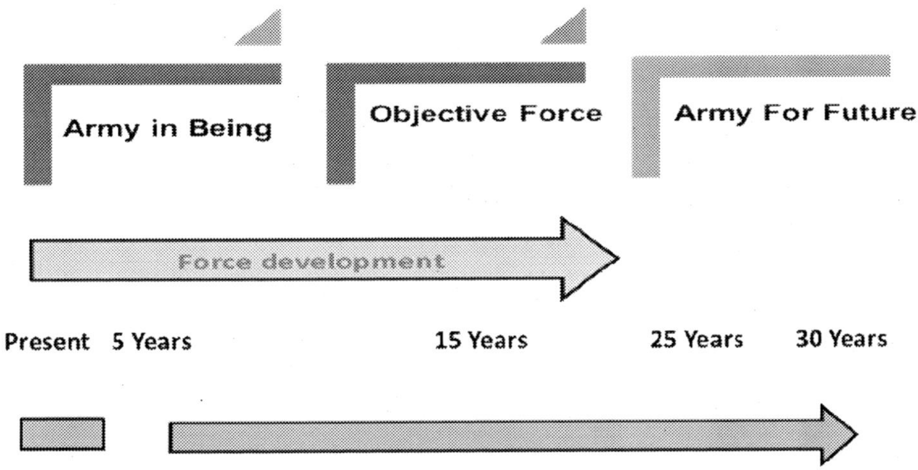

Figure 1 suggests that a nation should divide capability building and force development into three categories – i.e., existing force, objective force (that a nation should develop in the next 10-15 years) and future force (military that is required for future wars 25 to 30 years). Current threats are known and the contours of future threats can be assessed through strategic defence reviews, economic development parameters, the development of R&D, the development of doctrines, military modernisation plans and country-specific net assessment of potential adversaries. To put into practice such a model, resource allocation cannot be sacrosanct and needs to be adaptable instead. The budgeting process should also be a three tiered one as demonstrated below:

(i) There should be an annual budget with the provision of rolling over to the next year and it should cater for maintaining and consolidating current military capabilities.

(ii) The process of achieving objective force is linked to defence plans and the LTIPP (five to 15 years). This requirement cannot be met through the annual defence budget. However, yearly allocations based on approved defence plans could be considered as an alternate source of funding. Once the LTIPP is approved, it should receive budget support independent of the annual budget for capability building.

(iii) Investment in the development of the future army can be made through R&D and joint ventures for niche technology and infrastructure development. In a nutshell, linking the process of planning with resource allocation is the best way ahead. Defence plans and resource allocation should be made before the plan is put into effect.

(f) India's defence planning process requires streamlining and should cast aside unwieldy bureaucratic processes and reduce the number of advisory committees that currently exist in order to put in place a simple planning process. The recommended steps that should be adopted are as follows:

(i) On the basis of the strategic defence review, national political objectives, values and existing capabilities, the NSC should define national security objectives and strategy. After debating it in the NSC, apex political leadership should promulgate national security objectives and strategy. The PMO and the NSC should review objectives and strategy every three years based on the strategic defence review.

(ii) The CDS/Integrated Headquarters should formulate mission capability goals and lay down priorities for a force structure on the basis of threat/environmental assessment, national security objectives, strategy, access to technology, existing capabilities and capability mismatch.

(iii) The Services Headquarters should formulate defence plans on the basis of the parameters laid down by the CDS/Integrated Headquarters. The Services Headquarters should consider problems like capability mismatch, emerging threats, technology optimisation, force development priorities, resource constraints, indigenous defence industry potential/capabilities and military doctrines before finalising the defence plans.

(iv) The Integrated Headquarters/CDS should lay down the priorities of force development and prepare an LTIPP on the basis of service defence plans. The MoD in consultation with the Finance Ministry should work out the dedicated resources required for the implementation of the LTIPP and five-year defence plans. The Finance Ministry should also indicate the budget available for the five-year defence plans and how each year's allocation could be rolled over to the next year/five-year plan.

(v) Before the plan is approved by the government, the NSC should debate and discuss the rationale underlying critical projects and zone in on areas that need focus. Thereafter the apex decision-making body could approve the plan or ask the review to include or delete certain proposals that may not merit focus in the defence plan. Former US President Barack Obama had six rounds of deliberations with the Pentagon, the NSC and several think tanks before he approved the Military Doctrine in 2012. It is a bad idea to pursue, approve or reject such an important subject through file notings without consulting the end users (Services Headquarters). Ideally, the LTIPP and five-year plans should be personally signed by the Prime Minister to assure their sanctity and ensure that they are made binding for inter-government agencies and inter-ministerial groups.

(vi) On approval of the plan, the Finance Minister and the MoD should consult together and earmark dedicated resources for the plan over and above the yearly defence budget.

(vii) Once the resources have been earmarked it should be the MoD and Services headquarters' responsibility to ensure that the timelines in defence plans are met.

viii) The Defence Minister should review the implementation of the plans on a yearly basis, and the PMO/CCS should review the implementation of the defence plans after every two years.

Several defence planning models have been advocated by various analysts. However, given the specificity of the context, the following three sets seem most appropriate and can be adopted with certain modifications:

(a) The first model, shown in Figure 2, demonstrates the process of the LTDP. It is simple, satisfies all parameters and ensures the involvement of all stakeholders. It is also top down, determines clear responsibilities and accountability, covers all aspects of the planning process (from the political level to the services level) and has been tested by many transformational armies. (The

Figure 2: Process of LTDP[29]

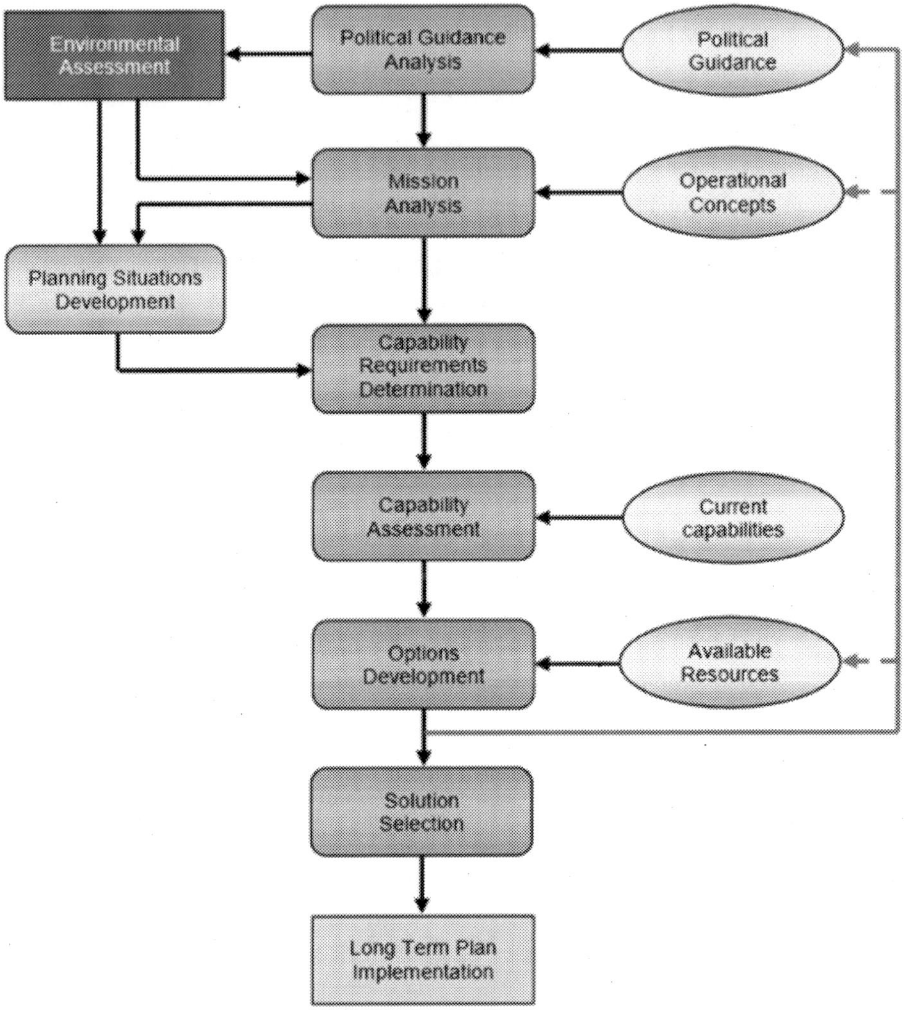

Defence Requirements Review of the North American Treaty Organisation uses a very similar model.)

(b) The capability-based model, shown in Figure 3, has been adopted by the NATO and the US with certain modifications based on the strategic defence review. It is essential to remember that grand narratives and political visions of desired capabilities aside, at the end of the day, defence plans are constrained by resources. The corner stone of this model is affordable capability.

Figure 3: Affordable Capability-based Planning Process[30]

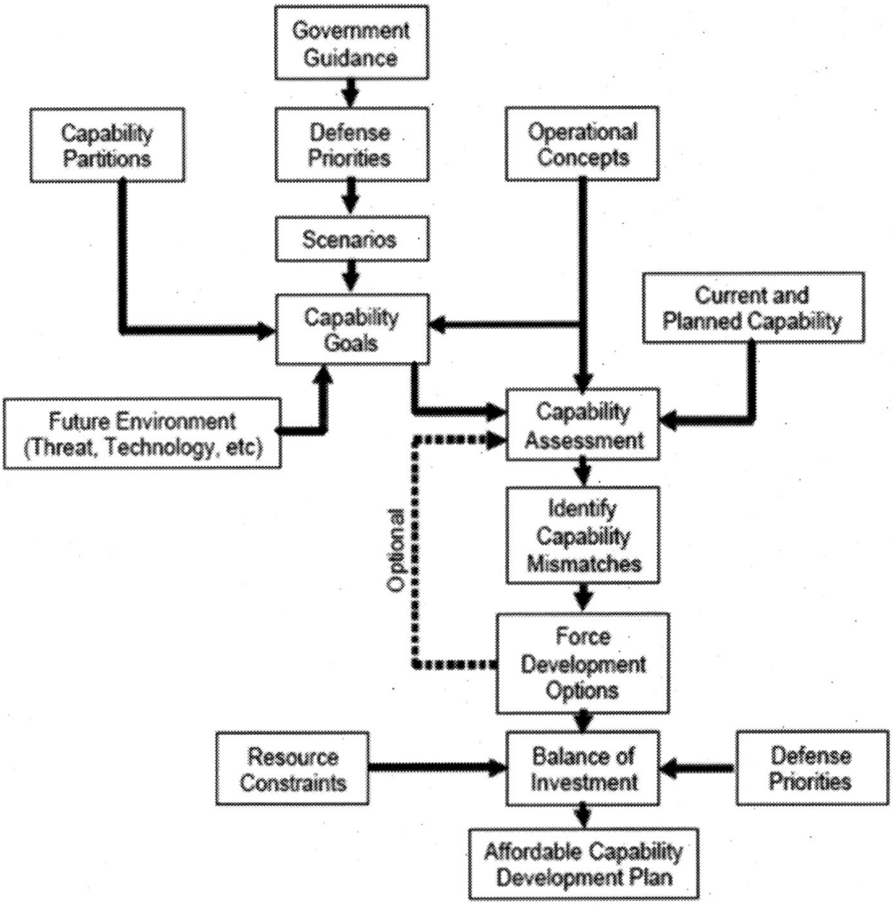

(c) General BM Kapoor (retd.) has recommended a defence planning process for India as shown in Figure 4. Though Gen Kapoor has also suggested an affordable capability based planning process, it appears to be more cumbersome compared to the other models, requiring feedback and consultancy at every stage of the process. While incorporating inclusivity and increasing consultancy and feedback are certainly desirable mechanisms, doing so at every single stage, might end up detracting from the model itself, thereby causing bureaucratic delays and feedback loops.

(d) The need of the hour is the adoption of a workable and affordable defence plan. The plan should be simple, manageable, with short,

Figure 4: Defence Planning Process for India

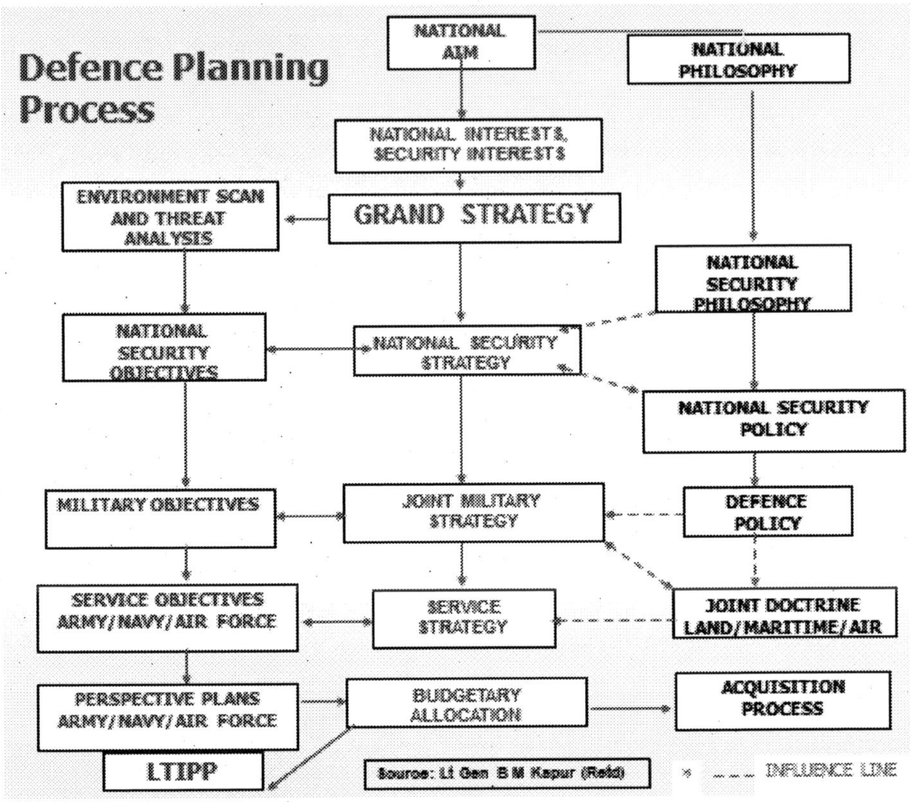

Source: Lt Gen B M Kapur (Retd).

synergized processes preventing bureaucratic red tape. The defence planning process should have the sanctity and approval of the apex political leadership of the government and should be binding on all stakeholders responsible for national security. The model recommended in Figure 4 is too complex and would require a long process of reform and restructuring. The author, therefore, recommends a combination of the models in Figures 2 and 3 as the most suitable option for India. The added advantage of such a customized model is that it can be tweaked based on the restructuring of the MoD and the creation of the CDS/ permanent chairman COSC. The suggested model is delineated in Figure 5.

Figure 5: Recommended Defence Planning Process for India

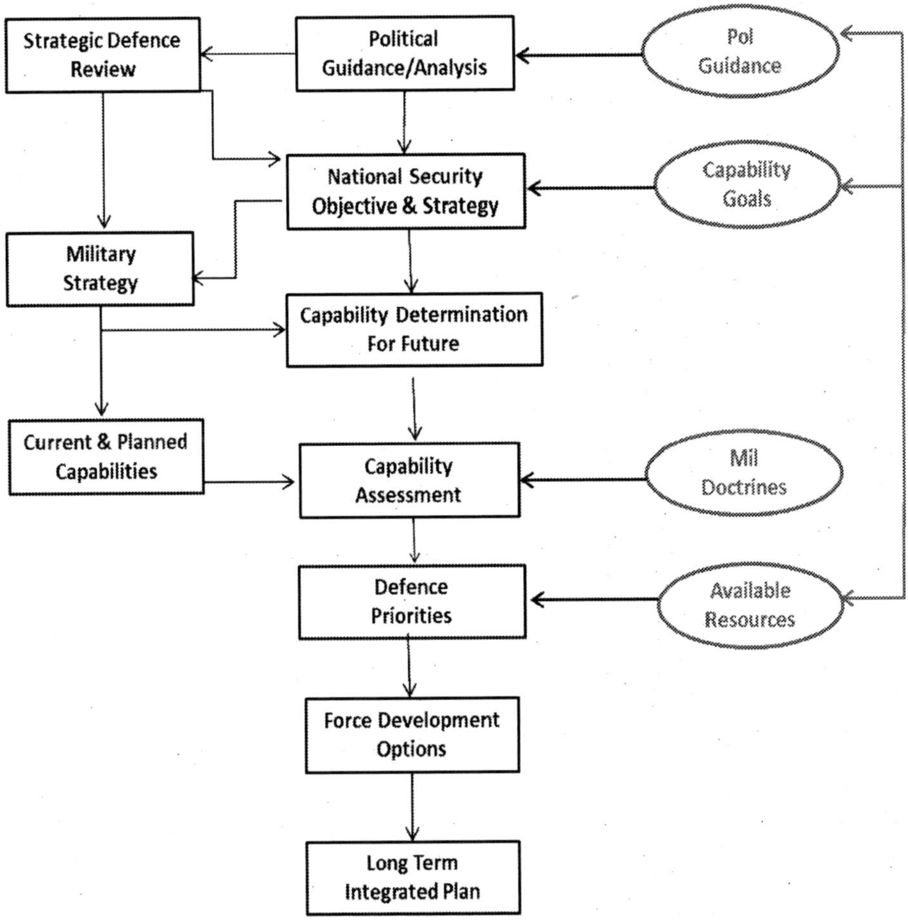

Conclusion

Security challenges today, are outpacing capability building process, and in such an environment, the question that arises is – how much is enough? A resilient defence planning process needs an interdisciplinary approach that includes environmental assessment, the articulation of national security objectives, a holistic national security strategy, cost assessment, capability mismatch and specific mission objectives for forces. Over and above defence planning, dedicated budget allocation and timelines for capability and force development are equally important to ensure the strict implementation of plans. The armed forces have no direct access to the apex levels of political leadership and continue to be deprived the opportunity to participate in the decision-making process of the NSC. This anomaly is hurting the nation; the 1962, 1965 and 1999 (Kargil) wars, along with the protracted conflict in Jammu and Kashmir have exposed the dysfunctional nature of the defence planning process. This is a tremendous cause for concern particularly since, in a country that lacks strategic culture the armed forces have a more vital role to play – as compared to civil bureaucrats[31] – in preparing to fight and win the nation's wars.

In 1961, after taking over as Secretary of Defense, Robert S. McNamara decided to take over the defence planning process and resource allocation from defence forces. He felt that capability building was a national responsibility and that the forces must focus on the development of their operational capabilities. Because the defence plans, resources allocation, programming and budgeting system are all integrated, the planning process will fail if it is not controlled by an appropriate apex authority. In India, the MoD can only assume such a role if the three Services and the DRDO are integrated with the MoD – as was recommended by the Subramanian Committee. Such a reformulation of the MoD and its associated wings' roles would require a complete restructuring of the current defence architecture and that appears to be a remote possibility under the given circumstances.

There is a need for the legislative institutionalisation of the NSC as a constitutional body to transform it into a decision-making authority because under the current charter it is a decision facilitating agency for the Prime Minister. Moreover, national security directives, national security objectives and strategy should bear the signature of the incumbent Prime Minister so that accountability is assured.[32]

NOTES

1. J.F.C. Fuller, *The Conduct of War, 1789-1961: A Study of the Impact of the French, Industrial, and Russian Revolutions on War and Its Conduct* (London: Eyre Metheun, 1972), 128.
2. Henrik Breitenbauch, "Defence Planning", *Academic Foresights*, No. 13, January-June 2015.
3. Stephan Frühling, *Defence Planning and Uncertainty, Preparing for the Next Asia-Pacific War*, Routledge, London and New York, 2016, P 192.
4. Dejan Stojkovic and Bjørn Robert Dahl, "Methodology for Long Term Defence Planning", Norwegian Defence Research Establishment (FFI), February 28, 2007.
5. Glenn A. Kent, *A Framework for Defense Planning*, RAND Corporation, Santa Monica, 1989, at http://www.rand.org/pubs/reports/R3721.html.
6. Upeka Premaratne, "Reconciling the Irreconcilable: The Use of Reasonable Consequentialism for the Conundrum of National Security and Fundamental Rights", KDU International Research Conference, September 8, 2016.
7. *National Security System Handbook*, Department of the Prime Minister and Cabinet,

August 2016, p. 8.

8. Ibid
9. Paul K. Davis, "Defense Planning in an Era of Uncertainty: East Asian Issues", in Natalie W. Crawford and Chung-in Moon (eds.), *Emerging Threats, Force Structures, and the Role of Air Power in Korea*, Rand Corporation, Santa Monica, 2000, pp. 25-47 at http://www.rand.org/content/dam/rand/pubs/conf_proceedings/CF152/CF152.chap2.pdf.
10. Gen. V.P. Malik, "Defence Planning in India", in Gen. V.P. Malik and Brig. Vinod Anand (eds.), *Defence Planning Problems and Prospects*, Manas Publications, New Delhi, 2006, P 21.
11. V.S. Shekhawat, "Challenges in Defence Planning", *Strategic Analysis*, 30 (4), October-December 2006, pp. 689-707.
12. *Handbook on Long Term Defence Planning*, Research and Technology Organisation (RTO) Technical Report 69, April 2003.
13. "The Use of Scenarios in Long Term Defence Planning", *Plausible Futures Newsletter*, April 10, 2007, at https://plausiblefutures.wordpress.com/2007/04/10/the-use-of-scenarios-in-long-term-defence-planning/ (Accessed January 28,2017).
14. Dejan Stojkovic and Bjørn Robert Dahl, No. 3.
15. Michael D. Hobkirk, Land, Sea or Air?: Military Priorities – Historical Choices, Royal United Services Institute, 1992, P 4
16. Colonel Bojan Zrniæ, "The New Trends in Defence Planning and Their Impact on the Defence Planning Systems in Transitional Countries", Issue 67, *Odbrana*, 2008.
17. Dejan Stojkovic and Bjørn Robert Dahl, No. 3.
18. Ibid.
19. Pawe³ Fleischer, "NATO Defence Planning Process. Implications for Defence Posture", *Securitologia*, 21 (1), 2015.
20. Admiral Arun Prakash, "National Security Reforms: Ten Years after the Kargil Committee Report", USI National Security Lecture, 2012.
21. "Nehru Wanted to Scrap Army: Former General", accessed from http://defenceforumindia.com/forum/threads/nehru-wanted-to-scrap-army-former-general.15710/
22. Jawaharlal Nehru, in Rajya Sabha, 1963, quoted in, "Why India Lost the 1962 Border War?", Canary Trap, at, http://www.canarytrap.in/2012/11/03/why-india-lost-the-1962-border-war(Accessed September 15, 2017).
23. Laxman Kumar Behra, "Defence Planning in India", *Journal of Defence Studies*, 4(3), pp. 132-3.
24. Vice Admiral Premvir Das (retd), "Is India Ready for War? No, Not Really", *rediff.com*, http://www.rediff.com/news/column/is-india-ready-for-war-no-not-really/20170816.htm, August 16, 2017
25. Craig Beutel, "Reviewing the Conduct of War, 1789-1961", review of *The Conduct of War, 1789-1961: A Study Of The Impact Of The French, Industrial, and Russian Revolutions on War and Its Conduct*, by J.F.C. Fuller, The Bridge, September 28, 2016, at http://thestrategybridge.org/the-bridge/2016/9/28/reviewing-the-conduct-of-war-1789-1961 (Accessed February 03, 2017).
26. Dr Subash Kapila, "India's National Security Council – A Critical Review", Paper

No. 123, South Asia Analysis Group, May 10, 2000.

27. Pravin Joshi, "Defence Budgeting System: Need for Change", *Strategic Analysis*, 29(4), October-December 2005.
28. Laxman Kumar Behra, No. 20.
29. Dejan Stojkovic and Bjørn Robert Dahl, No. 3.
30. "Guide to Capability-Based Planning", The Technical Cooperation Program (TTCP), Alexandria, 2004, p. 4.
31. Dr Subash Kapila, No 22.
32. Ibid.

7

Transformation: Military Force to Military Power

Vinod Bhatia

> *At a time when major powers are reducing their forces and rely more on technology, we are still constantly seeking to expand the size of our forces. Modernisation and expansion of forces at the same time is a difficult and unnecessary goal. We need forces that are agile, mobile and driven by technology, not just human valour.*
>
> – Prime Minister Narendra Modi, Combined Commanders Conference, December 15, 2015[1]

While addressing the Combined Commanders Conference onboard INS *Vikramaditya* in December 2015, Prime Minister Modi challenged senior military commanders to reform their 'beliefs, doctrines, objectives and strategies'. He identified six areas that required military reforms. These included restructuring the higher defence organisation, improving defence planning, synergising joint warfare, enabling manpower rationalisation (teeth to tail ratio), boosting defence procurement and specializing professional military education. The Prime Minister's directions can be seen as a challenge to the established structures, systems and organisations of India's military and the mind-set of senior military leaders.[2]

It is an established fact that nations always prepare to fight the last war. To assume that the armed forces are not prepared to combat future security challenges would be incorrect. However, the concepts, doctrines, capabilities and capacities that they currently possess to do so may not be adequate. The Ministry of Defence (MoD) and the armed forces have shied away from initiating reforms and disturbing the status quo. The resistance to structural and systematic changes – review of policies, procedures and processes to keep pace with future security challenges and addressing modern-day warfare needs – remains a major weakness. The armed forces are mandated to ensure the territorial integrity of our nation. This implies securing the various borders shared with other countries including – 3,488 km of the Line of Actual Control (LAC) along the India-China border, 772 km of the Line of Control (LoC) in Jammu and Kashmir (J&K), 126 km of the Actual Ground Position Line (AGPL) in the Siachen Glacier as well as a 7,516 km long coastline. India's unsettled and porous borders, that are being manned by the army, lie at altitudes of 4,500 meters and above, with woefully inadequate infrastructure and extreme climatic conditions, demanding ab-initio deployment of a large number of troops. The continuing proxy war being waged by Pakistan, the ever increasing and omnipresent threats from terrorists and the imperative to safeguard our national interests and assets in our areas of influence, necessitate the development of enhanced capabilities. Given the versatile nature and the multiplicity of threats to our national security across all domains, it is essential that a pragmatic and dispassionate analysis be carried out so as to derive desired military capabilities and enhance capacities. Furthermore, since the defence budget is limited, and will remain so, due to resources being deviated towards dealing with the national priorities of development and poverty alleviation, it becomes essential to utilise the limited resources provided efficiently. Furthermore, emerging security challenges also necessitate a manpower-centric deployment of troops for border defence along the LAC, in order to ensure the sanctity of the LoC by providing an effective counter infiltration grid on the LoC and counter-terrorist operations.

The MoD and the armed forces need to review and rebalance force structures to optimise combat power and synergise all assets to transform the armed forces from a 'military force to a military power' capable of securing the nation and its people against the full spectrum of conflict. This can only be achieved by a pragmatic approach in ensuring synergy, integration and jointness among the MoD and the armed forces both inter and intra-service. Further necessary steps that need to be taken include revamping the logistics support systems by integrating civil infrastructure and resources thereby reducing the teeth to tail ratio, inducting 'Force

Substitutors' and most importantly – engaging in a hard and dispassionate review of the effectiveness and efficiency of over six lakh non-combatants in various support organisations who are paid out of the defence budget.

The military needs change, it is time for reform to ensure a more effective, efficient, present relevant, and future ready military in order to meet multiple security challenges across the full spectrum of conflict, given the pragmatic but limited nature of the defence budget. The defence budget cannot be stretched beyond a point, which means the MoD and the armed forces have a tough choice for resource deployment. Reducing revenue expenses and increasing spending for capital pose the biggest challenges for the MoD right now.

Wars in today's context cannot be fought with outdated organisations and structures. There is a need for engendering jointness between the three services, as currently, the army, navy and air force conduct operations in stand-alone mode, with coordination and cooperation based on personalities. War is a joint endeavour, where all the elements of national power and all the resources of the union need to be synergised for fighting it. This truism is even more relevant in the present context, as war today is a complex phenomenon and this complexity is only going to increase in the future. The reasons for increasing complexity include technological advancements, the nature of modern war, emergent threats and challenges and the reality of nuclear weapons in the arsenal of our potential adversaries. Consequently, a joint force, that acts in an integrated manner is not just desirable but imperative. The complexities of the future security environment require India to be prepared to face a wide range of threats of varying levels of intensity. Success in countering these threats will require skilful integration of the core competencies of the three Services and their transformation into an integrated force structure. However, re-organisation by itself will not succeed in achieving such integration. What is required to ensure such a strategic structural change is a change in the collective mind-set – a change that makes every soldier, sailor and air warrior feel that he/she is a member of the Indian armed forces, and not just the Indian Army, the Indian Navy or the Indian Air Force. The Indian military is also among the least 'joint' major militaries in the world and there is a lot of scope for resource optimisation through in-house reforms such as enabling joint intelligence, planning, training, communications, logistics and force development prior to structured joint operations.

Despite the best efforts of countless dedicated people, the resources allocated for national security are rarely used to their full potential.

Departments and organisations, accomplish their core missions for the most part but they are ill equipped to integrate their efforts and to deliver efficient results on a sustained basis. Good people may sometimes rise above an inefficient system, but over time the limitations of the system make the task needlessly difficult. As large resources are involved in national security, there is little scope for inefficiency in managing the nation's defence. Today, the nation faces a mounting backlog of defence purchases, with finite resources and competing priorities. Under the circumstances, a constant push towards higher levels of efficiency is essential for safeguarding national interests. This is best achieved by aligning authority and ensuring accountability by appointing a single authority to ensure operational preparedness in the form of the much deliberated and delayed Chief of Defence Staff (CDS). For the present the Service Chiefs will continue to be responsible for operational readiness.

It is a national security imperative to appoint a CDS with the requisite authority and mandate. The envisaged role of the CDS could be as follows:

- (a) The CDS's primary role should be as principal advisor to the Prime Minister and the government (through the Defence Minister), on all matters pertaining to India's national security.
- (b) The CDS should provide an overarching 'strategic vision' and be responsible for all strategic perspective planning, as well as operational and contingency planning.
- (c) In peacetime, the primary task of the CDS is to focus exclusively on war preparedness with direct bearing on strategic operations.
- (d) In terms of war preparedness, the CDS should play a major role in the refinement and integration of operational plans, creating logistical means to sustain operational plans and ensuring the build-up of strategic reserves of arms, ammunition, military hardware, supplies and fuel requirements. In effect, he will be responsible for the financial planning, budgetary allocation and force structures of the three Services.
- (e) The CDS should prepare the annual Defence Intelligence Estimate and assess the requirements of defence intelligence to meet the existent threats overall.
- (f) The CDS should exercise operational command over the Strategic Forces Command, the Andaman and Nicobar Command and other bi-service or tri-service commands that may evolve in the future, like Cyber, Space and Special Operations Commands, until the formation of integrated theatre commands.
- (g) The CDS has to be viewed as the 'Head' of the Indian armed

forces in terms of providing strategic control, strategic direction and strategic vision.

(h) The CDS should play the primary role in the formulation of defence policies.

Another major weakness that currently exists is the lack of a promulgated and propagated National Security Strategy (NSS). This needs to be corrected as soon as possible and an NSS promulgated. This is a national imperative. A rational and well-structured National Military Strategy (NMS) can only flow from a well-defined, holistic NSS. Furthermore, the chain continues down the line as the National Military Objectives (NMO) can only be culled out from the NMS and the armed forces derive the desired military capabilities from the NMOs. Present capability building is mostly based on single service requirements that are at best coordinated at the Headquarters Integrated Defence Staff (HQ IDS) to 'Please all'. It is an important and a necessary dictate of the budget allocations that military capabilities are synergised in sync with the NSS.

Despite the creation of an Integrated Headquarters of the MoD (Army/ Air Force/Navy), the three Services continue to be merely attached offices with inadequate say in policy formation. There is an urgent and immediate need to correct this by ensuring the integration of the Services with not only the MoD but with all structures of the MoD, including the Defence Research and Development Organisation (DRDO), Ordnance Factory Board (OFB) and Defence Public Sector Undertakings (DPSUs). As of now, the latter continue to function in a stand-alone, suboptimal mode as a separate vertical of the MoD. For effective functioning of these organisations, there is a need for meaningful integration by posting service officers both at the apex and functional levels of these organisations. A DRDO lab will be more responsive if it is headed conjointly by a scientist and a service officer of equivalent rank. Similarly the general manager of certain Ordnance Factories should also be service officers. The shipyards and dockyards are headed by naval officers and their efficacy and ability to provide the navy with what it needs is well known. This needs to be replicated for Ordnance Factories.

Before analysing the rationale and requirement of the armed forces, a look at the present manpower strengths and budget is a must. The total strength of the Indian Army is approximately 1.2 million, the Indian Navy is approximately 80,000 strong, and Indian Air Force has another 140,000 taking the armed forces total to approximately 1.4 million and making it the world's fourth-largest armed force after China, Russia and the US. In addition to the 1.4 million strong military, the MoD also employs a little over 600,000 civilian employees of which 260,000 are embedded into the three Services and the remaining 340,000 form part of the 30-odd civil organisations of the MoD such as the Indian Ordnance Factories, DRDO, DPSUs, Controller General of Defence Accounts (CGDA), Directorate General of Quality Assurance (DGQA), General Reserve Engineer Force (GREF) and the Military Engineering Service (MES), among others. The question that emerges therefore is how do these figures stack up? Against a fighting element of approximately nine lakh soldiers – which includes Infantry, Mechanised Infantry, Armoured, Artillery, Engineers, Air Defence and Aviation, there are 450,000 uniformed personnel in the combat support services, in addition to approximately six lakh civilian employees, and hence the infamous and unaffordable teeth to tail ratio of 1:1. Given these statistics, there can be no doubt that the armed forces need to 'right size' particularly in order to meet the imperatives of raising the Special Operations, Cyber and Space Commands and to cater to the growth of Army Aviation, Electronic Warfare, Unmanned Aerial Vehicle (UAV) units and Control, Communications, Computers, Intelligence, Surveillance and Reconnaissance (C4ISR).

The overall ratio of revenue to capital expenditure is 64.67 : 35.33 percent. For the army alone, the ratio of revenue to capital expenditure is 81 : 19 percent; of which 73 percent of revenue expenditure is for pay and allowances, which seems rather disproportionate, and hampers modernisation. For far too long, the armed forces have looked for transformation and reforms within their own service. Effective reforms cannot take place without the direct intervention of the MoD. In sync with the Prime Minister's directions, former Raksha Mantri Mr Manohar Parrikar constituted the General Shekatkar Committee, which in itself was a positive and path-breaking initiative as it aimed to "enhance combat capabilities by rebalancing the defence expenditure" scrutinising all organisations and every person paid out of the defence budget. The committee submitted its report at the end of December 2016 and the report is believed to be all encompassing, doable, and includes transition management. The implementation of the Shekatkar Committee recommendations in totality would be a major contributory factor in transforming the Indian military force into a military power.

India is a "risen and responsible" power, however there is a need to achieve "strategic autonomy"; at present, India continues to be one of the largest exporters of arms and equipment. The DRDO, established in 1958, has a network of 51 laboratories with a 30,000 workforce that unfortunately comprises of only about 7,000 scientists, despite spending nearly 6 per cent of the defence budget. The DRDO has achieved success in strategic defence systems and some cutting-edge technologies but falls short in meeting the defence needs and soldiers' aspirations of tactical defence systems including small arms in the low-medium technological domain. The DRDO needs to cut manpower costs as each scientist cannot be supported by four administrative persons (a teeth to tail ratio of 1:4).

Similarly, there is an immediate requirement to revamp the Indian Ordnance Factories which have a huge strength of nearly 90,000 personnel, with most of the factories not being cost effective, forcing the captive armed forces to procure Ordnance Factory-produced products at exorbitant costs and thereby adding to the skewed defence revenue budget. The Indian Ordnance Factories need to be cost efficient and competitive, or the armed forces should be allowed to source their non-critical needs from the growing private sector. The case of various DPSUs is no better, with the same problems cropping up aside from marginally better cost effectiveness. One method for ensuring efficiency would be if some of the Indian Ordnance Factories functioned on the Government Owned Corporate Operated (GOCO) model. The Indian Ordnance Factories should no longer be seen as a tool for providing socio-economic benefits to the local population. It is a well-documented fact that the armed forces being captive customers are made to pay exorbitant rates for the equipment manufactured by them.

The DGQA functions directly under MoD's Defence Production. The control for contract awarding, ensuring cost effective and timely manufacture and quality assurance is under the secretary defence production. As there are no checks and balances this leads to issue of poor quality products with cost and time overruns. It has been reported that over 180 tank barrels have burst during practice firing leading to loss of life and limb. The DGQA, the Directorate General of Aeronautical Quality Assurance (DGAQA) and the Director General Naval Quality Assurance (DGNQA) should function under the HQ IDS/Chief of Integrated Defence Staff to the Chiefs of Staff Committee (CISC). The DGQA has a total manpower of approximately 11,000, but the technical staff – which forms the core competency of the quality assurance and quality checks is only about 3,500, the rest being administrative support staff, a ratio of 1:2.

The defence accounts department of the MoD in itself is an unproductive drain on the defence budget. Instead of being a watchdog and contributing to financial efficiency, the armed forces often are frustrated on account of the financial delays that take place as a result of archaic regulations, procedures and processes. The armed forces are subjected to both pre- and post-audits leading to cost and time overruns in the execution of various projects and contracts with little or no value addition. It is only twice in the last two decades that the capital budget has been fully spent. The capital budget should be a roll on budget wherein the unspent funds are carried forward to the next year. The 20,000 strong workforce of auditors have raised approximately 65,000 audit objections annually over the last five years, which translates to less than four per auditor per annum. This workforce can be reduced by about 85 percent without any adverse impact, and the CGDA can adopt "e-auditing"/ Computer Aided Audit Technique (CAAT), thus accruing major savings in manpower costs. As Bhartendu Kumar Singh, of the Indian Defence Accounts Service, in an article in the *Eurasia Review* points out, "The Accounts Branch of the Indian Air Force, for example, has 492 commissioned officers and 7,000 men catering to the pay matters of 1,60,000 officers and men in the Air Force. On a competitive note, the same can be provided by 300 people on the civilian side very easily."[3]

The MES is another white elephant manned by over 80,000 personnel with a budget of approximately 14,000 crore, spending over 70 per cent of the budget on salaries. The MES can easily be reduced to about 30 per cent of its present strength by outsourcing the maintenance services in all Cantonments and military stations during peacetime, leaving the MES to execute only capital works and maintenance contracts.

The National Cadet Corps (NCC) is an excellent organisation contributing to nation building and youth development. The growth of the NCC is hampered by a lack of resource in terms of instructors and staff. The MoD and NCC should expand, and the resource requirement can be met by resorting to re-employment of officers, Junior Commissioned Officers (JCOs) and Non-commissioned Officers (NCOs) from the areas where they are to be posted.

The present-day struggle world-over, is the retention of trained, experienced and quality manpower. Due to the varied terrain and multiplicity of tasks, the Indian armed forces need a judicious mix of young, experienced and trained manpower resources. This can be best achieved by enhancing the colour service of the soldier by two years. This will also result in recurring savings in the pension bill of around 13 to 15 thousand crore every year. A sum which can be better utilised for modernisation.

India is probably one of two mega nations in the world that is adding to its military might, by resorting to manpower accretions. The other nation is the US where the Trump administration has approved a 70,000 or

11 percent accretion to the army and marines, indicating a shift in the way they plan to meet future security challenges. China on the other hand has taken an alternative route, and post the September 04, 2015, military parade where China demonstrated its military might, President Xi Jinping surprised the People's Liberation Army (PLA) by declaring cuts of 3,00,000 troops.

The MoD needs to take a long hard look at the effectiveness and the teeth to tail ratio of various organisations functioning directly under its control – over and above the armed forces. A scrutiny of flab among the armed forces alone will not achieve the desired budgetary rebalance as is commonly believed. The army which is held guilty of excessive manpower and blamed for its major expenditure on manpower costs, is allotted 56 percent of the defence budget, with 1.2 million soldiers. It is a well-known fact that the Indian army soldier costs minimum and delivers the maximum.

The armed forces – particularly the army – need to look inwards too, and improve the teeth to tail ratio, by integrating the civil resources and infrastructure available, outsourcing certain services, and revamping policies, procedures and processes. The army also needs to review certain organisations that are suboptimal in today's environment and context.

The Corps of Electrical and Mechanical Engineering (EME) is the third-largest force in the army, next only to the Infantry and Artillery. Major savings can be affected by outsourcing the repair and servicing of "B" vehicles to the original equipment manufacturer's (OEM) service stations. The service stations are now located in most of our border areas and can easily be exploited – as is being done by the Assam Rifles. The maintenance of specialist vehicles should continue to be the mandate of the EME. The EME also needs to reduce the number of echelons of repairs. It is envisaged that major savings of up to 30,000 personnel can be effected from the EME alone by changing archaic procedures and outsourcing repairs without any adverse impact on combat effectiveness. The Army Base Workshops should be corporatized on the basis of the government-owned contractor operated model. Additionally, the many station workshops located in cities and major towns have become redundant establishments which can be disbanded, and their workload can be outsourced to civil service stations by the units.

The Army Ordnance Corps (AOC) also needs to modernise and cut down its long chain to enhance effectiveness, save time and manpower costs and add efficiency. It is unpardonable that in today's information age the army has been unable to capture the 4 lakh plus inventory, thus leading to unnecessary wastage and manpower costs. The vehicle depots and companies also need to be disbanded and the OEMs should be instructed to deliver the vehicles straight to the user units. Similarly, the ASC also needs to shut down butcheries and resort to procurement through trade. The number of integral transport units can be reduced, and vehicles can be hired through contracts, which will further reduce manpower, acquisition and maintenance costs. Particularly since provisions already exist to requisition civil transport during emergencies. The operational need for animal transport, similarly, needs to be reviewed as roads and tracks now connect a larger number of areas in the forward zone. This will also facilitate a reduction of the Remount and Veterinary Corps. Similarly, petroleum units can be done away with by resorting to direct dependency and hold of reserves by the trade.

The communications requirements manned by the corps of signals, can contribute to major redeployment of manpower for Cyber and Electronic Warfare, post review. The Air Formation Signal Regiment is an example where the same can be applied. The communications architecture should be theaterised and all stakeholders should be able to plug and play. The various dedicated signal regiments – from command, corps, division and brigades should be restructured to form theatre-specific communication groups, except the signal elements of the strike corps. The armed forces should move towards joint communications, optimising all resources including the civil ones.

As mentioned earlier, certain defunct organisations need to be closed without delay, such as the military farms, butcheries and stationery depots. This is merely an overview of the major manpower savings that can be initiated without any adverse effects and the requisitioned finances can be utilised for the modernisation of the armed forces by redeploying them towards emergent requirements such as Space, Cyber and Special Operations Command.

It is imperative that the MoD initiate the right changes and implement the recommendations of the Shekatkar Committee in totality, thus rebalancing defence expenditure and ensuring additional funds for the much-needed modernisation of the armed forces.

NOTES

1. http://pib.nic.in/newsite/PrintRelease.aspx?relid=133265
2. Ibid.
3. http://www.orfonline.org/research/rightsizing-the-military-the-need-for-a-comprehensive-examination/

8

Intelligence Reforms to Meet Future Challenges

Kamal Davar

Aside from being an inescapable ingredient in the successful pursuit of its statecraft, the intelligence edifice of a nation is a critical instrument of its safety and security as well. "Intelligence is the first line of defence", is unfortunately, a truism not widely accepted, but only acknowledged when nations or organisations are confronted with unexpected or catastrophic calamities. It is also a fact that most mishaps and security lapses are conveniently ascribed to intelligence failures even in cases where they were systemic shortcomings or leadership/organisational inadequacies. Conversely, credit for any strategic or tactical success is very rarely given to intelligence personnel as for obvious reasons, intelligence successes need to remain shrouded in secrecy. Practitioners of the craft of intelligence must remain silent warriors as there is "no place for drum beating in the business of intelligence".[1]

The question we must pose to ourselves now is that – as a rising regional and global power, does India have a responsive and strong intelligence structure in place? Threats today are increasingly diverse and pose formidable external and internal challenges to the nation's security and economic well-being. Currently, the nation is also challenged by both conventional and non-conventional threats emanating from the constantly changing nature of modern conflicts. These complex and multi-faceted threats span the entire spectrum of warfare, across all dimensions – land, sea, air, nuclear, space and cyberspace. Furthermore, another issue that has emerged in the last few decades is that these threats no longer emerge merely from enemy nations but also from suicidal, unpredictable, tech savvy and innovative non-state actors as well. All these factors taken together make the tasks that need to be performed by the intelligence agencies rather mind boggling and exacting.

Challenges for Indian Intelligence Agencies

The definition of security in today's world extends beyond military challenges/terrorism and includes not only defence but political, economic, social, energy, demographic and technological threats to a nation's existence as well.

India's strategic domain and area of interest spans the Strait of Malacca in the east to the Gulf of Aden in the west, thence running southwards along the eastern African coastline and down to the southern expanse of the Indian Ocean. Additionally, the entire Asia Pacific region (that is now increasingly referred to as the Indo-Pacific region) also impinges on our security calculus. India's land borders exceed 15,000 km, and it shares these borders with seven nations – China, Nepal, Myanmar, Bhutan, Bangladesh, Pakistan and including a small segment with Afghanistan (at present, this falls in the Gilgit-Baltistan region/Pakistan Occupied Kashmir [POK]). Furthermore, India also has a coastline that is 7,683 km long over and above its 1,197 islands and an exclusive economic zone (EEZ) that is over 2 million sq km in size. Aside from overt and covert threats, India also needs to take into account concerns that might arise from neighboring island nations such as Sri Lanka, Maldives, Mauritius, etc.

There are several specific and diverse security challenges confronting India, and these are likely to persist in the foreseeable future as well. One major example would be a rising and assertive China that is spreading its economic and security influence all around India's borders among other regions. Other significant emerging challenges that India faces today include a nuclearized Pakistan that is rapidly becoming an increasingly treacherous hotbed of terror. This development is particularly concerning since Pakistan remains pathologically anti-India in all its strategic formulations. Additionally, India faces indigenous as well as externally foisted insurgencies in Jammu and Kashmir (J&K) and some of our north-eastern (NE) states while the Maoist/Naxal threats – officially referred to as Left Wing Extremism (LWE) – also endanger normalcy in many districts in India's hinterland. The LWE is a serious concern across a wide, nearly contiguous territory, which has been dubbed "the Red Corridor". This corridor extends across the states of West Bengal, Bihar, Jharkhand, Chhattisgarh, Orissa and Andhra Pradesh.

Other threats that confront India include, inter alia, societal instability that occurs off and on, due to communal flare-ups; challenges to our communication and cyber networks; challenges relating to energy resources; nuclear and space threats; narco-terrorism; and financial laundering.

Over and above the threats mentioned above, there are also growing threats to India's vast coastline from problems such as maritime terrorism and the emerging rivalry between China and India in the strategic Asia-Pacific maritime commons. Threats also emerge from Pakistan based and supported terror tanzeems like the Lashkar-e-Tayaba (LeT), Jamaat-ul-Dawa (JUD), Hizbul Mujahideen (HUM), Jaish-e-Mohd (JeM). There are several other groups that are currently being sustained by Pakistan's sinister Inter-Services Intelligence (ISI) for anti-India operations that will only intensify in the near future. Additionally, challenges from global Islamic terror outfits like the Al Qaeda in the Indian subcontinent (AQIS) and the Islamic State are likely to emerge and multiply.

It will be amply clear to the nation's top security hierarchy that India's intelligence organisations have an increasingly exacting task ahead, if they are to keep the nation adequately and timely forewarned before any major setback occurs. As the former Indian Vice President Hamid Ansari succinctly expressed in his address at the K.N. Rao Memorial Lecture, "Good intelligence often has made the difference between victory and defeat, life and death. By the same token, faulty intelligence leads to failures of varying degrees."[2] Thus, intelligence organisations need to constantly monitor their performance but also, more importantly, focus on capability accretion in order to fulfil their onerous mission and remain one step ahead of the likely challenges confronting the nation. Reforms in the apex intelligence structures are thus called for, on a timely basis to analyse, assess and enhance their mission fulfilment capabilities.

Indian Intelligence: Defining Benchmarks

Post-independence, half-hearted efforts were made by some governments at the centre to review the adequacy of India's intelligence agencies, and as a result there were marginal improvements that took place. Among the defining benchmarks in Indian intelligence, the most significant one was the establishment of the Research and Analysis Wing (R&AW) in September 1968. This was a direct consequence of the inadequacies in intelligence found after the 1962 fiasco in operations against the Chinese and also the huge information void during the 1965 operations against

Pakistan. In fact, after the 1962 debacle, a review of the intelligence set-up led to the creation of the Directorate General of Security (DGS) under the Intelligence Bureau (IB) which was originally tasked for both internal and external intelligence gathering. The DGS was, however, taken away from the IB after the operations of 1965 and the Mizo Revolt in 1966, and placed under the R&AW thereafter, which was designated as the premier external intelligence gathering agency.

The next significant step in the evolution of Indian intelligence came about in the aftermath of the Kargil War in 1999, when Indian troops were caught off guard by the large-scale intrusion of Pakistani troops crossing the Line of Control (LoC) and occupying some of the Kargil heights in the Ladakh sector. The Kargil crisis led to a much required review of India's higher defence management (HDM) structures in totality – including but not limited to its intelligence architecture as well. The Kargil Review Committee (KRC), chaired by the widely respected strategic analyst K. Subrahmanyam, produced a comprehensive report that was vetted by a high-powered Group of Ministers (GOM). The GOM subsequently appointed four task forces to holistically go over and analyse various aspects of the HDM. The Task Force on Intelligence Reforms was headed by former R&AW Chief Gary Saxena, who after analysing the entire gamut of intelligence structures in India made some stellar recommendations that were incorporated in the final GOM Report, and subsequently approved by the Vajpayee government in 2000-01.

The KRC succinctly observed that "... there is no institutionalised mechanism for coordination or objective oriented interaction between intelligence agencies and consumers at different levels. Similarly, there is no mechanism for tasking the agencies, monitoring their performance... nor is there any oversight of the overall functioning of the agencies."[3] It also opined that "...the resources made available to the Defence Services are not commensurate with the responsibility assigned to them. There are distinct advantages in having two lines of intelligence collection and reporting with a rational division of functions, responsibilities and areas of specialisation... Indian threat assessment is a single process dominated by R&AW... Indian intelligence structure is flawed since there is little backup or redundancy to rectify failures and shortcomings in intelligence collection and reporting..." It further lamented that "Joint Intelligence Committee (JIC) reports don't receive the attention they deserve at the political and bureaucratic levels. The assessment process has been downgraded in importance."[4]

The Task Force on Intelligence recommended the establishment of an inter-services apex intelligence agency, namely a Defence Intelligence Agency (DIA) to synergise all intelligence aspects pertaining to defence intelligence and coordinate the functioning of the intelligence directorates of the army, navy and air force. Aside from this, the strategic intelligence assets of the three Services, (pertaining to satellite imagery and signals intelligence) were also placed under the DIA. The Task Force also recommended the creation of the National Technical Facilities Organisation (later re-christened the National Technical Research Organisation [NTRO]), a nodal agency that could procure and provide all forms of technical intelligence (TECHINT) for the nation. The DIA came into existence in March 2002, while the NTRO was established in early 2003. Some TECHINT assets, which belonged to the Aviation Research Centre (ARC) of R&AW, were transferred to NTRO.

The Task Force on Intelligence had also recommended the setting up of a Multi-Agency Centre (MAC) and a Joint Task Force on Intelligence (JTFI) which was to be set up under the IB. MAC was to collect and coordinate terrorism-related information, and the JTFI was to share information with the state governments. The Vajpayee government approved the recommendations on intelligence submitted to it through the high-powered GOM on May 11, 2001. It is pertinent to mention that the GOM Report also concluded that it was "neither healthy nor prudent to endow, notably R&AW with multifarious capabilities" for both human intelligence (HUMINT) and TECHINT responsibilities.[5]

Subsequently, while the then government approved the GOM recommendations, it also streamlined and established the National Security Council (NSC), National Security Advisory Board (NSAB) and various coordination groups for the macro-management of intelligence in a more cohesive manner. It also established the Intelligence Coordination Group (ICG), chaired by the National Security Advisor (NSA) that was tasked with the responsibility of overseeing and delineating the responsibilities of various intelligence agencies at the apex level.

Mumbai Terror Attack: 2008

Meaningful changes in the Indian intelligence edifice that were made post Kargil operations notwithstanding, the intelligence failures that were attributed to the dastardly ISI-supported terror attack in November 2008 brought the issue of intelligence competence to the fore once again. Lack of intelligence sharing and coordination between the IB and state police forces on the one hand and between the various central intelligence agencies on the other was highlighted. The government of Maharashtra established the Ram Pradhan Committee to recommend various measures to be undertaken to counter terror and streamline governmental responses to terror attacks. After some in-house deliberations, the UPA government announced the establishment of the National Counter Terrorism Centre (NCTC) and the National Intelligence Grid (NATGRID). However, owing to acute political and professional differences, the NCTC has not seen the light of day whilst the NATGRID, though functioning, has not achieved its desired objectives.

Nevertheless, there was a significant consequence of the 26/11 terror attack, and that was the UPA government establishing the National Investigation Agency (NIA) for the investigation of terror-related activities. The NIA is the only federal agency chartered to supersede the state's police forces in the investigation and prosecution of offenders for particular offences as required. Legally sanctioned, by an Act of Parliament, according to most security analysts, the NIA is carrying out its role effectively.

Naresh Chandra Committee and Other Task Forces

In June 2011, the second UPA government constituted a task force under the former Cabinet Secretary Naresh Chandra to carry out a holistic review of the nation's security preparedness and HDM structures. With respect to the intelligence reforms required, this Committee reportedly recommended the creation of a new post of Intelligence Advisor to the NSA. It also recommended the establishment of a National Intelligence Board for coordinating and overseeing the functioning of all civil and military intelligence agencies in the nation. As the Naresh Chandra Committee's recommendations are, inexplicably, still classified, no further mention of this report will be made in this paper.

In June 2009, the Pradhan-Haldar-Narsimhan Task Force also gave out its recommendations for improving intelligence organisations in the country. Additionally, the Federation of the Indian Chamber of Commerce and Industry (FICCI) also came out with a report on *National Security and Terrorism* (Vol 1, 2009). An interesting point that must be noted is that the L.P. Singh Committee that enquired into the role of the Central Bureau of Investigation (CBI) and the IB during the Emergency prescribed a detailed written charter for the IB that was not implemented.

In the last few years, many think tanks and some security analysts have come out with their recommendations for energising the Indian intelligence apparatus. However, most of these reports/recommendations have been crisis-driven rather than institutionalised reviews and have rarely been implemented/followed through.

Existing Intelligence Set-up at the National Level

Presently there are 14 intelligence agencies operating in India. Some of them are involved in intelligence collection, some have investigative roles, and some of these agencies have overlapping mandates and undefined boundaries. The lack of a single unified supervisory mechanism has affected the effective coordination of intelligence activities and intelligence assessments at the national level. Former Home Minister P. Chidambaram aptly summed up the intelligence scenario in India stating that:

> ...Intelligence elements are spread over different ministries: there is the IB which reports to the Home Minister; there is Research and Analysis Wing which falls under the Cabinet Secretariat and hence, reports to the Prime Minister; there are organisations such as JIC, NTRO and ARC which report to the NSA; and there is the NSC Secretariat (NSCS) under the NSA which serves the NSC. The armed forces have their own intelligence agencies, one each under the Army, Navy and Air Force and an umbrella body called the Defence Intelligence Agency. There are other agencies which specialise in financial intelligence. These are the Directorates in the Income Tax, Customs and Central Excise departments, the Financial Intelligence Unit and the Enforcement Directorate. The enforcement element of this architecture consists of the central armed police forces (CAPFs) such as CRPF [Central Reserve Police Force], BSF [Border Security Force], CISF [Central Industrial Security Force], ITBP [Indo-Tibetan Border Police], and SSB [Sashastra Seema Bal] and the para-military forces (PMF) such as AR (Assam Rifles) and NSG [National Security Guard]. What will strike any observer is that there is no single authority to which these organisations report and there is no single or unified command which can issue directions to these agencies and bodies.[6]

Current Roles of Existing Agencies

It is imperative to introspect and examine the role/responsibilities (not legally mandated but practiced nevertheless) of major intelligence agencies in the country and to analyse the streamlining/fine-tuning required for ensuring an improvement in their performance.

NSC

The NSC – established in 1999 – is a three-tier set-up functioning under the Prime Minister. Its members comprise of the ministers for Home Affairs, Defence, External Affairs and Finance, respectively. Initially, the JIC was merged into the NSC but in 2005 the two were de-linked and the latter was set up as a separate agency once again. Currently, the NSCS and the JIC are responsible for coordinating intelligence assessments, with the former concentrating on long-term policy and national security priorities, while the latter remains focused on immediate and short-term intelligence inputs.

JIC

The JIC is the apex intelligence assessment set-up of the nation. It comprises of representatives from all intelligence agencies. Its role is to review all the available information on political, economic, diplomatic, military and scientific matters that have a bearing on national security. The JIC has a permanent secretariat with specialists drawn from various disciplines. It functions under the Cabinet Secretariat and prepares national intelligence estimates and policy analyses for the Prime Minister and all the associated ministries, as required. The JIC does not collect intelligence on its own, but its analyses are based on inputs from different intelligence agencies.

IB

Established in 1887 as the Central Special Branch serving British interests in India and monitoring the Indian freedom movement, it adopted the name "Intelligence Bureau" in 1920 with its main mandate being political surveillance.

The IB functions as India's internal security agency and is directly under the Ministry of Home Affairs (MHA). It has a wide range of responsibilities. Within the country, it is responsible for all issues pertaining to terrorism, Left Wing Extremism (LWE), insurgencies in J&K and NE states, counter intelligence, narcotics problems, financial laundering, communalism, aviation security, VIP security, political instability and serious law and order threats in the states, etc. It operates at both the national and state levels and the IB personnel in the states are part of the State Special Bureau.

The GOM recommendations, as accepted by the then government in 2001, had designated the IB as the premier counter-terrorism agency that was tasked with the responsibility to create the MAC and Subsidiary Multi-Agency Centres (SMACs). The establishment of these centres was to enable the process of collating and analysing intelligence inputs from various sources. The SMACs are located at the state capitals and comprise of representatives from various security agencies. The NCTC, once raised, will be part of the IB. Additionally, the IB also carries out political intelligence internally, a role often criticised by political parties while in opposition but utilised relentlessly when in power!

R&AW

Since its establishment in September 1968, R&AW has been India's sole external intelligence gathering agency; not counting TECHINT inputs which are gathered by the DIA and the NTRO. R&AW also has its TECHINT arm, the ARC, whose major assets were allocated to the NTRO on its raising in 2003 after an acrimonious divide between R&AW and the NTRO. R&AW is exclusively tasked to collect, analyse and disseminate intelligence, employing diverse resources, on all aspects of national security concerning the external dimension of India. Functioning under the Cabinet Secretariat, it is directly accountable to the Cabinet Secretary and the Prime Minister. It collects intelligence on all nations bordering India, as well as the ones whose foreign and military policies and actions impact India's security.

R&AW's legal status is ambiguous as it is not an "Agency" but a "Wing" of the Cabinet Secretariat. Thus, R&AW is not answerable to the Indian Parliament which keeps it out of reach of the Right to Information (RTI) Act preventing access to classified information regarding its activities and budgeting, which thus remains a closely guarded secret.

DIA

Post the Kargil War, the DIA was established in March 2002 based on the recommendations of the KRC and the GOM Report. Its primary role was to "coordinate the functioning of different services intelligence directorates".[7] It was created to ensure better integration of the intelligence collected by the three Service directorates and also to serve as the principal military intelligence agency and collect, analyse as well as disseminate all defence-related information. The latter has been a weak area for the three Services for a while now, and hopefully, the DIA's endeavours to bridge this critical intelligence gap will bear fruit.

The DIA controls the strategic intelligence assets of the various Services, namely the Signals Intelligence Directorate and Defence Image Processing and Analysis Centre (DIPAC) for imagery intelligence (IMINT). Additionally, it also coordinates the functioning of all military attachés posted in various diplomatic missions abroad. The DG DIA is the principal military intelligence advisor to the Raksha Mantri and to the chairman Chiefs of Staff Committee (COSC)/Chief of the Defence Staff (CDS) whenever established.

MAC

The MAC and JTFI were created within the IB in 2003-2004. The MAC was tasked with coordinating all inputs related to terrorism from different field agencies and sharing them with the concerned states through the SMACs established at the state level. The MAC also works to synergise the state police's special or intelligence branches and bring about operational convergence between them and the central agencies.[8]

NTRO

As a follow-up of the GOM recommendations/KRC Report after the Kargil operations and bearing in mind the significant role of technology in the science of intelligence, the NTRO was established in 2003, along the lines of the US National Security Agency. The NTRO's roles is to plan, design, setup and operate major new TECHINT facilities. It was tasked to establish secured digital networks to disseminate and enable TECHINT/information flows to other intelligence agencies/governments in accordance with authorised guidelines and protocols. The NTRO has also been given the task of monitoring missile launches in countries of interest, aside from being responsible for defensive and offensive cyber operations.

The Chairman of the organisation is to be taken on rotation, from the IB, R&AW and the DRDO. Given the rapid convergence between technological advancement and effective intelligence gathering/processing, all major TECHINT facilities – as approved by the apex Technical Coordination Group (TCG) now fall under the ambit – of the NTRO.

NIA

Set-up weeks after the dastardly terror attack in Mumbai in November 2008, the NIA is now the premier central counterterrorism law enforcement agency of the nation. The NIA is now the only federal agency, (legally mandated by an Act of Parliament) that is able to supersede state police forces in the investigation and prosecution of those suspected of terror-related activities in the states without the permission of state governments.[9]

Economic Intelligence Agencies

The Central Economic Intelligence Bureau (CEIB) is the major internal intelligence gathering organisation when it comes to taxation and economic-related intelligence. It provides secretariat cover to the Economic Intelligence Council, a nodal body that coordinates the response of various government agencies (CBI, IB, etc.) to economic offences. The CEIB coordinates the work of the Directorate General of Revenue Intelligence (Customs), Directorate of Enforcement (Foreign Exchange), Directorate General of Anti Evasion (Central Excise), Directorate General of Income Tax and Narcotics Control Bureau.[10] However, the responsibility of collecting and collating data about the economies of hostile nations and the nation's economic competitors is undertaken by R&AW.

Directorate General of Military Intelligence (DGMI) and Other Service Intelligence Directorates (SIDs)

India's military intelligence set-up was established in 1941 and initially tasked to generate field intelligence for the Indian Army. Its original geographical mandate was to operate sources up to 50 km from the international boundary (IB)/LoC. It is tasked with generating pinpoint intelligence for small-scale operations and has counterterrorism responsibilities in the North East and J&K (particularly with respect to army operations within the region). With limited intelligence acquisition capabilities, it has largely depended upon the R&AW the IB, and the DIA to meet its strategic and internal intelligence requirements.

The Indian Army, the Indian Navy and Indian Air Force also have their own intelligence directorates that report directly to their respective Service Chiefs. For the most part, the three SIDs still act as the principal field and tactical intelligence collection agencies, except with regard to signals intelligence (SIGINT) and IMINT which are now the responsibility of the DIA.

Intelligence Units of PMF and CAPFs

The BSF (which, in peacetime, guards the Pakistan and Bangladesh borders) has its own intelligence set-up designated as BSF(G). The BSF(G) collates and analyses intelligence inputs from its units deployed on the IB as well as from its internal security deployments. It maintains a close watch on enemy deployments close to border areas and, more importantly, keeps a sharp lookout against narcotics and arms smugglers. State police forces and the IB also share relevant inputs with the BSF(G).

The Indo Tibetan Border Police (ITBP), that guards the border with China, coordinates intelligence collection between the IB and SSB. The Assam Rifles are also responsible for collecting intelligence inputs, and they work closely with the DGMI. The CRPF – which is the primary counterterrorism force of the nation – has also developed some capability for intelligence collection in Naxal-infested regions.[11]

Revamping of National Intelligence Infrastructure (NII)

Security crises that have been faced by the nation in the past, for many decades, clearly demonstrated the fact that India's National Intelligence

Infrastructure (NII) is far from optimal. It lacks unity of purpose and inter-agency coordination as well as accountability in the case of failures. Furthermore, the whole security architecture is embedded in antiquated practices that serve as roadblocks in its functioning. Many task forces appointed by various governments in the past have seen their sound recommendations getting obfuscated in the labyrinthine bureaucratic maze so characteristic of Indian governance. Additionally, the NII's outputs are virtually ad hoc and arbitrary in nature in the absence of specific requirements from intelligence clients. Instead of emerging from a synergized national strategy the outputs and recommendations usually stem from severe lacunae noticed during crisis situations. The twin troubles of parochialism and "turf wars" among central services, coupled with a lack of interest in the art and science of intelligence by national leadership in the overall strategic context have prevented the nation from establishing an NII to cater for India's aspirations both regionally and on the global stage.

Glaring Shortcomings in NII and Suggested Reforms

Reforms and Reviews of NII

Most major reforms/reviews conducted for the NII have been episodic, piecemeal, primarily after wars, and essentially crisis-driven. There has been a lack of holistic political guidance and governmental thrust. Furthermore, bureaucratic inertia and political indifference have been responsible for delaying the implementation of the sound recommendations that have been made by various task forces and committees. The central government, therefore, needs to undertake time-bound institutionalised reviews for the entire intelligence set-up every 10 years or so. A model that could be used as a template would be the Central Pay Commission and the regular reviews it conducts. Improvements, as suggested and approved, should then be implemented with alacrity and dedication.

Lack of Oversight and Accountability

India is one of the only democracies in the world where Parliament does not have oversight of its intelligence agencies. The ICG, established in 2001, and presided over by the NSA was mandated to provide systemic intelligence oversight at the apex level. It was tasked with overseeing the allocation of resources to intelligence agencies, approving annual tasking for intelligence collection and reviewing the quality of inputs provided by the agencies annually as well. It should be mentioned here that intelligence agencies are usually reluctant to submit to any oversight, as they are concerned with potential information leaks of sensitive operations as well as the lack of security knowledge in the political/bureaucratic hierarchy. However, there is a pressing need for strict accountability of intelligence agencies, but it must be undertaken with due caution and keeping security considerations in mind. Intelligence agencies cannot judge their own performance.[12]

Bearing the inescapable requirement of oversight in mind, a body with statutory powers comprising of eminent people with ministerial, defence, intelligence or security management backgrounds, should be constituted to monitor the functioning of the intelligence agencies, ensuring their accountability and financial probity.

Apex-level Management of Intelligence

Currently, the National Intelligence Board (NIB) with the Chairman JIC as its member-secretary constitutes the highest intelligence framework of the nation. Higher-level direction to the nation's intelligence fraternity is required in the areas of apex level tasking, ensuring coordination between agencies, facilitating oversight and supervision of the agencies. Above all, higher direction is necessary for the production of a clear-cut intelligence picture for crucial national-level decision-making in vital strategic matters. It is the near unanimous view of most intelligence/security professionals that the NSA, the Cabinet Secretary or the Principal Secretary to the Prime Minister will not have the necessary time or attention span to fully oversee the national intelligence endeavour in totality.

It is recommended that, along the lines of the US intelligence community, India should also appoint a Director of National Intelligence/ National Intelligence Coordinator who will work under the NSA. This appointment will ensure better inter-agency coordination, remove overlaps, eliminate 'turf-battles' and ensure optimal utilisation of scarce national resources, culminating in better intelligence products.

Legal Status for Intelligence Agencies

Barring the NIA, no intelligence agency in India has any legal status and the other agencies are functioning through executive orders issued by successive governments from time to time. In the world's largest democracy, it is only proper that intelligence agencies must function under the legislative enactments framed by the Indian Parliament. Operating outside the purview of any legislation makes them immune from financial, operational and administrative accountabilities and liable to misusing their powers or being unethically employed by governments in power. Intelligence agencies should work according to a written charter, sanctified by the law that lays down their duties and responsibilities.

The central government could consider a bill, similar to the one conceived by a former Lok Sabha member (Manish Tewari's Intelligence Services (Powers and Regulation) Bill, 2011), "to regulate the manner of functioning and exercise of powers of Indian Intelligence Agencies"[13] This bill should also consider the establishment of a high-powered National Intelligence and Oversight Committee headed by the Chairman of the Rajya Sabha. The committee should comprise of the Prime Minister, the Speaker of the Lok Sabha, the Home Minister, the Leaders of Opposition in the two houses and two Members of Parliament each with the Cabinet Secretary as the Secretary of the Committee. This Committee should also appoint an Intelligence Ombudsman and a National Intelligence Tribunal to investigate complaints and deal with various administrative issues of the various agencies.

Quality of Human Resources in Intelligence Agencies

The overall quality of personnel manning intelligence agencies is far from desirable. It can be attributed to unresponsive recruitment policies and an absence of the necessary impetus and vision accorded to specialised training essential for intelligence operatives. Indifferent intelligence cadre management and a shortage of specialised personnel to man diverse skills appointments in the agencies prevent intelligence organisations from producing intelligence mosaics for their consumers on time and with the required clarity. It must also be appreciated that investigation and law enforcement work is different from the acquisition of information and analysis of intelligence – even though the overly police culture that pervades our intelligence agencies, at times, clubs these skills together.

Intelligence agencies today require far larger numbers of personnel with regional expertise, linguistic, technological and cyber skills, etc. Agencies like R&AW, IB, NTRO lack considerable military expertise as well. While a system of deputation exists, military officers are reluctant to be posted to these agencies. In the absence of a position of equivalent rank in the agencies, military officers are compelled to work at a level which is often lower than their Service rank. Additionally, the agency that they are sent to keeps them employed in insignificant appointments, which is naturally not taken well by the armed forces officers on deputation.

It is recommended that direct recruitment for the intelligence community (along the lines of the recruitment and promotion policies for the civilian/police bureaucracy) needs to be introduced by establishing a separate and distinct cadre for intelligence personnel. The well-established Union Public Service Commission (UPSC) route could be suitably utilised for proper recruitment to the National Intelligence Services which should develop into a full-fledged career service. With respect to information technology (IT), technical and linguistic skills the system of "short service commissions" (as is prevalent in the armed forces today) can be given to suitable youth who will be available to bridge the gap existing today.

Another area of expertise that can be exploited is the use of private contractors for specialised tasks that can be implemented after necessary security clearances are obtained. In order to prevent any leakage of information. Their post-employment credentials can also be monitored. Outsourcing or intelligence contracting, as a concept, is a common practice with western nations especially the US who are utilising it extensively to bridge their intelligence gaps in nations like Afghanistan, Iran, Pakistan and Iraq, among others. Furthermore, cross postings between civil and military intelligence agencies, in far larger numbers, must be ensured for better integrated intelligence outputs. All intelligence agencies must endeavour to develop a dedicated core of expert analysts who – despite huge information overloads – are experts at Open Source Intelligence (OSINT) that provides, by most estimates, over 80 percent of intelligence gathered from all sources.

HUMINT

It has been observed that, for the last few years, reliance on HUMINT is decreasing due to increasing advances in penetrative technology available to intelligence agencies. This anomaly needs to be addressed as in intelligence operations, HUMINT will always remain a point of significance. HUMINT skills must continue to be fostered, along with the ability to mount covert operations and these skills need to be sharpened for employment as and when required. It takes years to cultivate and sustain sources in enemy territories/organisations and this age-old proven skill cannot be tossed aside so callously. It needs to be given its due. Apart from civil intelligence agencies, the DIA should also develop its expertise in HUMINT by discreetly employing its military attachés abroad whilst developing sources amongst the large number of military diplomats from foreign nations posted in New Delhi. Currently, the military attachés are not mandated for any espionage activities but they form a potential pool that can be tapped into if trained in the right way. Additionally, both the civil intelligence agencies and the DIA/SIDs must fine-tune their training of trans-border operators for intelligence acquisition. Linguistic prowess in neighbourhood languages such as Mandarin, Pashto, Dari, Persian, Sinhalese, Burmese, etc. should also be rapidly built up.

Counterterrorism and Counter-insurgency

A void in national architecture continues to exist in place of a well-equipped, coordinated mechanism that can thwart emergent threats and cater to counterterrorism and counter-insurgency operations. The need for a National Counter Terrorism Centre (NCTC), modelled on a variant of the US Homeland Security Department, was proposed in the wake of the 2008 Mumbai terror attacks. Given the manner of power sharing in India and the nature of the centre-states relation, it is hardly surprising that the NCTC has not become operational to date. This can be attributed to some states feeling that the NCTC will go against the spirit of genuine 'federalism' and trample over their constitutional rights.

Additionally since, law and order is a 'state subject' under the Constitution, some states (particularly the ones that belong to parties, other than the party in power at the centre) feel that the centre may misuse its powers by having organisations like the NCTC, ostensibly raised to combat terrorism, but utilised to destabilise state governments. While some of these concerns are valid, it is also a fact that states, by themselves, do not have either the intelligence or the combat capabilities to take on terrorists adequately. Thus, the centre must get all states on board and establish the NCTC for effective counterterrorism and counter-insurgency operations. Additionally, as felt by many well-meaning citizens, law and order should be placed in the 'Concurrent List'.

National Intelligence Grid (NATGRID)

Immediately after 26/11, a project to centralise data from multiple sources for better intelligence inputs and analysis was formalised. NATGRID aims to synergise both – intelligence and operations – to counter all threats emerging against the nation. While some progress can be seen in the fact that it has been established, the desired effects have not been achieved owing to resistance from some quarters regarding the sharing of data. NATGRID endeavours to link 21 databases, and make them accessible to 11 agencies in order to facilitate real-time tracking of inputs – including professional as well as personal transactions such as travel, banking and insurance.

Reportedly, India's Central Monitoring System and National Cyber Coordination Centre will, enable the government to access all phone calls and Internet-related data 24/7 in real time.[14] However, the centre must put into place legislative authorisation for this large-scale invasion of privacy. It must place penalties against the misuse of data thus obtained to ensure guarantees against misuse. A delicate balancing act between security considerations and the right to privacy will need to be practiced.

TECHINT and Overcoming Technology Obsolescence

Intelligence organisations, are heavily dependent on technological aids for intelligence collection and data mining. Security organisations, therefore, have to keep abreast of the technological obsolescence of their specialist equipment, which inevitably occurs. Purchases of critical technologies – whether through 'off the shelf' markets abroad or through the 'Make-in-India' programme – need to be ensured to help India keep up with emergent threats from a rapidly modernising China and other Non-State Actors. The TCG should be given the power to oversee all programmes for cost-effective and constant update of the nation's TECHINT resources to avoid wasteful expenditure and duplication. Additionally, better coordination between the DIA, NTRO and ARC in all aspects of TECHINT including SIGINT, electronic intelligence (ELINT), communications intelligence (COMINT), IMINT should be ensured, and these vital organisations must not function in "silos". Also, streamlining of certain TECHINT roles are required as there exists some overlaps and duplication in roles both in COMINT and IMINT of the NTRO and ARC. It is the considered opinion of many intelligence experts that currently the NTRO has too much on its plate and cyberspace activities could be taken out of its fold and allotted to another new set-up.

Meanwhile, secure, firewalled common databases for dissemination of real-time intelligence and effective data mining by own intelligence agencies should be established. With effective technical support of the NTRO and the DRDO, it should form part of the NATGRID format. Intensive research and a futuristic approach will be required for intelligence preparations for the impending battles in the nuclear, space and cyberspace domains.

Cyber Security Architecture

Cyberspace is now as relevant a strategic domain as the other naturally occurring domains of land, air, sea and space. India is becoming increasingly exposed to hostile cyber-attacks that can cause electronic paralysis through various adversarial acts that can cause telling damage to critical infrastructure, compromise the integrity of data banks, etc. The

Indian Armed Forces must be geared to fight future wars in cyberspace, whether in standalone skirmishes or in conjunction with kinetic battles. The Internet is being increasingly "weaponised". This can be seen in the way it is being used for the recruitment of terrorists, the proliferation of radicalised agendas, the disruption of financial networks and electricity grids, etc. "Integrity of India's digital networks can affect the strategic trajectory of a nation: cyberspace can be used to mould, even determine political outcomes; spur or stunt the growth of its economy."[15]

The criticality of both offensive and defensive operations in cyberspace will become more pronounced with the passage of time. India thus needs a national cyber security strategy and, importantly, a National Cyber Agency. The much discussed Inter Services Cyber Command – as suggested by the armed forces and some security analysts – is therefore, the need of the hour, and such an organisation will be able to synergise all cyber activity both in the military and civil sectors. Alternatively, a National Cyber Security Agency interfacing the cyber requirements of the armed forces and civil establishments could also be established.

Maritime Domain Awareness

After the Mumbai terror attacks in 2008, major restructuring of maritime intelligence was undertaken with the establishment of the National Maritime Domain Awareness (NDMA) and the National Command Control Communication Intelligence (NC3I) network. This led to the setting up of the Information Management and Analysis Centre (IMAC) which is connected to coastal radar stations – including those deployed in our island territories. The IMAC collates, fuses and disseminates intelligence about suspicious or unusual activities in India's maritime peripheries. The Government of India must continue to add more technical prowess to these institutions, and ensure seamless coordination between all agencies involved in maritime surveillance – including the Indian Navy, Coast Guard, DIA, etc. These organisations thwart challenges arising from information overload and therefore need to ensure that their vital equipment does not succumb to cyber-attacks or electronic paralysis engineered by enemy agencies.

Doctrinal Document

The absence of a doctrinal document has led to the various agencies that are involved with national security and intelligence affairs and their respective ministries, working at cross-purposes at times. Thus it is essential to issue a classified National Strategy/Security Doctrine, for both the long and medium terms according to which the concerned ministries can draw out their time-bound action plans. Additionally, the NSA could also give out his directions/priorities for the Annual Tasking Plans in conjunction with the Director of National Intelligence (DNI), the NIB, the ICG and the TCG. It is a painful fact that hardly any domain in the Indian Government is truly integrated. Let us make a beginning towards synergy and synchronisation by effecting collusiveness in the vital realm of intelligence.

Strengthening Defence Intelligence

A major abiding gap in India's intelligence needs, since independence, has been the huge void in military intelligence regarding the operational requirements of India's armed forces. There has been an endeavour to address this strategic-cum-tactical anomaly by establishing the DIA in March 2002 as a follow up of the centre approving the KRC/GOM reports after the Kargil conflict. Having functioned for 14 years now, it is evolving on the right lines to fulfil its mandate and provide the necessary strategic and tactical intelligence cover to the three Services. However that being said, much more needs to be done by the government, the MOD and the three Services Headquarters themselves, to ensure that the DIA can meet its chartered responsibilities. The abundant skills and resources of armed forces personnel, in intelligence activities, have remained woefully underutilised. Some measures to re-energise military intelligence are enumerated below:

(a) As the premier coordinating intelligence agency for the three Services, the DIA will only be able to carry out its role when the SIDs report directly to it. The DIA must be made the single-point contact for the government on all aspects of defence-related intelligence. The current loose arrangement between the DIA and the SIDs is unsatisfactory and unworkable.

(b) As recommended for all civil intelligence agencies, the mandate and charter of the DIA also needs to be legislated by an Act of parliament.

(c) Furthermore, the charter for all military related external intelligence acquisition should now be handed over to the DIA and this role should therefore be taken away from R&AW that has not been able to fulfil this responsibility satisfactorily. The latter can continue with its emphasis on diplomatic, political, economic intelligence activities, etc. The DIA should also build up its capabilities using HUMINT sources abroad. However, both the DIA and R&AW should share intelligence with each other with sincerity.

(d) To improve the effectiveness of the military intelligence apparatus, the creation of a Defence Intelligence Corps is sine qua non. This Corps should have personnel from all the three Services, suitably trained in modern intelligence acquisition skills, regional and linguistic proficiency, overt and covert operations, analysis, intelligence tradecraft, etc. Some of these personnel should also be cross-posted to civil intelligence agencies for missions abroad.

(e) India must make greater use of its highly professional and articulate armed forces officers in defence diplomacy – especially in nations around the globe that have military/quasi-military governments.

(f) The Military Intelligence School, Pune, should be upgraded to a Defence Intelligence School. The necessary resources and expertise – including resources and expertise from friendly foreign nations – should be provided to it to impart intelligence skills to the Indian intelligence community.

(g) The DIA will be able to fulfil more than its mandate once the critically required institution of the CDS, to whom it will directly report, is established by the government. It is militarily and strategically inexplicable that the world's third-largest armed forces are working without the office of the CDS.

Conclusion

India's rise as a major regional power and global player will only be possible if it strengthens the structures of comprehensive national power adequately. Given the changing nature of warfare, new realms of intelligence have a major contribution to make in edifying these frameworks of security. The strategic craft of intelligence is a veritable force multiplier and India needs to accord the necessary significance to it. Bold and structurally transformative intelligence reforms are, thus, the need of the hour.

NOTES

1. Lt Gen. K. Davar, "Drum-beating Has No Place in the Business of Intelligence", interview by Josy Joseph, Rediff.com, April 15, 2003, at http://www.rediff.com/news/2003/apr/15inter.htm. (Accessed on May 15, 2003.)
2. Vice President M. Hamid Ansari, "Intelligence for the World of Tomorrow", Fourth R.N. Kao Memorial Lecture, New Delhi, January 19, 2010.

3. *From Surprise to Reckoning: The Kargil Review Committee Report*, Sage Publications, New Delhi, 2000.
4. Ibid., 23
5. Manoj Shrivastava, *Re-Energising Indian Intelligence* (New Delhi: Vij Books, 2013).
6. Home Minister P. Chidambaram delivering the 22nd IB Centenary Endowment Lecture at New Delhi on December 2009, quoted in, Manoj Shrivastva, *Re-energising Indian Intelligence*, (New Delhi: Vij Books, 2013), p. 29.
7. *Group of Ministers Report: Reforming the National Security System*, 2001, Government of India, New Delhi, p. 104.
8. MAC Executive Order issued by the Ministry of Home Affairs (MHA), December 31, 2008.
9. Official website of the NIA, at http://nia.gov.in/about-us.htm (Accessed on May 15, 2017).
10. Sunil Saini, "Intelligence Reforms", Bharat *Rakshak Monitor*, 3(4), January-February 2001, p. 14.
11. B.P. Routray, "Intel Wing for the CRPF: Not the Right Move", CLAWS, July 17, 2001.
12. B. Raman, *Intelligence: Past, Present and Future*, Lancer Publications, New Delhi, 2002, p. 10.
13. Congress leader Manish Tewari quoted in, Manoj Joshi and Pushan Das, "India's Intelligence Agencies: in Need of Reform and Oversight", *ORF Issue Brief*, No. 98, July 2015.
14. Manoj Joshi and Pushan Das, "India's Intelligence Agencies in Need of Reform and Oversight", *ORF Issue Brief*, No. 98, July 2015.
15. Arun Mohan Sukumar and Col. R.K. Sharma, "The Making of India's Cyber Security Architecture", in Sushant Singh and Pushan das (eds.), *Defense Primer: India at 75*, Observer Research Foundation, 2016, p. 68.

9

Inter-ministerial and Inter-departmental Coordination

Shakti Sinha

Introduction

Most Indian strategic analysts – particularly those with a background in the Defence Services, but not limited to them – trace the suboptimal outcomes of India's security investments to major problems in civil-military relations. They refer, particularly to a perceived lack of role of the defence forces in policymaking and in the reported imposition of bureaucratic control instead of political control.[1] According to Admiral Arun Prakash, a former naval chief, and one of India's pre-eminent soldier-scholars, it would be wrong to say that the security system has worked well. In his words, the system consists of a "deeply flawed approach ... and we are fortunate to have muddled through crisis after crisis".[2] In the same vein, Stephen Cohen and Sunil Dasgupta have stated that "the price of extraordinary civilian control of the military in India is military and strategic inefficiency".[3] Former Army Chief General V.P. Malik has further argued that in the appointment of the Service Chiefs, the bureaucracy should not be involved even in processing papers which should instead go straight to the political leadership.[4]

The fact that there are issues with civilian interface with higher defence management cannot be denied. Even if the diagnosis, and hence solutions are disputed, the situation is complicated.[5] Given these circumstances, drastic measures are required to change the narrative, since the country cannot afford to perpetuate such a dysfunctional national security architecture. The focus of this study is to suggest institutional measures that would lead to greater coordination across ministries, departments and agencies in order to obtain optimal outcomes in the task of defending the nation and its interests. In fact, since resources will always be limited and traditional challenges are now being supplemented by new ones – like cross-border terrorism, cybercrimes, money laundering, forged currency and illegal migrations – we should be looking at going beyond coordination to obtain synergies.

While this study is not about the organisation of higher defence management per se, it would be impossible to suggest institutional innovation aimed at bringing about greater coordination and synergy across government structures, without referring to how the higher defence management structure is currently organised and the steps that can be taken to make things better. It is also necessary to identify the points where intervention is required horizontally while trying to keep vertical flow issues to a minimum so that the focus of the reform is not lost. To that extent, it is necessary to explain the background and point out areas of suggested reform.

Present Structures

A quick recap of the existing architecture will be instructive for analysing and implementing reforms. Like other parliamentary democracies, India vests the executive powers of the state with its elected representatives – a cabinet that is led by the Prime Minister/Chief Minister – who are collectively accountable to the legislature. Since the executive holds office so long as it enjoys the confidence of the legislature, the former has substantial discretion in policy formulation and execution that is not available to directly elected executives who have to seek legislative scrutiny and approval far more intensely. This point that must be kept in mind when looking at the structure of parliamentary oversight over the functioning of defence forces in India. Furthermore, in the spirit of reforms one must keep in mind the limitations of what we can learn from how the US Congress operates vis-à-vis its US armed forces.

The Second Schedule of the Government of India (Transaction of Business Rules), 1961, allocates responsibility for different subjects to different ministries and departments. The Defence Ministry is charged with all matters relating to the 'Defence of India'. Furthermore, different departments – Department of Defence, Department of Defence Production,

Department of Defence Research and Development and the Department of Ex-Servicemen Welfare – have been created to handle specified functions and further streamline the process. Though the President of India is the Supreme Commander of the Armed Forces, the powers of the president are exercised by the Defence Minister. It is clearly laid down that "all business allotted to a department specified under The Government of India (Transaction of Business Rules) 1961 shall be disposed of by, or under the general or special directions of, the Minister-in-charge".[6] The rules further state that in cases where ministers need to consult with/seek the concurrence of other ministries they can be referred to the cabinet or its committees.

As criticism of the existing system, it is often stated that the Transaction of Business Rules make the Defence Secretary "responsible for the Defence of India".[7] The factual position, as we see, is quite different. According to the Transaction of Business Rules, the Defence Secretary, like all secretaries in other ministries, "shall be the administrative head thereof and *shall be responsible for the proper transaction of business and careful observance of these rules* in the department"[8] (emphasis added). In other words, he is to ensure that all proposals and routine business, are to be processed according to the rules so that due diligence and fiduciary concerns are taken care of and secretariat functions are performed across organisations, big or small. The issue therefore is to identify what institutional coordination mechanisms are needed to make sure that the ministry is better able to meet the needs of the three Services and facilitate decision-making that would ensure that the Services have clear directions and are acting according to the national objectives decided by political executives.

The Service Headquarters function outside the ministry. Over the years, particularly after the acceptance of the recommendations of the Kargil Review Committee, the financial and administrative delegations to the Service Chiefs, and the heads of lower formations have increased substantially. The posting of integrated finance advisors in the Service Headquarters reduces the need to go the Ministry of Defence (MoD) for most cases other than major procurements. In the absence of an overarching national security policy or even an operational doctrine, the Services determine their own policies and priorities. An example of this is the Indian Maritime Doctrine – both the 2009 and the 2015 versions (Ensuring Safe Seas) that emerged from the naval headquarters, the latter clearly propounded by the then Chief of Naval Staff, Admiral Robin Dhowan. Along the same lines, even human resource policies – including criteria for promotions and contents of training programmes – are handled autonomously with the ministry accepting the recommendations made by the Service Headquarters.

Gaps

It is necessary to identify the areas and pressure points where specific reforms and interventions across ministries, departments and agencies are critical and should not be delayed. Larger structural issues like the establishment of a single-point military advisor (Chief of Defence Staff [CDS], permanent chairman of the Chiefs of Staff Committee), the integration of Service Headquarters in the MoD and the establishment of joint commands are relevant, but out of the context of this chapter. Therefore, no specific recommendations will be made with regard to these issues as they are being addressed elsewhere in the volume. The focus here will be limited to process improvement and human capacity accretion.

The first gap that needs to be addressed institutionally is the lack of a national security doctrine. It is often said that Indians have no strategic culture.[9] While this is clearly an exaggeration, what is undeniable is that Indian systems are geared to working tactically, responding to crises, studying issues ad nauseam and making incremental changes. This is not always a weakness, as explicated by former Prime Minister P.V. Narasimha Rao, who said that occasionally not taking a decision is also a decision. However, the need for wider ownership in a democracy, especially one as big and diverse as India, cannot be over-stressed. Information asymmetries in an uneven system with islands of excellence and a large hinterland of mediocrity means that often policymakers are unsure about the quality of information available or about the ability of the system to implement policies as conceived. This means that ad hoc measures and reactive responses prevail over planned/detailed long-term strategies, including, arguably, the decision to test nuclear weapons that came before any "thought of doctrine, strategy and structures for command and control".[10] Despite having powerful armed forces and a nuclear deterrent, India has "failed to put in place an effective national security architecture" that can manage its deteriorating strategic environment.[11] India needs to reform/amend/innovate its security architecture to enable it to develop a National Security Doctrine. Any such doctrine that gets implemented would need to be dynamic and draw on the expertise of the defence, internal security, economic, agriculture and human resources, sectors to develop a composite architecture.

The second key gap that prevents the optimal utilisation of our massive investments in our armed forces is the lack of jointness across the Services

– and arguably even within individual Services. The dissonance between the Service Headquarters and the civilian-led and staffed MoD is a recurring theme in any discussion on defence reforms. What however falls by the wayside is how this lack of coordination among the three Services has been detrimental for military effectiveness. Anit Mukherjee has studied this failure using four basic attributes of military effectiveness, namely (i) Quality, (ii) Responsiveness, (iii) Skill, and (iv) Integration, and his unequivocal conclusion is that the Indian armed forces function in silos.[12] This has led to a particularly deleterious effect on several aspects of military preparedness including but not limited to – procurement, indigenous development of defence platforms, absence of interoperability, lack of joint training and an inability to bring the full force of the military in battle.

The third gap, is the lack of expertise in the MoD that has led to a situation where it is essentially seen blocking decision-making instead of questioning the Services and collaborating with them to achieve national security targets. It has also failed to develop appropriate policies that would lead to improved military effectiveness. The frequent changes to promotion criteria – that the MoD approves unquestioned – have led to litigation, and affected force morale adversely. And while the MoD has to approve the introduction of new courses, it has not been able to ensure that the course content for senior officers has the necessary coverage of India's Constitution and its working, or adequate components of civil faculty.[13]

The fourth gap that requires a much higher level of coordination across ministries, departments and agencies, is military aid to civil authority. With the establishment of the National Disaster Response Force (NDRF), this issue is soon becoming history as far as humanitarian assistance and disaster responses are concerned. However, it is becoming more complex to establish such coordination in other circumstances – particularly in areas affected by insurgency/left-wing extremism – since the army often operates along with Central Armed Police Forces (CAPF) and the state police. The complexities these authorities face range from a lack of clear objectives, to issues of command and control, all of which are made worse by serious interoperability issues. There have been successes that need to be built upon, modified and tried out elsewhere. But there are nevertheless a lot of challenges that need to be considered as well. For example, problems like illegal migration across national borders and surveillance of maritime territory – particularly across coastal areas – increases the complexities and challenges involved since the number of agencies having responsibilities and legal jurisdictions increases. Despite the substantial investment in asset accretion and manpower, post the Mumbai attack of

2008, coastal security arrangements still have grey areas and gaps that can be exploited by anti-national elements and cross-border terrorists.

Way Ahead

The standard global response to demands for improved coordination across jurisdictions that is adopted by civilian as well as military bureaucracies is to set up inter-agency committees and joint control rooms. As a response to an emergency situation, this is natural and works, but in the long run, there are issues of sustainability and such coordination mechanisms more often than not lack accountability and responsibility. There is also the danger of falling back into a state of ennui once the initial pressure for action has passed and things settle down. On rare occasions where the agenda has been focussed, and there has been regular monitoring by superiors and/or stakeholders; joint committees have succeeded in moving beyond the emergency situation. Hence, the approach isn't completely futile, but it would be wrong to solely depend on contingencies for modernisation. A healthy balance would require re-jigging institutional design – ranging from incremental to the revolutionary – without discounting the emergency response approach. Again, there are no hard and fast rules to the process of Defence reformation. In different situations, bottom-up, top-down and broad horizontal participatory approaches have worked. One could either have a clear picture of what one wants to achieve and the way to go about it, or one could "cross the river by feeling the stones", to quote Deng Xiaoping.[14] This study recommends a series of actions, neither simultaneous nor sequential, that would help reform institutional mechanisms to bring about greater inter-ministerial, inter-departmental and inter-agency coordination.

In a structure that is as hierarchical structure as the defence, change must begin from the top. Before going into the detail, it is worth mentioning that the apex body dealing with national security and defence matters below the full Cabinet is the Cabinet Committee on Security (CCS). Headed by the Prime Minister, its members include the Home Minister, Finance Minister and the Defence Minister, with other ministers invited where necessary. Traditionally, the Deputy Chairman of the Planning Commission (now Niti Aayog) is a permanent invitee, being the top policy advisor to the government. Additionally, whenever defence issues are discussed, the three Service Chiefs and the Defence Secretary are also invited, with the Chiefs invited to express their opinions – this author has personally witnessed this many times. It should be noted that within a parliamentary democracy with ministerial responsibility, this is as participatory as it can get.[15] Therefore, no changes are suggested in either the composition or the functioning of the CCS. The recommendations proposed in this study begin at a level below the cabinet.

Firstly, a case can be made for the establishment of a National Security Council (NSC) whose membership goes beyond those charged with defence forces and includes those responsible for economic development, food security, energy security, internal security and other key sectors as well. It could coordinate and involve more help as and when required. Furthermore, it need not always meet as a body but create subject as well as ad hoc committees with specific responsibilities. The approach for such an establishment would need to be "governmental as a whole" and not sectoral. The advisory adjuncts should be broad in composition, have no operational or executive responsibilities, and should support the NSC in planning long-term strategy and in developing policy responses to specific issues/emerging situations. Functional ministries are simply unable to think beyond sectoral perspectives, and this is made worse by the turf battles that all bureaucracies are prone to. A National Security Advisory Board (NSAB), with diverse representation across sections – military, civilian and governmental – that is not anchored in any ministry and has no functional responsibility, would have the potential to develop into an extremely useful institution that could help improve India's defence capabilities and performance. Appointments to bodies like the NSAB should not be seen as sinecures or restricted to retirees. A balance between specialisation and rotation would keep the body agile and pro-active and help it plan, propose and draft policies and approaches with a horizon of 10-15 years.

Secondly, a restructured MoD that integrates the headquarters of the three Services à la the Pentagon is a desirable goal but that would require having a single point military advisor to the government. Before we get there, there are a number of steps that need to be taken to increase the efficiency of the MoD, and equip it to give clear directions to the Service Headquarters and to monitor implementation. While the Defence Minister's Committee – where the three Chiefs and the Defence Secretary participate – never took off as a formal body, it nevertheless provides a platform where issues can be discussed informally without an agenda and its utility should not be underestimated. There is certainly a lot of merit to the suggestion of formalising its procedures to ensure that action in processing specific proposals could be monitored, preventing items from falling between the cracks. In fact, in the immediate aftermath of the 1962 War, the government set up a Defence Coordination and Implementation

Committee (DCIC) to restore the wherewithal that the army needed in the shortest time possible. It was chaired by the Defence Secretary and its members were the three Service Chiefs, Secretary Defence Production, Director (Intelligence Bureau, IB) and the head of Military Intelligence.[16] This functioned for years but slowly lost its relevance and changes in the Warrant of Precedence overtook its original composition. The main point is that committees often have a limited shelf life, so over-reliance on them could be a limiting factor in bringing about positive change.

A reform that cannot wait and must be brought about immediately is the improvement of the expertise quotient of the civil bureaucracy posted in the MoD. This is an issue that concerns not just the MoD but many other ministries, departments and agencies that are staffed by the generalist civil bureaucracy as well (not just those belonging to the Indian Administrative Service). The key issue that arises is how to balance the need for general management skills with those of domain expertise. Clearly, the latter cannot take a backseat in many jobs that need working expertise and technical skills. The MoD should be allowed to have officers posted to it without waiting for comprehensive civil service reforms. It should be able to hold them for longer and more frequent tenures, and also ensure compulsory participation in courses run by military training institutes (besides the prestigious National Defence College). Without completely detracting from the essentially generalist nature of the bureaucracy, at the middle level there should be mini-cadres specialising in security affairs, economic subjects, agriculture and rural development, human resource development, etc. This would aid in developing the critical expertise necessary to becoming an excellent staff officer, without compromising the chances of getting a promotion at the highest level. This would be a good way to facilitate the specialisation of a level needed to better appreciate proposals sent by Service Headquarters. Another proposal, suggested for years, that merits serious consideration is the posting of serving military officers (Colonel, Brigadier, Major General and equivalents) at different levels in the MoD. They would bring in much needed expertise to the ministry. There is a potential downside to this which is that there could be pressure on them from their respective Service Headquarters to clear its proposals. And if they are expected to merely 'rubber-stamp' the Headquarters' proposal, there would be no value addition in their presence in the MoD. However, this issue would potentially sort itself out once a decision on the CDS is taken. In the meantime, a practical way forward would be to form a joint task forces on specific subjects/issues, staffed by the MoD and Service Headquarters. These should be time bound, and not permanent bodies, that would soon deteriorate into routine discussions. Nomination to these bodies – based on the task at hand – should be by name so that the tendency for downward delegation to the lower levels is checked. These task forces would enable the sharing of experiences and perspectives, and make for more-informed policies that are owned by both the MoD and Service Headquarters. It would also have the benefit of preparing the grounds for eventual integration of Service Headquarters into the MoD.

Thirdly, there is the need to better equip military officers to work at the MoD and even in their own headquarters. True to the objective control norms identified by Samuel P. Huntington, India has chosen to "insulate" the military from the messy political life outside. This has enabled the military to remain a professional force which makes the country proud, and feel safe. However, the dissonance with the MoD in particular and the wider civilian set-up outside causes considerable disquiet. While all the recommendations in this chapter and in the rest of this volume attempt to address it, a specific suggestion being made here is to better acquaint military officers about the structure of government, as it is, and especially about the functioning of ministries. Service Headquarters' issues with the MoD are repeated across governments in varying degrees. Leaving structural reforms aside, what is suggested is that higher command military training institutions place more emphasis on explaining the structure of government to their officers, so that they are better placed to deal with the MoD. Staff functions, beyond the Flag Officers, are performed by Service Headquarters/commands, etc., that process proposals sent by lower formations. Every formation has men detailed for procurement, logistics, maintenance and other non-line functions. Hence, when suggestions are made that the Defence Minister should function without the assistance of the MoD, or that the military would like political control but not bureaucratic control, they reveal a gap in perception that adversely affects the smooth running of defence establishments. A related suggestion would be that, like in the US, Indian military training institutions should have permanent civilian faculty for courses on political science and the Constitution, and non-military aspects of strategy (economic issues, recent history and developments, energy, etc.). This would help in both, widening perspectives and better equipping military officers both to handle the MoD, as well as increasing their employment prospects post-retirement which are otherwise constrained for no fault of theirs.

Fourthly, there is also the issue of integrating the functioning of the Service Headquarters, which would bring about synergy between the three Services. Given the changing nature of warfare in the twenty-first century and the need for integrative action, it is an issue that will have to be addressed sooner rather than later. Such an action would be necessary to make the position of a CDS – as the single point military advisor to the government – meaningful, and is important but is not being elaborated here. Some intermediate steps are being recommended that would bring about better coordination, even if synergy is still some distance away. These are primarily based on the author's experience of interacting with the erstwhile Fortress Command (1983-85) and later with the Andaman & Nicobar Command (ANC; 2009-12) and very detailed discussions with Lt Gen. Naresh Marwah (retd).[17] The failure of the ANC, created in the post-Kargil restructuring exercise, to acquire the necessary assets for it to adequately address its tasks is a reflection of how much inter-service coordination is lacking, and how the Defence Ministry should help break these self-contained silos. Even the assets acquired/created for it specifically like an army brigade are deployed elsewhere in the country.[18]

The ANC should start integrated logistics and procurement functions, breaking out of single service silos. This would save costs and resources since process duplication would be avoided. The establishment of a Joint Signals Node would help prepare the base for the interoperability required to fight the emerging challenges that India faces in the Indo-Pacific. Nationally, "existing inter-service structures such as National Defence Academy, Defence Services Staff College, College of Defence Management, and National Defence College" should be strengthened to "further nurture better understanding of other services".[19] The training institutions of different services catering to similar activities should either be combined or have higher levels of cross-training. Technical subjects like communications/telecom should have combined institutions in order to take advantage of economies of scale in attracting the best faculty and acquiring the latest technology. It would also help promote interoperability. Another suggestion that should be implemented immediately is to extend the scope of cross-service postings on staff functions, which are at present extremely limited and restricted to improve liaison. Cross attachments at formation levels (units, ships, squadrons) should be increased to help develop an understanding of other Services and facilitate battle-front jointness.

The *fifth*, and final, set of recommendations deals with military aid to civil authority. This is a complex and contentious issue and rather than suggest how to proceed with the Armed Forces Special Powers Act, important as it is, this study will suggest how to improve Army-Civil Administration-CAPF interactions. The basis for these recommendations would be in terms of improved army-CAPF partnership in combating left-wing extremists (LWEs) and cross-border terrorists. The CAPF include the Border Security Force (BSF), Central (earlier Crown) Reserve Police Force (CRPF), Indo-Tibetan Border Police, Sashastra Seema Bal (SSB), Assam Rifles, Central Industrial Security Force (CISF) and the National Security Guard (NSG), which are controlled by the Home Ministry.[20] While the numbers may seem unimaginably large and unprecedented,[21] they have specified geographical jurisdictions and were created in response to different episodes/incidents. Other than the CISF, these forces are largely involved in guarding the border. However, both the BSF and CRPF are also used for supporting state police forces to handle exceptional breakdown of public order. Along with the Assam Rifles, both BSF and CRPF are also essential in the fight against LWEs and cross-border terrorists that attack sensitive establishments. The army has traditionally responded to the call of state governments to support their efforts to handle complete breakdown of civil order, and in anti-insurgency operations in the North East. The area of concern that remains is that these forces work under their internal command and control systems during times of peace; however in times of external hostility, their operational commands get transferred to the army despite the fact that their normal standard operating procedures (SOPs) and command structures are completely delinked from the army. A similar issue also arises from the fact that at higher levels the CAPF are manned by posting officers of the Indian Police Service, whose organisational ethos and operating principles are also completely different.

To achieve true synergy, it is important for these forces to combine their training facilities so as to achieve higher levels of professionalism and operate on broadly similar levels of capability. (It must be made sure that organisational identities would be respected to avoid creating uncertainties regarding promotions and career growth paths.) More importantly, the army needs to be closely associated with designing training modules for the same, and in helping run them. This would ensure that the CAPF personnel are better prepared for neutralising terrorists and extremists, and would enable a seamless transition towards working under the army in warlike situations. The Indian military has exercises with several foreign militaries, they should also carry out joint exercises with the CAPF to ensure familiarisation and facilitate greater coordinated action during war.[22] Approaches to higher levels of staffing raise substantial controversies, with former serviceman and commentators arguing for an end of the Indian Police Service deputation culture. If these forces were engaged purely in guarding the borders or in fighting LWEs/armed infiltrators, such an approach would be perfectly justified. However, the

CAPF are regularly called upon to act in support of state police forces when there are large-scale incidents of breakdown of civil order. Senior officers should therefore be equally equipped to handle stone-pelting mobs as they would be in handling Pakistani infiltrators at Pathankot and Uri. The via media lies in extending deputation periods and encouraging multiple deputations from state Indian Police Service cadres. This process is similar to the IB's "hard core" cadres which though drawn from state cadres continue in the IB for long durations. This, along with joint training in the armed forces, would help professionalise the CAPF and facilitate greater synergy among the different units as well as between the CAPF and the army.

State governments should also pro-actively work with local military formations in facilitating the acquisition of lands for defence needs, sorting out the many issues of conflict/disagreement between local civil administration and local military formations, and mediating disputes with the local community. The grievances of soldiers should be addressed as soon as possible and settling them should be made a priority. Since most of such grievances are land-related, and hence sensitive, the earlier practice of encouraging zonal/regional civil-military cooperation should be revived. While the fears of descent to falling back into traditional patterns of non-engagement are real, the attendance of the Defence Minister and Service Chiefs at these events would motivate the states to proactively meet the needs of the Services, as well as the individual servicemen/ servicewomen. Another recommendation to ensure synergy is that the state police, the IB and the army should have a congregated intelligence base and must maintain constant communication so that if the need to deploy the military in fighting LWEs/cross-border terrorists arises, the state police, the IB and the army would have been sharing information well before the actual intervention and would be better equipped to handle the crisis. The actual operations should be predicated on the articulation of clear political aims, running a unified command and operating a common control room. Failure to do so would lead to sub-optimal results. Finally, with respect to maritime security and coastal management, there should be a move towards the inclusion of agencies like the state forest department, and the regional environmental offices of the central government. Despite the differing objectives of different agencies, the development of new inter-ministerial platforms would be a welcome step. Placing Global Positioning System (GPS) devices in country boats run by local fisherman by the Coast Guard enhances coastal security and motivates local users to act as eyes and ears of the government. Such cross hierarchical and cross departmental reforms need to be implemented and built upon.

Conclusion

India's ambition of emerging as a leading power would require the country to substantially overhaul its governance systems and structures, and generate long-term economic growth similar to China's developmental model. The current tendency of acting in silos, refusing to see the other sub-systems perspective and the refusal to adapt to changing demographic scenarios prevents the country from taking its anointed place in the sun. Thus, India needs to accept that there are no free lunches and that it cannot achieve the position of power it aspires to simply by riding on the shoulders of America – irrespective of the strategic convergence between the two countries. India now needs to put its money where its mouth is, and step up its strategic profile in the Indo-Pacific. For example, the Andaman and Nicobar Islands are capable of accepting more tourist flows than governmental estimates currently indicate, and the islands also have the economic potential to serve as a feeder to the traffic flows through the Malacca Straits. Investing in the economic and military improvement of these island bases would enable greater synergy that would be conducive to improving the security of the country. But for that, the government would need to strategize carefully, decide its goals and act with full force to achieve them.

As of now, there are substantial gaps between the capabilities and perceptions of different stakeholders. The common aim for all parties involved should be to work towards improving synergy and integration. While the larger issues of principles remain to be addressed, there are several intermediate steps that can be taken to help achieve greater coordination and resolving some foundational disagreements. Such steps are necessary for the development of appropriate paths towards building a common understanding. Through this study an attempt has been made to identify a number of parallel steps that can be taken to improve outcomes in the security sphere.

NOTES

1. See, for instance, Maroof Raza, "Civil Military Relations in India and Pakistan: An Analysis", *The Journal of USI of India*, CXXIV, January-March 1994; V.K. Nayar, "Civil Military Relations", *The Journal of USI of India*, CXLV (), July-September 2015; Stephen Cohen and Sunil Dasgupta, *Arming without Aiming: India's Military Modernization*, Penguin, New Delhi, 2010.
2. Arun Prakash, "National Security Reforms: Ten Years After the Kargil Committee Report", USI National Security Lecture 2012.
3. Cohen, Stephen, above cited
4. Robin David, in an interview with former Army Chief General V.P. Malik,

"Remove Bureaucrats from Selection of Army Chief ... Cabinet Committee on Security Should Decide", *On the Bounce, The Times of India* blog, December 26, 2016, at http://blogs.timesofindia.indiatimes.com/On-the-bounce/remove-bureaucrats-from-selection-of-army-chief-cabinet-committee-on-security-should-decide/.

5. A completely different perspective emerges from other scholarly studies by Srinath Raghavan and Anit Mukherjee, both of whom have served in the Indian Army and have acquired solid academic credentials. See, for example, Srinath Raghavan, "Soldiers, Statesmen, and India's Security Policy", *India Review*, 11 (2), 2012; Anit Mukherjee, "Civil-Military Relations and Military Effectiveness in India", in Rajesh Basrur, Ajaya Kumar Das, and Manjeet Singh Pardesi (eds.), *India's Military Modernization: Challenges and Prospects*, Oxford University Press, New Delhi, 2014.
6. https://cabsec.gov.in/files/allocation/transaction_businessrule.pdf
7. Government of India (Transaction of Business Rules) 1961.
8. Ibid.
9. George K. Tanham, *Indian Strategic Thought: An Interpretive Essay*, Rand, Santa Monica, 1992, at http://www.rand.org/content/dam/rand/pubs/reports/2007/R4207.pdf.
10. V.K. Nayar, No. 1.
11. Arun Prakash, "India's Civil Military Dissonance: Playing with Nation's Security", *India Defence Review*, January 29, 2016.
12. Anit Mukherjee, No. 4.
13. Ibid.
14. Clemons, Steve, '*China's Steve Jobs Debate and Deng Xiaoping*', The Atlantic, Nov 7, 2011, accessible at https://www.theatlantic.com/international/archive/2011/11/chinas-steve-jobs-debate-and-deng-xiaoping/248080/
15. The National Security Council is the closest equivalent to the CCS in the US. Under President Trump, The Joint Chief of Staff and the Director of National Intelligence are no more on the Principal's Committee, its highest ranking body.
16. Sumit Ganguly, "From Defence of the Nation, to Aid of the Civil: The Army in Contemporary India", *Journal of Asian and African Studies*, XXVI (1-2), 1991.
17. Lt Gen. NC Marwah, the longest-serving commander-in-chief of the Andaman & Nicobar Command (CINCAN), was kind enough to share with me a document ("Challenges of Jointmanship") he has been working on. I am deeply grateful to him and acknowledge his ideas, some of which I have listed here.
18. Shockingly, the ANC has not been able to construct even its own headquarters since it is unable to persuade the navy, the largest defence landowner in the islands, to part with the land required for it.
19. Personal discussions with Lt Gen NC Marwah (retired).
20. The Special Protection Group (SPG) is kept out as it is a specialised security force charged with protecting the Prime Minister, ex-Prime Ministers and their families. Unlike the CAPFs, it functions under the Cabinet Secretariat (Security) and not Home Ministry. Earlier the Rajasthan Armed Constabulary (RAC) had border protection duties, but those have been taken over by the BSF. Though the Assam Rifles has been listed, it is effectively an infantry establishment staffed by the army, and can hardly be considered as a CAPF.

21. Narender Kumar, "Internal Security Needs a Relook To Deal With Emerging Challenges", Centre for Land Warfare Studies (CLAWS), Issue Brief, No. 88, December 2016.
22. The shocking incident in Chhattisgarh when the air force component left a downed helicopter in LWE territory with an injured policeman inside deep inside a forest is a pointer to the lack of preparedness among the non-infantry sections of the Indian military in acting in support of civil authority.

SECTION III

DEFENCE BUDGET AND PROCUREMENT

10

Defence Budget: Optimising Planning and Utilisation – I

Anjan Mukherjee

The Armed Forces require large budgetary allotments to modernise, train and sustain themselves. It is a daunting task for the government to make adequate financial provisions for the armed forces. This has resulted in continual slippages in resource allocation culminating in large gaps in military modernisation and procurement programmes. It is well-known that the Indian subcontinent is among the most tense regions in the world where the Indian military is a stabilising factor. Keeping in mind that the Indian military operates in the most variable terrain – ranging from high Himalayas to desert, plains, marshy terrain, jungles, sea coast and oceans – it requires adequate budget allotment and the optimal management of resources to ensure desired levels of national security. Therefore, given the myriad challenges of higher financial allotment and the difficulty of planning the augmentation of wide-ranging capabilities for the armed forces, there is a need to have a professional assessment of inter-service and intra-service resource allocation and its efficient management. The ultimate aim should be to ensure modernisation of the armed forces in a time-bound manner as well as to sustain operational capabilities at desired levels.

Optimal management of the budget is closely linked with the efficient management of all resources in the armed forces. Therefore, resource management has become one of the essential verticals of budget management. In real terms, it includes the transformation of management policies, structures and processes relating to all the resources earmarked for the defence – including but not limited to budget and finance – in a fully transparent, accountable and focused manner. Resource management has a substantial impact on areas like operations, logistics, infrastructure, acquisitions, training, financial management, support services, project management, etc. With the expanded responsibilities of resource management, there is also a need to undertake dynamic policy initiatives especially for defence acquisition, which is well-documented in the Defence Procurement Procedure (DPP) 2016 and Defence Procurement Manual (DPM) 2009.

Procurement and Acquisition

Procurement and acquisitions represent one of the most important activities of the Ministry of Defence (MoD) as well as the Service Headquarters and subordinate formations and units. It is evident that, the elaborate policies that have been laid down in the DPP and DPM notwithstanding, the entire process of procurement and acquisition is significantly delayed at every stage. This results either in a sizeable reduction of capital outlays at the Revised Estimate (RE) stage of the budget, or the surrender of the Capital Budget at the last moment. Despite being aware of the evolving situation, the Finance Ministry takes away a large chunk of the defence capital acquisition budget every year. During the financial year (FY) 2013-2014, the Finance Ministry took away over Rs. 10,000 crore from the defence capital budget. Similar exercises have been undertaken by the Finance Ministry in the subsequent years as well. This is an unacceptable situation as it directly affects the country's defence preparedness.

It should also be mentioned that the Comptroller and Auditor General (CAG) report that was tabled by the Parliament in February 2014 raised the issue regarding the sub-optimal management of the Indian Navy's 'Warship Refits', wherein only 18 per cent of the 152 refits for frontline destroyers, frigates and other warships, commenced as per norms, and 74 per cent of the rest were completed with a total delay of 8,629 days. The CAG report also pointed out that a ship overdue for refit cannot be part of an optimal solution to Indian security needs and thus represents a gap in Indian military preparedness. While many a study on the subject has been undertaken in the three services to mitigate similar problems, very little success has been achieved so far. Recent times have witnessed substantial cost overruns and imbalanced budget management has resulted in delays and inadequacies. Can the nation accept such wastage of its resources and finances anymore?

Financial Management

The Finance Commission legislates the sharing of resources between the central and state governments which is known as *vertical devolution*. Resource sharing between states is known as *horizontal devolution*. These were further progressed by the Planning Commission and implemented by the Finance Ministry and the other associated ministries. However, it should be noted that the 13th Finance Commission recommendation is for 2010-15, whereas the 12th Plan period of the Planning Commission is for 2012-17. An analysis of the effect of divergent expenditure in the period covered between the Planning and Finance Commissions indicates that this has resulted in serious impediments towards long-term planning. The funding for many ongoing defence projects has been affected as well. The Goods and Services Tax (GST) regime, introduced in July 2017, will have major implications for financial management in the three Services; these implications need to be studied.

With a large quantum of nearly obsolete equipment currently owned by the military – which is a fall-out of years of slippage in modernisation plans – it is estimated that the average growth of expenditure between 2014-15 and 2016-17 will have to be at an annual rate of nearly 30 per cent, as opposed to the recent years that have witnessed a growth rate of approximately 7.5 per cent per annum. With the revenue budget growth galloping and the admissibility of One Rank, One Pension (OROP) for ex-servicemen, the provision of adequate budgetary support for growth on a year-to-year basis appears to be very difficult, if not impossible. It is high time that the central government engages in a detailed assessment of the same and takes hard decisions to restore India's military power through rapid modernisation.

Budget management in the services also face the challenge of "overkill" in the planning and financial management aspect of the three services. The Indian Air Force (IAF) has stated that their long-term capital acquisition plans have been prepared based on the assumption of 15 per cent annual growth in the capital budget on a year-to-year basis. The IAF is reportedly processing schemes valued at 110 per cent above the available budget so as to ensure full utilisation of the budget. The army and the navy too are not far behind in this regard. Such suo moto initiatives could result in an imbalance and make budget management more difficult. Hence, there is a need to holistically analyse the areas of concern prior to initiating course corrections. Some of the issues that need to be considered while undertaking corrective analysis are:

(a) Availability of budget versus inescapable necessities
(b) Committed liability vis-à-vis new procurement funding
(c) Extension of equipment life versus operational necessities
(d) Prioritisation in procurement
(e) Indigenisation versus imported equipment
(f) Expansion of the armed forces versus management of future challenges through 'restructuring and technology'

To understand the parameters governing defence budgeting in India, it would be pertinent to refer to Article 114 of the Constitution of India which states:

> The number of funds sanctioned by the Parliament under various grants should not exceed the provision of the Appropriation Bill of that FY. Thus, the funds provided should be spent for the purpose allocated and the unspent funds will be returned to the Consolidated Fund of India.[1]

It is from this statutory guideline enshrined in the Constitution of India that the Government of India's accounting system is structured. Accordingly, the accounting system followed by the Government of India is not an "accrual" but "cash-based" system. In the cash-based system, expenditures that are transacted in the form of cash and other monetary transactions are recorded in the accounts while receipts are recorded when actual receipts are received by the collecting agencies. It means that the exchequer's cash outgo, receipt and accounting must tally at the end of any transaction process. The entire budget of the department must also close and tally at the end of the FY. Over-expenditure is not permitted and the remaining amount in the case of under-spending is required to be credited to the Consolidated Fund of India thus becoming the property of the Parliament of India, with the Finance Ministry as its statutory manager.

The expenditures undertaken by the departments of the Government of India are bound by General Financial Rules (GFR). Ministries and departments are free to come up with their own standard operating procedures (SOPs), regulations and financial management procedures to adhere to the GFR in "letter and spirit".

Limitations of Cash-based System

- Only financial transactions pertaining to the FY are recorded and maintained.

- Committed liabilities incurred during the year do not get transparently recorded in subsequent years.
- Token allotment for a project during the FY can become a huge outgo in subsequent years.
- Earlier foreign currency parameters for imported items and cost as worked out in the Long-term Integrated Perspective Plan (LTIPP) change drastically during the FY, resulting in uncontrolled outgo from the budget allotment. For example, the US dollar value for imported defence procurement in the 12th Plan was pegged at Rs. 54, while its present value is around Rs. 65. As of now payments in US dollars are being made at the current exchange rate. Similarly, the contracted exchange rate of rouble is around Rs. 35 for payments of committed liabilities from Russia, whereas the actual rate is between Rs. 5 to Rs. 9 at present. Thus, substantial unplanned foreign currency expenditure tends to be incurred from the defence budget.

Budgetary Process for Defence

- It is a top-down process which commences with the issue of the budget circular by the Budget Division of the Finance Ministry.
- The circular contains guidelines for the preparation of the next FY's budget estimates (BE) as well as the current FY's RE. The modified appropriations to balance budgetary allotments are managed by the ministries themselves.
- The MoD (Finance) issues similar circulars to the three services, the Coast Guard, Defence Research and Development Organisation (DRDO) and attached departments and offices.
- Defence services and the MoD departments/attached offices compile the requirement of their funds for the forthcoming FY and send it to the MoD (Finance) for allocation.
    - o Projections in respect of Locally Controlled Heads (LCH) are formulated by the defence services in consultation with Command Headquarters/PCDA/IFA.
    - o Projections of Centrally Controlled Heads like Pay & Allowances, MGO, ASC, ASC, ACG, Army Commander Special Powers Funds and Modernisation are formulated by the Service Headquarters and forwarded to the MoD.
    - o These projections are compiled, analysed, discussed and vetted by competent authorities, and then forwarded to the Finance Ministry. This exercise in the MoD (Finance) is based on projections, priorities, availability of resources, etc.

- A similar exercise is undertaken in the Finance Ministry and allocation is made to the MoD.

Problems in the Present System

- At the higher levels in the Service Headquarters, MoD (Finance) and more so in the Finance Ministry, the budgetary process is merely an annual mathematical exercise wherein a standard nominal hike is made in the next year's budget. This results in a serious mismatch in budget management at functional levels.
- Parking of funds for later withdrawal by the Finance Ministry, is followed by its attempts to hide higher allotment to some other sector. These actions disturb the services' entire budget management system.
- No strategic defence priorities or programmes ever get discussed as part of BE planning.
- The services are never called to present their case for budget priorities by the Finance Ministry. Only the MoD (Finance) is authorised to discuss budgetary issues with the Finance Ministry, and they primarily concentrate on the technical issues of budget management.
- Thus, the entire focus of the present budgetary process is on resource allocation and not on "capability enhancement and efficiency of expenditure" in defence forces.
- In effect, since budget estimates and allocations are annual in nature, there exists neither the space nor the flexibility to integrate this allocation with strategic, operational, tactical requirements and match them with priorities of modernisation. These constraints have a severe impact on balanced capacity building in the armed forces.
- Due to the absence of an outcome budgeting process, it is difficult to point out the quantitative co-relation between the increase or decrease in allocation and its bearing on the operational efficiency or readiness of the defence services. For example, as we procure weapon platforms like guns, tanks, aircrafts and ships, we need to simultaneously procure ammunition, missiles, and rockets for the same, otherwise the procured weapon systems only remain partially effective. Thus, the concept of outcome budgeting gets defeated.
- Defence Public Sector Undertakings (DPSUs) and the Ordnance Factories Board (OFB) – which are under the MoD (Defence Production) – work out their pricing formula for goods in an arbitrary manner, which must be accepted by the indenters. In this

manner, the government and the indenters are forced to support inefficiency. As the government has invested billions in these institutions, it must keep a constant check on the cost of investment (COI) and the return on investment (ROI). This is never done. So, we continue with the non-scientific bookkeeping method of utilising valuable DPSU resources.

An Analysis of Defence Budgets

Figure 1: Defence Expenditure as a Ratio of GDP: 1986-87 to 2015-16[2]

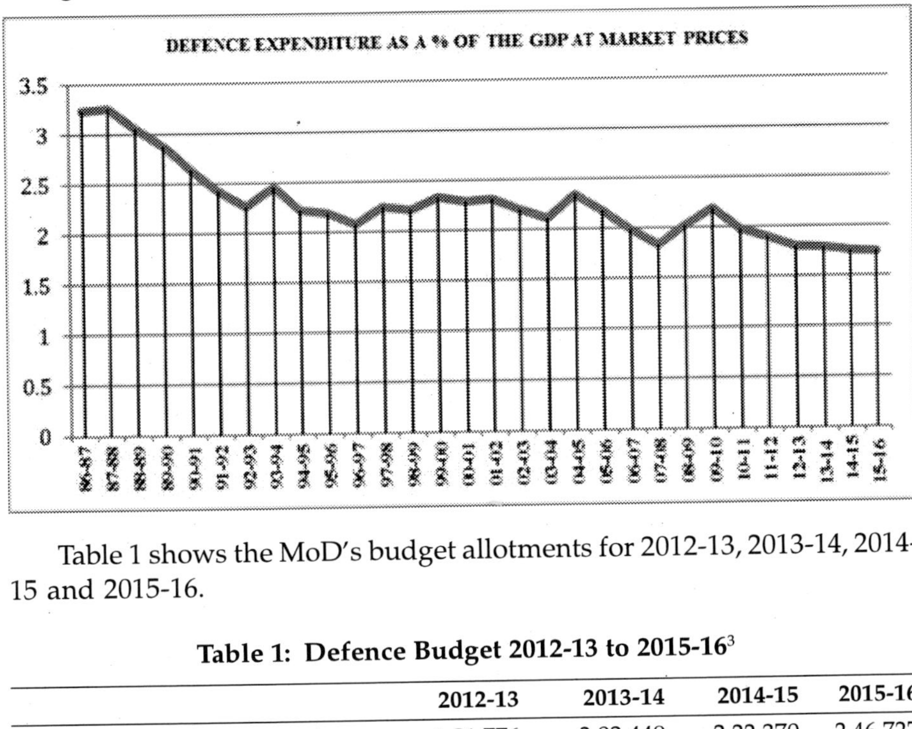

Table 1 shows the MoD's budget allotments for 2012-13, 2013-14, 2014-15 and 2015-16.

Table 1: Defence Budget 2012-13 to 2015-16[3]

	2012-13	2013-14	2014-15	2015-16
Defence Budget (Rs. in crore)	1,81,776	2,03,449	2,22,370	2,46,727
Growth (%)	6.36	12	9	10.95
Revenue Budget (Rs. in crore)	1,11,276.65	1,24,799.79	1,40,404.8	1,52,139
Revenue Growth (%)	6.22	12.15	7.70	8.36
Share of Revenue Expenditure in Defence Budget (%)	61.22	61.27	60.01	62
Capital Expenditure (Rs. in crore)	70,499.12	78,872.20	81,965.2	94,588
Share of Capital Budget in Defence Budget (%)	38.78	38.73	39.99	38

Table 2 shows the defence budget's vital statistics for 2015-16 and 2016-17.

Table 2: Defence Budget: Vital Statistics[4]

	2015-16	2016-17
Share of Defence Budget in Central Government Expenditure (%)	13.9	12.6
MoD's Budget (Rs. in Crore)	3,10,079.6	3,40,921.98
Growth in MoD's Budget (%)	8.72	9.95
Share of MoD Budget in GDP (%)	2.29	2.26

- The cascading effect of restricted financial support from the government has resulted in an army with no reserves (or an almost nil war wastage rate of reserve), serious deficiencies in ammunition and general stores items, as well as dwarfed modernisation initiatives.
- Budgets are often connected either to the wholesale price index (WPI) and the consumer price index (CPI), indicating the purchasing power of the rupee; or the gross domestic product (GDP) indicating the percentage of defence allotment when compared to the gross revenue of the government. If the hike of 6.36 per cent during the FY 2013-14 is considered, then with a WPI of nearly 6.8 per cent which was accompanied by the swift escalation of oil prices (which had reached nearly US$ 90-95 per barrel), as well as the rapid depreciation of the Indian rupee, the overall defence budget allotment works out to approximately (–)1.5 per cent. This without

Figure 2: New Procurement vs Committed Liabilities[5]

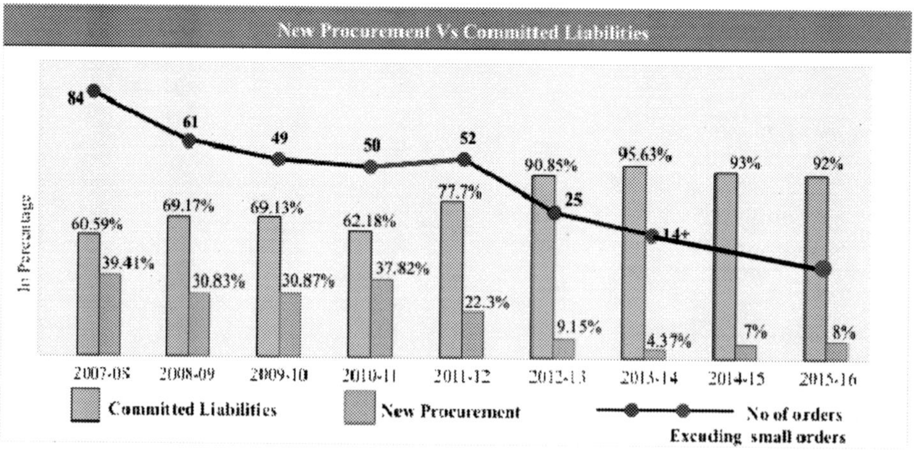

considering the withdrawal of over Rs. 10,000 crore that was made by the Finance Ministry at the end of the FY.

- One of the lesser known aspects of the grim financial situation faced by the armed forces during that FY was the substantial increase of product prices by the DPSU due to the depreciation of the value of the US dollar and the subsequent increase in the cost of raw material. It severely hampered the modernisation and reserves build-up of the armed forces.
- At the level of higher political leadership, major procurement schemes both at the Defence Acquisition Council (DAC) and the Finance Ministry were delayed. Thus, the armed forces could barely manage committed liabilities from the capital modernisation budget. Revenue shortfall increased as well. The miscommunication and resultant confusion culminated in the armed forces surrendering some of their budget allotments.
- An important point to note is that the army is a revenue budget heavy organisation. This can be attributed to the tremendous amount of manpower that they possess. The navy and the air force on the other hand are capital budget dominated organisations. The ratio for revenue to capital expenditure for the army is 80:20, while the ratio for the navy and the air force is nearly 50:50. Thus, capital modernisation is inbuilt in the annual budgets of the navy and the IAF. The army, on the other hand, has to struggle with the same due to negligible committed liabilities and deficient capital modernisation cases being cleared by the government. As a result of this deficiency, only small payments are being made from time to time. The details of modernisation cases that are being considered for the army and have finally been cleared are discussed below.

Defence Budgeting: Planning Commission Approach Paper for 12th Plan

The Planning Commission has linked the GDP to the likely availability of capital and revenue segments of the defence budget. The Approach Paper recommends that the revenue component should grow at 7.5 per cent (the distributed effect of the army's allotment being higher) and the capital component by 15 per cent. The Planning Commission has estimated GDP growth between 6.5 and 7 per cent, after taking into account 6 to 8 per cent inflation. Accordingly, the Planning Commission paper recommended a plan-wise defence budget as follows:

- 12th Plan — Rs. 11, 49,561 cr. – including the 7th Central Pay Commission (CPC)

- 13th Plan Rs. 22, 67,575 cr.
- 14th Plan Rs. 38, 88,437 cr.

An internal study within the army indicates that the revenue budget component of the critical deficiencies in the army for the FY 2017-18 and 2018-19 should be approximately Rs. 43,000 crore. This includes nearly Rs. 19,500 crore to replenish ammunition stocks. However, these figures are likely to rise due to several reasons such as constantly fluctuating dollar exchange rates, the seventh CPC's effect on the DPSU/OFB and its corresponding effect on inflation, the implementation of the Goods and Services Tax (GST), etc.

The armed forces require investments towards capacity building and modernisation urgently. Unless future budgets incorporate these concerns, the potential of the armed forces to deliver as per the nation's expectation would be severely affected.

Adequacy and Management of the Defence Budget

The present defence budget is pegged at 1.60 per cent of the GDP. Is it adequate for defence preparedness as well as modernisation?

Prior to the FY 2010-11, the previous four plan periods witnessed an average growth of approximately 2.1 per cent of the GDP along with an average rate of WPI inflation at around 7 to 8 per cent. The gradual decline in defence budget allocation has been observed since 2010. The defence budget for the FY 2013-14 was 1.79 per cent and for 2014-15, it was 1.78 per cent. It continues to be the same for the FY 2015-16 and 2016-17.

India, which is gradually becoming a front-line state – with its land and maritime borders active – cannot continue to deliver with budgetary allotments that are merely 1.78 per cent of the GDP. Under the present economic conditions in the country and the likely strengthening of the economy due to GST, it is felt that a sustained increase in the budget allotment of 2.1 to 2.3 per cent of the GDP is necessary to meet national

Table 3: Defence Spending as % of GDP in Other Countries (Approximate)[6]

• China	2.0
• Russia	4.4
• France	2.3
• USA	4.4
• Pakistan	4.2
• UK	2.5
• Average of the above nations considered together	3.3 per cent

security commitments. Delegating the task of managing the Revenue Budget to the Services is an idea that often comes up. Would it be a beneficial step?

The constitutional requirement for management of government funds dictates that government funds need to be spent as per laid down rules, and such expenditures must be audited. Accordingly, the government has well-established departments to advise the CFA. This task is usually undertaken by the Defence Finance Department and the Audit Department that reports to the CAG, who is an independent constitutional authority and reports to the parliament.

The management of revenue and capital budget allotments is actually exercised by the respective services through their finance departments without external interference. For example, in the case of the army these allotments are overseen by the DGFP. The services have not surrendered any revenue budget in recent times except for some small amounts under the pay and allowance head, wherein claims of all ranks and corresponding payments had to be rolled over to the next FY due to technical and audit issues. These are many small amounts which add up to less than Rs. 500 crore. This kind of roll-over will take place even if the services run the revenue budget. The problems of the services are twofold:

- They want to get out of the IFA and pre-audit cycle, however this request is constitutionally unacceptable.
- Many cases pertaining to both revenue and capital budgets get stalled in the MoD, PCDA, IFA and local audit levels. This is due to a lack of proper knowledge among the personnel regarding the nuances of financial management and related documentation. This cannot be learnt by *on the job training* any more, when the budget of the army itself is more than the annual budgets of many states in India.

The problem arises due to the non-availability of a Finance Cadre in the three services. In the army, the availability of trained financial personnel is non-existent, despite a Financial Cadre having being approved during the Army Commander's Conference in October 2012. Later, however, the Military Secretary Branch felt that such a cadre would be unmanageable due to its small size and, hence, the decision was not implemented. Furthermore, the accounts departments of the IAF and the navy are not the same as the MoD's Finance Department and are not allowed to control, manage and execute substantially large government finances. If the aim of the query relates to delegating audit and IFA functions to the armed forces, it should be clear that the Constitution and GFR prohibit expenditure, accounts and audit functions being undertaken by the same department. Therefore, under the present dispensations the status quo will have to be maintained.

Another contentious issue is the institution of a non-lapsable defence modernisation fund. Will such a step be helpful? While it is a good idea, it may be difficult to roll out and implement. The problems envisaged are as follows:

- The cash-based financial management system in the government does not permit the creation of a non-lapsable fund as a general policy. In the past, the Finance Ministry has permitted small non-lapsable funds on a case-to-case basis. It is known that as a policy the revenue budget is funded from the government's revenue collection of the previous year, and the capital budget is mostly funded by the bonds and long-term monetary instruments picked up from the market by paying. So, the capital modernisation funds have an execution period which cannot be overlooked as capital funds of the government need to be quickly deployed to commence returns.
- However, for specific national level projects, a non-lapsable fund can be earmarked if sanctioned by the Finance Ministry. But when the capital modernisation procurements of the services take four to five years, or more – mostly due to our retrograde systems and procedures – then what case can the services make for increased fund management powers for capital modernisation?

Large amounts of unspent funds are surrendered year after year. What measures can be taken to minimise the surrender of funds? The issue has been deliberated in great detail at various forums. There are a few key aspects to this vexing issue:

- The Finance Ministry's agenda shows higher initial allotment of the defence budget, whereas it wishes to provide less. This indicates that the Finance Ministry has not been satisfied by providing a low 1.78 per cent of GDP as the defence budget. Now, to withdraw the previously earmarked amount, the Finance Ministry micro manages the capital procurement cases by returning the files with minor observations and pushes it to the next year. The money saved is taken away during the last quarter of the FY. The entire exercise is undertaken as a previously laid down plan.
- Government parks funds in the defence budget, and moves it back when necessary.

- Revenue budget funds are not surrendered; in-fact the government has to make additional allotments during the RE stage.
- Due to non-specialist finance and procurement personnel, the pace of trials, documentation and the completed staff work to clear the laid down checks, procedures and audits get delayed substantially, resulting in higher unspent balance which is finally surrendered.

Way Ahead

There is no denying that there is substantial scope to improve resource management within the armed forces. Some of the issues that merit immediate consideration are:

(a) Perspective plans for modernisation and procurements should be formed with members from the DPSUs and DRDO. Experts from all these organisations should be encouraged to participate in the deliberations. Indigenisation should be given greater priority as well.

(b) All major projects need to have life-cycle costs that should include operational and maintenance costs in addition to capital acquisition costs.

(c) Unspent funds that remain with the DPSUs need to be monitored, and their efforts at arbitrarily increasing costs to adjust to budgetary constraints should not be permitted. Such practices increase the inefficiency in the system.

(d) Personnel costs in DPSUs must be monitored and reduced. The productivity of workers and installed machines needs to be quantitatively analysed and reviewed periodically, in order to obtain better returns on investment.

(e) Revenue expenditure should to be restricted, and there also needs to be a substantial increase in the capital procurement stage of budgetary allotment. Admittedly, this is easier said than done, since the revenue expenditure – particularly the army's – is galloping. Furthermore, the OROP will lead to additional pressure on the revenue budget of the MoD.

(f) The timely clearance of capital acquisition projections is necessary, as is the cost overrun that can occur sometimes due to delays. These overruns may be very expensive as in the case of the 155 mm 39 cal Ultra-Light Howitzer where the US Government has increased the cost of the project substantially due to a delay in project finalisation. If this trend remains unchecked, similar situations are bound to occur in the case of other large acquisition projects as well.

(g) Ammunition procurements and weapon systems overhaul that might cost over Rs. 10 crore should be moved from the revenue to the capital budget and brought under the ambit of non-lapsable funds. The government should explore the viability of opening up ammunition production to the private sector for indigenous manufacture. Such an act of privatisation might help provide alternatives to foreign suppliers and competitive costs. However, such privatisation would need to be coupled with strict security measures.

(h) A workable link should be established between the services budget, and the DRDO, DPSU, and other government establishments that are dealing with the services. Such a link should be based on good corporate practices with specific attention to budgetary allotments.

(i) "Life-cycle cost" is one of the key elements of resource management. It is worth noting that expenditure undertaken on operations and the maintenance of major equipment during its potential lifetime can dwarf the initial acquisition cost. It is, therefore, necessary to holistically consider issues such as:

  (i) total technical life,
  (ii) calendar life,
  (iii) mean-time between failures,
  (iv) mean-time to repair,
  (v) turnaround time,
  (vi) time between overhaul, etc.

These issues need to be considered while upgrading/purchasing major equipment and monitored holistically so that unnecessary fund drainage can be avoided. If implemented in a fully networked and online environment, it can substantially reduce thousands of crores on spare parts, equipment and maintenance.

Conclusion

The quantum of budget for the three services is very large and its management is becoming increasingly complex day-by-day. If budget allotments are managed in a professional and efficient manner, it will be possible to reduce expenditures and streamline processes, thereby achieving higher efficiency. The management of the defence budget is not merely limited to accounting. New processes that involve better policies, checks and procedures need to be implemented. There needs to be improved internal auditing of deployed finances as well as efficient deployment and redeployment of budgetary allotments to achieve optimal results. Whether the outcome budgetary process is followed or not, the Director General of Financial Planning (DGFP) of the army and his counterparts in the other services need to deploy and re-deploy financial allotments in a scientific manner so as to achieve the best output for their respective services. Hence, the time of ad hoc un-trained appointments in the Finance Divisions of the three services is over. There is an urgent need to establish a Finance Cadre in the army and the other two services. The personnel for the same would need to be trained in premium financial institutions such as the National Institute of Financial Management (NIFM), Faridabad, with special focus on job effective curriculum. Additionally, they should be encouraged to attend refresher courses from time to time. There is also a need to identify critical operational shortfalls and address them on priority. To ensure that important operational shortfalls are not lost sight of, institutional memory is necessary. The civilian counterparts in the MoD (Finance) have an upper hand due to their strong institutional memory. Unless the Headquarters of the three services get over this problem, they will not be able to put up their arguments in a convincing manner. Therefore, it is necessary that the finance department appointments in the services are classified as high-tech and the staff posted in these positions are given longer tenure, akin to the officers and staff in the MoD (Finance).

In order to ensure the smooth functioning of the Finance Divisions in the three services, coordination between the budget allotting authority and the actual user needs to improve. This can be best achieved by ensuring that the entire process of budget management becomes fully automated. Given recent technological proliferation, specific professional software can be acquired or developed for the process. The Service Headquarters needs improved communication and coordination between the budgeting/purchase/procurement for modernisation/budget head expenditures/audit/CGDA/PCDA/respective IFA in a seamless manner. Perhaps a fortnightly clean cash system between various budget holders may help with the process.

The government needs to empower the defence industry base in the private sector under the Make in India and Skill India initiatives.

Ordnance inventories need to be reduced. The holding of stocks in the Ordnance Depot should also be reduced substantially. There is a need to introduce modern supply chain management technologies like Just in Time, six Sigma process and other logistical chain systems that are being followed for delivery of stores by e-tailing organisations like Amazon. To achieve this concept, there is a need to improve storage infrastructure in order to avoid wastage.

The completion of any major project usually involves huge delays due to convoluted decision-making and repetitive due diligence issues. In order to avoid delays, the CFA's financial powers should be enhanced in tune with inflation. Currently there exists a substantial amount of inefficiency within the services while dealing with large finances. This is due to the lack of knowledge, attitude problems and a fear of the unknown coupled with a tremendous amount of hesitation regarding document signing. Therefore, the entire process of financial planning and budget management should be an integral part of the overall planning process. In case the overall management of the defence budget at the Finance and Defence Ministries cannot be changed to an outcome budget system, the concept can easily be introduced within the services instead. This will require prior consideration at the time of planning for the next FY budget and a focused internal distribution of funds to achieve preconceived aims.

There is a need to institute a more comprehensive establishment to conduct technical and user trials of new weapons and equipment under the vice chiefs of the three services. The present system is inefficient and far too personality based. It is recommended that the General Staff Qualitative Requirement (GSQR) evaluation and the trial team should be part of the same group and they should be domain specialists. Furthermore, any deficiency in GSQR compliance should not lead to a delay in the finalisation of the case for years. Therefore, an empowered standing committee with members from all the stakeholders and the DRDO should be established. This committee should be responsible for getting into the details of the problem and providing considered opinions for proceeding ahead.

Under the present conditions, perhaps a two to three years' roll-on capital modernisation budget should be considered. Along with it the three services should also move from a part manual-part automated inventory, accounts, budget, auditing and financial management systems to a fully integrated and automated system.

The higher CFAs like the army commanders and their counterparts in the navy and the air force, as well as the Principal Staff Officers (PSOs) in the Service Headquarters should be provided with fully qualified and trained financial advisors (Col./Lt Col. and staff) who can help them correct and complete all financial documentation that needs to be sent to the IFA. This will substantially cut down the time required to complete any finance and resource-related cases.

NOTES

1. Constitution of India available at http://lawmin.nic.in/olwing/coi/coi-english/coi-4March2016.pdf
2. MoD Annual reports available at http://mod.nic.in/documents/annual-report
3. Ibid.
4. Ibid.
5. Compiled from various Press Releases of MoD/PIB.
6. As compiled from various newspapers.

11

Defence Budget: Optimising Planning and Utilisation – II

Amit Cowshish

The *Merriam-Webster online Dictionary* defines optimisation as "an act, process or methodology of making something (as a design, system or decision) as fully perfect, functional or effective, as possible".[1] Optimising planning and utilisation of the defence budget, therefore, requires identification of the deficiencies in these processes and the steps required to address them.

Planning and utilisation are two distinct, albeit inter-related, activities. While there is a fair amount of clarity about what needs to be done to optimise utilisation of the defence budget, such clarity eludes the process of optimising defence "planning". This lack of clarity gives rise to the question whether optimisation of planning refers to the process of securing higher allocation for defence or does it refer to making the most of whatever allocation is made every year, or to both?'

Ideally this question should not arise as the budget allocation is a given for the Ministry of Defence (MoD),[2] and there is very little that the MoD can do to get it increased before the budget is passed by the Parliament or during the course of the financial year. But there is a scope to *plan* the process of securing higher allocation of resources in the long run and to prevent the reduction in allocation when the estimates are revised by the Ministry of Finance (MoF) as a part of the budgetary process. Such planning has to be based on pragmatism, as well as credibility of the estimates based on which the allocation is sought, and not on self-serving rhetoric.

Any discussion on the optimisation of planning generally revolves around the impact of inadequate funding and ends up with a fervent plea for higher allocation for defence. Merely asking for more funds is of little help. In the short to medium term time frame, the government's resources are going to remain limited. Simultaneously, it will continue to face serious challenges in raising its income and the demand from other sectors will continue to grow. All this has to be factored in while considering options for optimisation of the defence budget.

The endeavour in this chapter is to explore the possibilities that exist to *plan* for the prevention of the withdrawal of funds by the MoF, as well as to secure a gradual and realistic increase in allocation for defence, while simultaneously dealing with the question of making efficient use of the given outlays.

Optimisation of Planning

Securing Higher Allocation for Defence

The need for optimising the process of planning for securing higher allocation for defence arises because the current budget invariably falls short of the requirement by two commonly applied yardsticks. First, the annual allocation is consistently lesser than the requirement projected by the MoD to the MoF during their pre-budget discussions. Second, the allocation is always well below three per cent of the gross domestic product (GDP), which is considered by many, including the Standing Committee on Defence (SCoD), as the ideal level of funding.

Gap between projection and allocation: That the allocation is always less than the projection is indisputable. In 2016-17, for example, the army asked for the allocation of Rs 1,53,521.96 crore, but received only Rs 1,39,700.43 crore[3] in the budget estimates (BE) at the beginning of the year. It was the same with the other two services: the navy asked for Rs 48,725.87 crore but received Rs 39,424.88 crore, and the air force asked for Rs 66,995.01 crore, against which it received only Rs 53,451.25 crore.[4] There has been a similar mismatch in the previous years as well as in 2017-18.

This mismatch is sufficient to conclusively establish that adequate funds are not being provided to meet the requirements of the armed forces. However from the point of view of *planning,* it raises an important question: Does the difference between projection and allocation represent realistically and accurately the extent of the shortfall?

Back-of-the-envelope calculations based on various SCoD reports show that in 2014-15, the gap between the overall projection made by the MoD and the actual allocation was around Rs 80,000 crore; while in each of the two subsequent years, it was close to Rs 40,000 crore. Gaps of this magnitude cannot be bridged during the pre-budget discussions between the defence and finance ministries, particularly since the demand is not based on any commitment made by the MoF. In fact, the projections are invariably out of tune with the indication of how much is likely to be available in a given year. The demand is also seldom, if ever, fully backed by irrefutable data.

The only inescapable conclusion that can be drawn is that the projections are not realistic. This assumes significance because the execution of any annual expenditure plan, based on the assumption that the amount demanded will actually be available in its entirety, is bound to present insurmountable difficulties. Therefore, the question that the planners need to ask themselves is whether making such unrealistic projections serves any purpose? And if not, would it not be better to synchronise annual projections with the likely availability of funds without banking on additional allocations which may or may not come through during the year?

Need for accuracy in projections: Wide fluctuations in the estimated and final cost of acquisition programmes and other projects on the one hand; and the underutilisation of funds provided for capital expenditure on the other, raise questions about the accuracy of projections. The first problem can be attributed to a weak regimen of costing, coupled with the lack of sanctity attached to the initial estimation of the cost of the projects and the absence of any mechanism to enforce accountability for resultant cost and time overruns. This underscores the need for ensuring accuracy of budgetary projections. While it is true that estimates cannot be precise but these have to be credible enough to be taken seriously by the MoF.

Costing – the Achilles heel: Costing is arguably the weakest link in the process of budget estimation as well as subsequent expenditure management. While the MoD does have the benefit of professional cost accountants working for it, they have been unable to perform the function with as much professional finesse as they are capable of because the requisite wherewithal has not been made available to them. It would not be wrong to say that costing in defence, as a discipline, is yet to mature. It requires careful nurturing, particularly if the MoD is serious – as indeed it ought to be – about life-cycle costing.

Costing of military equipment is complex. It requires the creation of the product and country specific historical and current databases on price, inflation, etc., as well as the development of defence-specific techniques for costing. It is unfair to leave the whole complex process to a few individuals in the ministry. More importantly, a greater sanctity needs to be attached to the estimation of cost than is the case at present. Capital-intensive acquisition and infrastructure development programmes are often approved on the basis of a tenuous estimation of cost, resulting in final costs being substantially higher than the estimated costs. Although to be fair, cost-escalation is also attributable to several other reasons, such as changes in the scope of work or the tax structure.

Underutilisation of the capital budget: The other related factor which impinges on the credibility of projections made by the MoD is the persistent underutilisation of funds allocated for capital expenditure. The fact that large sums remain underutilised is ironic considering that the annual allocation is invariably less than the requirement projected by the MoD.

The capital budget comprises two notional segments. A large proportion of the allocation is spread over budget heads which cater to the procurement of equipment, weapon systems, various platforms and other capabilities usually associated with the modernisation of the armed forces. The remaining funds are largely spent on acquisition of land and civil works.

The malady of underutilisation afflicts all these budget heads to varying extents. In 2016-17 the total allocation for capital expenditure of the three services came down from Rs 85,878.20 at the BE stage to Rs 74,413.28 crore at the revised estimates (RE) stage with all the three services contributing to this decrease (see Table 1).

Considering that the assessment of likely expenditure at the RE stage is more realistic, it can be presumed that the MoD actually ended up underutilising Rs 11,464.92 crore out of the budget allocated at the beginning of the year 2016-17 for capital expenditure. This has been the case in the previous years as well.

Table 1[5]: Capital Budget: 2016-17 (Rs in crore)

Service	BE	RE
Army	27217.31	24230.47
Navy	25003.24	19740.66
Air Force	33657.65	30442.15
Total	85878.20	74413.28

Non-lapsable defence modernisation fund: Some analysts believe that the problem of underutilisation could be addressed by creating a non-lapsable defence modernisation fund and the entire unspent balance could be transferred to this fund at the end of the financial year. A tentative step was indeed taken by the National Democratic Alliance (NDA) government in 2004 when the then Finance Minister Jaswant Singh, announced the establishment of a non-lapsable Defence Modernisation Fund of Rs. 25,000 crore to "commit availability of funds for the purpose" while presenting the interim budget for 2004-05.[6]

It is not as if the fund did not get established because the NDA lost the general elections following the presentation of the interim budget. Had that been the sole reason, the present Bhartiya Janata Party (BJP) government would have set it up by now, particularly because the SCoD has also been persistently recommending it. There is also no constitutional impediment in creating such a fund, which is evident from the fact that a somewhat similar non-lapsable pool of resources for the development of the north-eastern region has been in existence since 1997-98.[7] Clearly, there are other more complex reasons why the fund has not been set up so far.

One way of operating the modernisation fund could be to withdraw the unspent balances from the exchequer and park them in a separate account to be used some time in the future. In a manner of speaking, this will amount to setting aside some money (unspent balance in this context) out of the borrowings, keeping in mind the persistent revenue deficit that the successive governments have not been able to wipe out. It would not be financially prudent to keep a part of the funds, borrowed by the government idle, for use in the future.

Alternatively, it could be a notional transfer of unspent balances to the modernisation fund. The problem with this alternative is that the MoF will need to raise the money in the year in which it is required to be taken out of the fund. Moreover, the Parliament's approval for the appropriation of any amount out of the modernisation fund will also be required in the year in which the amount is to be spent. This will undermine the utility of the fund.[8]

The SCoD has dismissed these arguments in the past, and eventually its perseverance has made the MoD change its mind once again about the creation of a non-lapsable fund. The ministry sent a proposal to the MoF on February 09, 2017 for the creation of the fund, although the MoF continues to remain reluctant to set it up. This change of heart on the MoD's part has been praised by the SCoD, but given the MoF's stand on the subject, it will take some doing to set up the fund[9] and, more importantly, derive the intended benefit from it.

Reduction of allocation at RE stage: contrived or real?: While the reduction of capital outlay at the RE stage cannot be disputed, many argue that this reduction is not because of the MoD's inability to utilise funds, but due to the manipulation of these funds by the MoF, which plays a critical role in sanctioning all capital acquisition contracts where the negotiated cost is more than Rs 2,000 crore (raised from Rs 500 crore in 2017).

The argument is that the MoF delays the process deliberately with the aim of making sure that the MoD is unable to utilise the allocated funds which can then be withdrawn at the RE stage to meet the fiscal deficit target set for a given year. However, statistics do not support the view that the annual fiscal targets cannot be met by the MoF unless it withdraws money from the MoD.

The same argument is advanced to explain occasional reduction at the RE stage under certain revenue budget heads. Considering that the financial power for sanctioning revenue expenditure is fully delegated to the MoD and the services down to the lowest echelons, the inability to spend the allocated amount, at least under the revenue segment, cannot be attributed to any external factors such as the bureaucratic machinations by the MoF. The situation is, however, somewhat different in the case of utilisation of the capital budget.

Preventing Reduction of Allocation for Capital Expenditure at the RE Stage

The view that the underutilisation of funds is actually manipulated by the MoF is unsubstantiated. Even if it is true, the fact remains that the amount authorised by the parliament for appropriation during the year does not get fully utilised. Whatever the reasons for underutilisation,[10] the MoD needs to address this problem through better planning. This has to be its first priority as it is possible to prevent to underutilisation of funds.

One of the arguments given by the MoF is that it withdraws the portion of the allocated amount that is likely to remain unspent, as per the assessment made during its consultation with the MoD at the RE stage. That such a mutual consultation does take place is certainly true, but whether the assessed amount that is likely to remain unspent is determined through mutual consent, is questionable. The official position of the MoD has been that it can always spend the money if it is not withdrawn, but it cuts no ice with the MoF because the MoD is unable to substantiate this claim.

The impression that the MoF manipulates acquisition proposals so as to be able to withdraw a substantial amount at the RE stage, as well as the impression that were it not for the withdrawal, the MoD would have spent the money, needs to be dispelled. Better expenditure management by the MoD leading to the creation of contractual commitments in the first six months of the year would make it virtually impossible for the MoF to withdraw funds at the RE stage.

It is equally important that the MoD officials, who participate in pre-budget discussions with the MoF, are better equipped with irrefutable facts and figures in order to establish without an iota of doubt that the entire funds allocated for the year stand committed. The role of the services and the other departments in providing the MoD with all the necessary details is critical in this exercise. Incidentally, some analysts used to hold the view that the civilian bureaucracy was unable to convince the MoF during the pre-budget discussions to meet the projected requirement completely. Although now the service officers participate in the pre-budget discussions, it has not made a difference in so far as the mismatch between the projection and the allocation.

Viability of Higher Allocations for Defence

The question whether it is viable for the government to make higher allocations for defence is moot as it is inextricably linked with generation of substantially higher revenues for meeting the requirement of not just the defence but also of the other sectors, including health, education and infrastructure development. What is important from the point of view of defence planning that it is not based on unrealistic assumptions about future increases in the defence budget.

A more immediate issue that has cropped up in the context of planning is the replacement of the Planning Commission by the Niti Ayog which has vowed to foray into defence planning as well. This has created uncertainty regarding what shape the present three-tiered structure of defence planning will take in future. Both the 15-year Long-term Integrated Perspective Plan (LTIPP) 2002-17 and the 12th Defence Five-year Plan 2012-17 are due to be replaced with new ones from April 01, 2017. What will be the basis of revising these plans, what role will the Niti Ayog play in that revision, and to what extent, are questions that cannot be answered at this stage. These questions continue to be relevant although media reports suggest that the armed forces are now ready with the 13th Five-year Defence Plan.[11]

There is a need to draw lessons from the past experience in defence planning. While the problems with defence planning are manifold, one problem which impacts the subject being discussed is the financial moorings of the defence plans. The unrealistic assumption about the availability of funds that characterises annual projections stems from the assumptions that underlie the 15-year and the five-year defence plans. The LTIPP 2002-17, for instance, was based on the assumption that the allocation for defence during this period would be equivalent to three per cent of the GDP – a level that has perhaps never been reached in the recent past and is unlikely to be reached in the near future. The 13th Five-year Defence Plan apparently envisages an outlay of Rs 27 lakh crore.[12] This will require the allocation to be more than doubled beginning 2018-19. The question whether this is practical is moot.

This is a very difficult problem for the MoD to tackle entirely on its own. Protestations by successive finance ministers in their budget speeches about no stone being left unturned for the nation's defence and security are not compatible with the persistent discordance between the MoD and the MoF on the question of annual allocation. The financial viability of defence planning is a larger issue that needs to be resolved at the highest level in the government.

This situation has come about because, by all accounts, the MoD has been reluctant in involving itself in defence planning throughout the process, leaving it largely to the services and other departments. This has to change. Not just the MoD, but the MoF, National Security Council, Ministry of External Affairs and other associated departments need to be fully involved in the process of developing defence plans. All of them need to come together from the beginning until the end of the planning process, if the problems besetting defence planning are to be fixed.

Optimisation of Utilisation

This brings us to the next part of the discussion. While all the issues related to the optimisation of budget planning cannot be addressed in a short while, there are many things that can be done to optimise the utilisation of the allocated resources. The formulation and management of the defence budget should not be seen as some kind of a blue-collar, plebeian task to be handled by the MoD's Finance Division. The Department of Defence in the MoD needs to involve itself in the formulation and execution of the annual budgets[13] for it is the MoD as a whole and not just its Finance Division that is responsible for overall defence preparedness.

Involvement of Department of Defence

The involvement of the Department of Defence[14] would mean that the DoD would need to lay down the targets to be achieved during the year keeping in mind the availability of funds, issuing guidelines to be followed by all budget centres while assessing their requirement, application of standard costing techniques and a host of other things. These are small steps that can be taken immediately, pending the resolution of larger issues related to efficacious planning.

A point needs to be made at this stage regarding the general impression that defence planning suffers because there is no long-term assurance of funds. While this is true – and it is doubtful if there can actually be any "assurance" of funds – it would be incorrect to say that the MoD has no indication of the funds likely to be made available in the long run. The annual growth in the defence budget that needed to be taken into consideration for the purposes of planning was known before the formulation of the 11th and 12th five-year defence plans.[15]

More recently, the medium-term fiscal policy statement of 2016 clearly indicated that the government estimated its total defence expenditure to be 1.6 per cent of the GDP in 2017-18 and 2018-19.[16] It has indeed turned out to be true for the year 2017-18, and there is no reason to suspect that it will be any different in 2018-19 as there is no revised forecast in the medium term fiscal policy statement of 2017.[17] It is unlikely, though, that the MoD's projections for 2017-18 took this fact into account.

The choice really is between planning expenditure – both in the long run and on an annual basis – based on unrealistic assumptions on the one hand and with due consideration of the financial realities on the other. Continuous remonstrance regarding the inadequacy of allocation has not helped all these years and it is unlikely to help in future.

Outcome-oriented Budget Management

There is a need to ensure that expenditure leads to planned outcomes. This requires a restructuring of the defence budget in order to make it possible to allocate funds for specific acquisition schemes, programmes, projects and operational activities. It should be known right in the beginning of the year what portion of the funds are being allocated for the procurement of ammunition, bulletproof jackets, or even various types of aircrafts, and what the intended outcomes would be in quantifiable terms.

These outcomes should form the benchmark for evaluating performance at the end of the year. This approach was recommended by the SCoD in 2016. Though the recommendation was related to capital acquisitions, it can be extended and applied to critical activities funded from the revenue budget.[18] It is inexplicable why no significant steps have been taken as of now, to move towards an outcome-oriented management of the defence budget.

An outcome-oriented management of budget outlays pre-supposes a need-based delegation of financial powers. The existing scheme of delegation of financial powers is inefficient. The authority to spend needs to be delegated to the working-level functionaries who are responsible for producing the intended outcomes. This does not entail any risk because the delegates will be able to exercise these powers only as per the prescribed rules, regulations and standard operating procedures, and subject to availability of funds and a reasonable system of checks and balances.

While a distinction needs to be made between the financial powers for capital and revenue procurements, with the former being concentrated at the higher echelons in the government and the Services Headquarters, there is no reason why the retention of financial powers for revenue expenditure at the higher echelons should not be more of an exception than the rule.

For example, while the officers commanding workshops, repair depots or dockyards need not be given full power to spend on, new machinery or land acquisition; they ought to be given full financial powers to incur expenditure on buying spares, outsourcing or running their own establishments, all of which are critical for discharging the responsibility cast on them.

The reluctance to delegate financial powers to the lower echelons to incur revenue expenditure is inexplicable. This issue revolves around less than a third of the revenue budget, the rest of which is spent on pay and allowances, hardly entailing the exercise of any financial powers. The tendency to tie down whatever powers are presently exercised by the lower functionaries to a plethora of terms and conditions negates the very purpose of delegation.

One of these conditions, which has emerged as a sore point in the system is the need for the competent financial authorities (CFAs) to whom the powers are delegated to seek the concurrence of integrated financial advisors (IFAs) before sanctioning any expenditure beyond a certain threshold within the overall limit up to which the financial powers are delegated to them. These advisors are perceived to be a hindrance by the CFAs. This system has thrown up serious issues that have remained unresolved over the years.

It would, however, be wrong to pin the entire blame on the IFAs. The system gives CFAs the authority to overrule the advice of the IFAs. Theoretically there should be no hesitation in exercising this authority if CFAs have the courage of their conviction but in practice the IFAs are seldom overruled. There is a need for the MoD to step in and resolve this issue, to the satisfaction of both, so that the delegation of powers serves its intended purpose.

The effective delegation of financial powers and an outcome-oriented management of the budget are contingent upon several factors. These include removal of ambiguities in, and updating of, rules and regulations at regular intervals of two or three years, laying down of standard operating procedures., removal of procedural bottlenecks and the creation of a forum for quick resolution of all issues arising from the exercise of these powers.

This does not necessarily imply that procedures need to be diluted. That is simply not possible; public money has to be handled with due care and in a transparent manner. The problem, quite honestly, is also not so much with the existence of procedures per se, but due to the difficulties caused by the lack of clarity and the grey areas in these procedures. This has impacted decision-making, which has been the bane of efficient expenditure management all along. The answer lies in instituting a system of collegiate decision-making and crisis management.

Rationalisation of the Demands for Grant

An outcome-oriented management of the budget would require rationalisation of the structure of demands for grant to ensure that the categories under which the allocation is made are conducive to outcome-oriented monitoring. The demands for grant presented by various ministries and departments to the parliament were restructured in 2016. This resulted in the number of demands for grant presented by the MoD to the parliament coming down from eight to four. The structure of these demands for grant was again tinkered with in 2017. But all this is unlikely to be of much help as this exercise has not led to the creation of outcome-oriented budget heads. If anything, it has only resulted in further obfuscating the defence budget.

In 2016-17, for example, the outlay for the National Cadet Corps was separated from the army's revenue and its capital outlays. In 2017-18, it is back to the fold, while the outlay for the Jammu and Kashmir (J&K) Light Infantry – a regular regiment of the Indian Army – continues to be outside the army's budget. Similarly, outlay for Joint Staff continues to be a part of the navy's outlay, though it does not function under the administrative control of the Chief of Naval Staff.

Similarly, the allocation of funds under the "stores" budget head does not provide a clear idea about the allocations made for the procurement of ammunition to cover up deficiencies in the war wastage reserves. Nor does the allocation of funds under the "other equipment" budget head – under the capital segment of the budget – provide a clear idea about what is being procured.

There are many such incongruities which only create further confusion in the management of the defence budget. The removal of these incongruities will not necessarily lead to the availability of more funds for the services, but it will certainly facilitate better management of budget outlays by the financial planning directorates. Rationalisation of the demands for grant should be based on outcome-oriented reclassification of budget heads under which allocations are made, both under the revenue and capital segments, as is already being done to a limited extent under the capital segment of the budget.

Rationalisation of Expenditure

Given the current level of defence spending, it is important to make sure that the entire expenditure being incurred by the MoD is really justified. At the SCoD's behest, the MoD had set up a committee in 2008 to review defence expenditure.[19] The committee's report contained several recommendations to rationalise expenditure but those recommendations were not pursued seriously. There is a need to revisit this issue with as much objectivity and dispassion as can possibly be ensured by the MoD, based on the recommendations of the other committees set up since then.[20]

To be sure, it is not all about reducing the size of the armed forces. This is a very sensitive issue by any stretch of imagination and while there is a strong case for it – with more than half the total defence budget being spent on pay and pensions – there are several other organisations and activities which also need to be subjected to a zero-based review. The fierceness of the response to any suggestion to carry out such a review comes in the way of any serious attempt to rationalise expenditure. Nevertheless, this has to be done by picking up a specified number of activities and organisations every year for independent zero-based review of their continued utility.

There is also a need to look at long-term measures, such as the creation of a logistics command to optimise the administrative cost of providing logistical support to the services (as also Coast Guard and Border Roads Organisation) and improving efficiency. This concept also needs to be extended to the operational domain through the creation of theatre commands, as also to all other activities that are presently being carried out in a fragmented manner.

Defence procurements are another case in point where the responsibility is presently being shared by the MoD, the respective services, HQ Integrated Defence Staff, Directorate General of Quality Assurance and several other agencies. This fragmentation is fraught with redundancies and undermines efficiency and accountability. A committee was set up by the MoD last year to recommend the modality of setting up a compact defence acquisition organisation. While the committee has submitted its report,[21] it is going to be of little use unless some bold decisions are taken by the MoD.

Generation of Higher Revenues and Reduction in Expenditure

This issue has not received as much attention as it deserves. There is a need to explore the possibility of generating higher revenues through the exploitation of the idle capacity of the assets held by the MoD. As of now, all the receipts and recoveries related to rents and tariffs, sale of ordnance stores and dairy products, services provided by the armed forces, etc., are credited to the Consolidated Fund of India (CFI) and subtracted from the gross amount allocated under various demands for grant.

There is a case for the recoveries made against the expenditure incurred by the services/other MoD departments from their annual allocation for providing goods and services to outside users being ploughed back into the defence budget by accounting for it as reduction in expenditure. However limited it may be, this will mitigate the hardship caused by the allocated sums being spent for providing goods and services that have nothing to do with operational preparedness of the armed forces. There is also a need to explore the possibility of greater commercial exploitation of the idle assets, including research and development laboratories, and the proceeds being ploughed back for the maintenance of those very assets and other infrastructure.

Rationalisation of Administrative Costs

More cost-effective ways will need to be found to reduce administrative and establishment costs. This will require outsourcing on a larger scale under clearly set out policy and procedure. The adoption of performance based logistics – shutting down or leasing out money guzzling facilities should also be considered. This would require the adoption of a government-owned-company-operated model for running defence establishments that necessitates public-private partnerships, mandatory electronic payments, multitasking by personnel, zero-based review of all cost-prohibitive activities, pooling of assets (including infrastructure), jointness in training, real-time accounting and reporting, adoption of accrual accounting, and the creation of databases for financial management, including life-cycle cost estimation. While it is not as if nothing has been done to promote some of these measures, but the disjointed focus on these initiatives has produced sub-optimal results.

Measures not Meant Just for the Services

All these measures are not meant for the services alone. These should be applied in equal measure to all the other departments under the MoD's administrative control. There is a great deal of potential for the optimisation of expenditure there. To illustrate this point, in his budget speech for the year 2017-18, Finance Minister Arun Jaitley announced "a comprehensive web based interactive Pension Disbursement System for Defence Pensioners" to "receive pension proposals and make payments centrally". This, he said, "will reduce the grievances of defence pensioners".[22]

There is no reason why the pension sanctioning authorities should not take on the responsibility for disbursing pensions electronically. This will save on the expense of running more than 50 Defence Pension Disbursement Offices all over the country (which are funded from the overall defence budget); and also relieve the banks of the pension disbursement workload presently being grudgingly borne by them.

The centralised disbursement of pension – by no means an impossible task – will result in a more accurate and timely disbursement of pension, over and above saving establishment costs. However, the success of the arrangement will depend on the establishment of a strong grievance redressal mechanism. There are several such potential pockets of rationalisation that could be looked into.

Several other measures could be added to this representative list of areas which merit focused attention by the MoD. These ideas are not being talked about for the first time, and it will be unrealistic to expect any miraculous effect even if these are implemented but there are no quick-fixes to address the problems besetting the planning and utilisation of the defence budget. Optimisation is not rocket science. All it requires is the acknowledgment of financial constraints by all concerned and, more importantly, determination on the part of the civilian and military leadership to follow through on the steps – some even quite drastic – that need to be taken to fix the problems.

NOTES

1. "Optimization", *Merriam-Webster.com*, Merriam-Webster, at https://www.merriam-webster.com/dictionary/optimization.
2. For the purpose of this chapter, the MoD includes armed forces and other departments under the administrative control of the Ministry of Defence, unless the context requires specific reference to one or more of them.
3. The figures for the army include allocation for the National Cadet Corps, Military Farms, Rashtriya Rifles and Ex-servicemen Health Scheme.
4. Standing Committee on Defence (16th Lok Sabha), Report No. 20, May 2016, pp. 8, 21 and 51, at http://164.100.47.134/lsscommittee/Defence/16_Defence_20.pdf (Accessed on February 10, 2017).
5. Defence Services Estimates 2016-17
6. Interim Budget 2004-2005, Speech of Jaswant Singh, Minister of Finance, paragraph 27, February 03, 2004, at http://indiabudget.nic.in/ub2004-05(I)/bs/speecha.htm (Accessed on March 07, 2017).
7. See "Non-Lapsable Central Pool of Resources", Ministry of Development of North Eastern Region, at http://mdoner.gov.in/node/728 (Accessed on March 07, 2017).
8. For a more detailed analysis, see A. Cowshish, "Would a Non-lapsable Defence Modernisation Fund Work?", *IDSA Comment*, Institute for Defence Studies and Analyses, February 10, 2017, at http://idsa.in/idsacomments/would-non-lapsable-defence-modernisation-fund-work_acowshish_100217 (Accessed on March 07, 2017).
9. For details, see Standing Committee on Defence (16th Lok Sabha) Report No. 31, March 2017, Part I, Paragraph 1.17 to 1.25, and Part II, Paragraphs 10 to 15.
10. It is not within the scope of this chapter to examine the causes of underutilisation, but a number of scholarly articles are available on the subject.
11. Rajat Pandit, "Forces seek Rs 27 lakh cr over next 5 years for def projects", *The Times of India*, July 16, 2017 at http://timesofindia.indiatimes.com/india/forces-seek-rs-27-lakh-crore-over-next-5-years-for-defence-projects/articleshow/59613786.cms (Accessed on July 16, 2017)
12. Ibid.
13. As of now, the requirement is worked out by the services and other departments, aggregated by the Finance Division of the ministry and communicated to the MoF with the minister's approval. It is generally only at this stage, when the projections are to be submitted to the minister for approval, that the Department of Defence gets involved at the level of the defence secretary.
14. There are four departments in the MoD, besides the Finance Division. These are the departments of Defence; Defence Production; Defence Research & Development; and Ex-servicemen Welfare. On account of the tasks allocated to it, the Department of Defence commands pre-eminence.
15. No evidence to that effect is probably available in the public domain. This statement is based on personal knowledge of the author who was associated with defence planning while serving with the MoD between 2005 and 2012.
16. Medium Term Fiscal Policy Statement 2016, paragraph 66, at http://indiabudget.gov.in/budget2016-2017/ub2016-17/frbm/frbm2.pdf (Accessed on February 15, 2017).

17. Fiscal Policy Strategy Statement, at http://indiabudget.gov.in/ub2017-18/frbm/frbm3.pdf
18. Standing Committee on Defence (16th Lok Sabha), Twenty-second Report on Demands for Grant for 2016-17, May 2016, pp. 58-59, at http://164.100.47.134/lsscommittee/Defence/16_Defence_22.pdf (Accessed on February 16, 2017).
19. The report is not in the public domain.
20. One of the recent committees was headed by Lt Gen DB Shekatkar (Retd) which, among other things, has recommended a leaner military. See 'A leaner military is on the cards', *The Hindu*, March 25, 2017 at http://www.thehindu.com/news/national/a-leaner-military-is-on-the-cards/article17664580.ece (Accessed on July 21, 2017)
21. Sushant Singh, "Create Unit Outside Defence Ministry to Fast-track Defence Deals: Panel to Tell Govt", *The Indian Express*, February 03, 2017, at http://indianexpress.com/article/india/create-unit-outside-defence-ministry-to-fast-track-defence-deals-panel-to-tell-govt-4505063/ (Accessed on February 7, 2017).
22. Union Budget 2017-18, Budget Speech, paragraph 126, at http://indiabudget.gov.in/ub2017-18/bs/bs.pdf (Accessed on February 17, 2017).

12

Indian Defence Industry: A Reform Agenda

Laxman Kumar Behera

The story of the Indian defence industry is one of great disappointment. Despite having several associated bodies and a huge workforce engaged in research, development and production, India continues to be the world's largest arms importer.[1] Successive past attempts to reverse the fortunes of indigenous arms production have met with limited success. Past failures notwithstanding, one more attempt is currently being made by the National Democratic Alliance (NDA) government led by Prime Minister Narendra Modi, through its ambitious "Make in India" programme. Under the programme, a host of initiatives have been taken/are being contemplated by the Ministry of Defence (MoD) with the objective of making India self-reliant in terms of defence requirements. The question that still looms large, however, is: can the new initiative change the fortune of an industry that has been marred thus far by a host of legacy issues? Issues such as policy conservatism, structural inadequacy, gross inefficiency of the entities directly responsible for research and development (R&D) and production and the slow pace of governmental decision-making.

This chapter attempts to examine some of the fundamental weaknesses of the Indian defence industry, in order to provide certain policy prescriptions aimed at improving India's domestic industrial base. In doing so, it also attempts to engage in a broad survey of the performance of the industry and critically examine the initiatives undertaken under the much-touted Make in India programme.

Indian Defence Industry: How Much is Made in India?

The Indian defence industry is largely dominated by government-owned/ controlled entities, with the private sector playing a peripheral role.[2] The dominance of the public sector is ensured through the nine giant Defence Public Sector Undertakings (DPSUs) and 41 Ordnance Factories (OFs) that are under the administrative control of the MoD's Department of Defence Production (DDP). There are also 50-odd research laboratories under the umbrella of the Defence Research and Development Organisation (DRDO), the MoD's premier R&D agency. Together, these three (DPSUs, OFs and DRDO) have more than 190,000 direct employees on their payroll, including over 7,400 scientists. There is a clear division of responsibility among these entities. While the DRDO is largely responsible for technology development, the DPSUs and OFs are more concerned with production. In 2015-16, their combined value of production was Rs 51,000 crore, of which Rs 38,000 crore (or 56 per cent) was by the DPSUs.[3]

In comparison to the DPSUs and OFs, the private sector is a nascent player. It was barred from defence production till 2001, when the government, in a major policy decision, decided to throw open the sector to private investment. The government opened out the defence sector to foreign companies as well and these companies could own up to 26 per cent equity stake in any defence joint venture. (The FDI cap has been increased to 100 per cent by the Modi government. See more on this later.) Post the 2001 liberalisation policy, private sector companies have shown a great deal of interest in investing in the defence sector, which can clearly be discerned by the 340-odd industrial licences obtained by them. These licences have been obtained by around 200 companies, of which 50-odd companies have reportedly commenced production, although there is very little official information regarding the same in the public domain.

The vast set of public and private companies has, however, been unable to meet the crucial 70 per cent goal of self-reliance in defence procurement set to be achieved by 2005 by a high-level committee that was set up under the then Scientific Advisor (SA) to the Defence Minister, Dr Abdul Kalam. A 2013 study by the Institute for Defence Studies and Analyses (IDSA) estimates self-reliance at around 40 per cent during the period 2006-07 and 2010-11.[4] The situation does not seem to have changed in any significant manner during the post-study period. In the three years following the study, the MoD spent a whopping Rs 82,496 crore on capital procurement from foreign sources.[5] Additionally, there is an equally significant amount of outflow of foreign exchange (FE) in the form of what is now widely known as India's indirect arms imports. These indirect imports are undertaken by the DPSUs and OFs in the form of parts, components and raw materials for the purpose of their production. In four years, from 2011-15, the utilisation of FE by the nine DPSUs alone amounts to a staggering Rs 60,238 crore, indicating the huge import dependency implicit in whatever little is being made in India.

What Ails India's Defence Industrial Base

Archaic Model of Defence Production

The biggest stumbling block for India's defence production is the archaic model that is rooted in the mind-set of 1940s and 1950s. Soon after India's independence, the policymakers thought it would be wise to give monopoly rights over certain core sectors of the economy to the state. The monopoly was responsible for the creation of the Central Public Sector Enterprises (CPSEs) – that encompasses the nine DPSUs – and some departmentally run industrial houses like the OFs. The legal basis for them to operate was provided through the first-ever Industrial Policy Resolution of 1948 and its revised version of 1956, both of which were articulated under the aegis of India's first Prime Minister Jawaharlal Nehru. Under the Nehruvian model of state-led industrialisation, the task of producing defence items was exclusively entrusted to the DPSUs and OFs.

At the time of independence, the justification provided for limiting defence production to the public sector was that the private sector (at the time) was not financially and technological capable enough to meet the requirements of the armed forces. Over the years, however, while the private sector has emerged as a force to be reckoned with, the public sector is rapidly losing its importance. There is a growing realisation that PSUs, given their inefficiency, have been a drag on the Indian economy. The state of affairs of these public-sector giants is perhaps best reflected in the 1991 Industrial Policy Statement released by the Narasimha Rao government, which took the bold step of demolishing the "licence-permit-quota raj" system that was prevalent in many industrial sectors.[6] The policy statement rightfully observed that:

> After the initial exuberance of the public sector entering new areas of industrial and technical competence, several problems have begun to manifest themselves in many of the public enterprises. Serious problems are observed in the insufficient growth in productivity, poor project management, over-manning, lack of continuous technological upgradation, and inadequate attention to R&D and human resource development. In addition, public enterprises have shown a very low

> rate of return on the capital invested. This has inhibited their ability to re-generate themselves in terms of new investments as well as in technology development. The result is that many of the public enterprises have become a burden rather than being an asset to the Government. The original concept of the public sector has also undergone considerable dilution. The most striking example is the takeover of sick units from the private sector. This category of public sector units, accounts for almost one third of the total losses of central public enterprises. Another category of public enterprises, which does not fit into the original idea of the public sector being at the commanding heights of the economy, is the plethora of public enterprises which are in the consumer goods and services sectors.[7]

In view of the 1991 Policy Statement, the government made a plan to disinvest 20 per cent equity in select CPSEs. This disinvestment cap has been reviewed several times since then and one of the most important reviews was carried out in 1993 by an expert committee under C. Rangarajan. The report recommended that the government's share, – in sectors that are not exclusively reserved for CPSEs, – could either be divested completely or brought down to 26 per cent. A second recommendation was that the government's equity share in sectors that are reserved for the public (such as the defence industry), could be brought down to 51 per cent. This second recommendation didn't, however, get immediate acceptance by the government, even though it has undertaken a certain degree of disinvestment (including strategic sale[8]) from companies in the non-reserved sectors. Until recently, successive governments have continued with the policy of retaining majority holding in all the key CPSEs, which include the DPSUs.

In an important decision taken by the Modi government in October 2016, the Cabinet Committee on Economic Affairs (CCEA) has approved a plan to sell certain PSUs to strategic buyers.[10] Among the PSUs approved for strategic sale is BEML, one of the two publicly listed DPSUs. (See Table 1 for the shareholding pattern of BEML and Bharat Electronics Ltd, BEL.)

Table 1: Shareholding Pattern of BEL and BEML[9]

	Central Government (%)	Public		Total
		Institutions (%)	Non-institutions (%)	
BEL	75.02	18.53	6.45	100
BEML	54.03	28.31	17.66	100

As per the plan, the government's equity stake in the BEML would reduce from 54 per cent to 26 per cent, effectively resulting in the company's privatisation.[11]

The important question that emerges therefore, is whether the BEML's eventual strategic sale is an indication of the fate of the other DPSUs. While it is too early to predict the government's next move with respect to the rest of the DPSUs, it is important to note that when the Rangarajan Committee gave its recommendations in 1993, the DPSUs along with the OFs were the sole producers of defence items. But with the 2001 opening up, they no longer enjoy the monopoly they were privy to, prior to liberalisation. By the logic of the Rangarajan Committee, the equity shares of the DPSUs could be completely divested or brought down to 26 per cent through disinvestment. For this to happen, the first step that the government needs to take is to list the seven unlisted DPSUs in the various stock exchanges and then plan further disinvestment.

It is worth noting that while there has been some movement on the issue of DPSUs, virtually no action has been taken for improving the management of the OFs, which continue to function as a department-run organisation. As discussed earlier, the running of businesses by the government – either directly (OFs) or indirectly (DPSUs) – has not proved successful thus far. Every possible performance parameter that one can use to evaluate the functioning of these entities would testify that they are grossly inefficient, and drastic measures are needed to resurrect them.

Gross Inefficiency of the DPSUs and OFs

Until 2001, the DPSUs and OFs had a near monopoly over India's arms production. Even in the post-2001 period, this monopoly is still intact as the private sector is yet to make a dent in the industry because of various factors. Similar to several other sectors, the monopoly of the DPSUs and OFs has also bred inefficiency, which is reflected in their functioning and performance. Measured in terms of innovation, productivity, export success and timely execution of orders, they are gross underperformers.

Given that the armed forces are captive customers of the DPSUs and OFs, there is no incentive or necessity for the latter to innovate their products. Over the years, they have confined themselves to producing items based on designs and technologies supplied by others. The lack of focus on innovation is amply visible from their poor R&D spending. The combined R&D spending of the nine DPSUs in 2014-15 was Rs 1722 crore, a mere five per cent of their turnover. Moreover, most of the R&D spending is primarily incurred by two entities, HAL and BEL with others spending less than one per cent. The situation is worse in the OFs. In 2014-15, they spent only 0.5 per cent of their sales on R&D. The utter lack of R&D investment is representative of the stagnation in the industry and unless drastic changes are made, future innovations seem unlikely as well. Suffice it to say that the Ordnance Factory Board (OFB) generated less than 15 per cent of its turnover from its own developed products.[12]

The combined labour productivity of the DPSUs, on the whole, is less than a quarter of some of the leading global companies. This gross mismanagement of the labour force is also evident in the OFs, that employ two supervisors for every three direct industrial employees.[13] In essence, the poor labour productivity is a burden on the budget of the armed forces, effectively reducing their purchasing capacity and hampering capability development.

Exports, a key indicator of the global competitiveness of any enterprise, is non-existent in the DPSUs or OFs. Compared to the fact that their global peers generate 20-80 per cent revenues through exports, the DPSUs and OFs cumulatively receive barely 3 per cent through exports. Not only have the DPSUs and OFs failed to market their products in the global market but they have also failed miserably at sustaining whatever little success they had. The lack of success and the subsequent inability to raise revenues through exports has further prevented these entities from scaling up and deriving the benefits of the economies of scale for lower units cost of purchase for the armed forces.

In a report presented to the parliament in July 2016, the Comptroller and Auditor General of India (CAG) had castigated the DPSUs for their "inordinate delay in supply of critical weapons and equipment ... during XI Army Plan (2007-12)", hampering the "modernisation and capability enhancement plan of the Indian Army".[14] The CAG observed that contracts that were worth upto Rs 30,098 crore and amounted to 60 per cent of total value of contracts signed by the MoD with the DPSUs, were delayed. Furthermore, in his other reports, the CAG has also castigated the OFs for severe delays in supply to the armed forces. In a report presented to the parliament in December 2015, the supreme auditor had observed a shortfall of 61 per cent in the OFs' achievement of targets.[15] Such poor levels of target achievement coupled with the aforementioned unsatisfactory performance indicators reflect the gross inefficiency of these entities. These reflections do not bode well for India's aspiration of becoming self-sufficient in the matter of defence production.

Inefficiency of DRDO and its Separation from Production Agencies

If the Indian defence industry has not performed well, the DRDO, which has a monopoly over technology and product development, must assume the lion's share of the blame. It is widely known that the DRDO has not performed optimally. Time and cost overruns in key projects undertaken by the organisation coupled with failures in developing key technologies in a time-bound manner are among the reasons why the organisation has been subjected to widespread criticism in the past. Some of the problems facing the organisation are lack of organisational reforms, poor accountability, meagre resources and poor human resource management.[16]

If the above-mentioned weaknesses have hampered the DRDO's own R&D efforts, the organisation itself is also responsible for inhibiting wider R&D, especially by the industry, which has become notorious for its miserly attitude towards innovation. To understand the gravity of the issue, one needs to travel back to the organisation's birth in the late 1950s. The DRDO was created in January 1958 at the instructions of the then Defence Minister, V.K. Krishna Menon.[17] The organisation was created by merging two entities: the Defence Science Organisation (DSO)[18] and the Technical Development Establishments (TDEs), both of which were functioning under the same administrative head who was also responsible for production. In hindsight, the merger of these organisations, especially the TDEs, into the DRDO was not a smart move as it not only robbed the industry of a close R&D support base, it also forced the industry to overlook R&D as an integral part of its functioning, resulting in a production base devoid of its own technology. Considering that a credible in-house R&D by the industry is the most effective way of shortening the time period for the commercialisation of any technology, it is imperative that this historical neglect dating back to 1958 is corrected at the earliest.

As mentioned earlier, although the TDEs were separate entities, they were nonetheless under the same administrative head as the production agencies. Furthermore, since they were situated closely along with the production centres, they were quite helpful and provided timely assistance in terms of inspection, modifications and development. The arrangement was efficient and had some useful contributions in the areas of explosives and weapons.[19] The separation of the TDEs, however, diluted the unified control over development, production and inspection, much to the detriment of indigenisation efforts. Moreover, the dilution of functions brewed discontent from the very beginning of the DRDO's creation and was evident in the development of the famous Ishapore Rifle, in which the R&D and production agencies moved in opposite directions, causing unnecessary delay and bitterness. The difference between them has remained as large as ever. With the DRDO failing in developing key technologies/products in a timely manner and the production agencies doing very little R&D on their own, critical technologies which could have been otherwise developed indigenously through a synergistic approach have ended up being imported.

Realising the pitfalls of segregating R&D from production and inspection and its harmful effect on the users, the first Chief Controller of the DRDO, Major General B.D. Kapur, had strongly suggested that the R&D organisation should be merged with the production agencies. Ironically, the suggestion which was accepted by the government was not implemented due to strong resistance from the DRDO, which had a first full-time scientific advisor (SA) as its head by then. Opposing the breakup of what had come to be called an "empire", the SA ensured that the crucial linkage between R&D and production remained as broken as ever. Unfortunately, same attitude continues to remain a strong force against reform implementation even today. The recommendation of the Rama Rao Committee – appointed by the Manmohan Singh government to suggest measures to overhaul the DRDO's functioning – to merge few DRDO labs not engaged in mainstream defence technology with other public-funded institutions – has also been thwarted by the same force.

Separation of Procurement from Indigenisation

If the separation of R&D from production has been a major problem in India's industrial defence development, the separation of procurement from production has also been an equally contributory factor. For a long time until the announcement of the Defence Procurement Procedure 2011 (DPP-2011), India's procurement was synonymous with import which was, in fact, a default option for the procurement authorities to acquire any capital equipment for the armed forces. The change in the DPP-2013 (which prioritised domestic procurement over direct import for the first time), has though removed this rampant import bias to a certain extent, the apathy towards the domestic industry continues to loom large.[20] This apathy stems from the way acquisition and production functions are distributed between the two distinct power centres in the MoD. It is rather interesting to note that although a mere brick wall separates the offices of the Director General (Acquisition) and Secretary (Defence Production) – the latter is responsible for indigenous arms production by both state and private entities – the two are yet to find common ground. While the former is keen on awarding contracts (so as to utilise the allocated resources) irrespective of the source of supply, the latter is interested in obtaining contracts for the domestic industry, particularly the state-owned/controlled DPSUs and the OFB. Since the basic objectives of these two high offices are not necessarily driven by indigenous-centric procurement, the focus on indigenisation has become subservient to acquisition. It is primarily because of the inherent conflicts of interest between these two high offices that the domestic industry has not received the necessary attention it deserves, and India continues to figure among the top arms importers in the world.

Compared to India, some of the advanced defence manufacturing countries have placed both the production and procurement functions, under one centralised agency. One country that has benefited the most from such a centralised system is France, which has now become a major manufacturer and exporter of defence items. At the core of the French system lies the Direction Générale de l'Armement (DGA), one of the three pillars of the French Ministry of Defence. The agency is responsible for a wide range of functions pertaining to the procurement, design, development, production and testing of equipment. Created in 1961 by President Charles de Gaulle, it has promoted a very high degree of indigenisation and a robust and controversy-free procurement system. Such is the credibility of the DGA that the French authorities do not hide their pride in saying that others have attempted to copy their success.

It is worth noting that in its 2005 report, the Kelkar Committee, set up by the government to suggest measures aimed at enhancing self-reliance in defence, had suggested the potential creation of a DGA-like agency in India. The recommendation – which led to the setting up of an expert committee under then Director General, IDSA, Narendra Sisodia, – did not, however, see the light of the day as the government did not act upon the expert committee's report. The dumping of the Sisodia Committee report to cold storage notwithstanding, another committee was set up by the Modi government to look into the structural aspects of procurement, among other issues.[21] The report of the committee, which is yet be made public, reportedly contains suggestions for the creation of an "independent organisation" outside the MoD. The committee is also believed to have suggested the hiring of legal, financial and technical experts to man the proposed organisation.[22] While these recommendations, (if accepted and implemented), might expedite the procurement process, it is unlikely that they will bridge the existing gap between the processes of acquisition and production as both these functions are undertaken by two different departments without a common focus on indigenisation.

Lack of Users' Interest in Indigenisation

In the Indian scheme of things, the users, that is the armed forces, are widely perceived to be reluctant participants in indigenisation efforts. The reluctance has, inhibited the growth of indigenous R&D and production. Apart from the inefficiency of the domestic R&D and production agencies, there is a historical context as to why the users have been less enthusiastic on indigenous efforts. At the time of independence, India inherited the British system in which the Indian Army was responsible for "defence production, inspection, R&D and all inter-related and inter-acting activities".[23] However, soon after independence, these were transferred to civilian authorities and placed under the control of the MoD. This loss of ownership led to a "battle royal" between the users and the authorities responsible for R&D and production. Little has changed since then to bridge this gap and give a sense of ownership to the users over domestic weapons programmes intended to be used by them. As a result, the users seem to have developed a deep-rooted tendency to ignore the domestic options for easier import options. It is a constant complaint by the R&D and production establishments that users tend to bypass the domestic options by asking for products that have stringent technical requirements that are beyond current indigenous development capabilities. For example, B.D. Kapur notes that during the development of the Ishapore Rifle, the General Staff gave conflicting and stringent specifications that even the best guns available in the world at that time did not possess.[24] In a recent report, the CAG also spoke about the Indian Army's imposition of as many as eight stringent parameters on the MBT Arjun, as opposed to the parameters set for the imported Russia T-90 tanks which were quite relaxed.[25] The CAG also mentions the Indian Air Force's lack of enthusiastic participation in the development of the Light Combat Aircrafts (LCA) that are being developed by the DRDO. The supreme auditor observed that the IAF's non-involvement with the design team prevented "better appreciation of mutual perception, including appropriate trade-offs in performance, weight, time frame, cost, technological complexity and operational consideration of LCA ... [and] impacted the LCA developmental timelines".[26]

Make in India Initiative

With the Modi government coming to power, "Make in India" has become the main economic mantra aimed at reviving India's moribund manufacturing sector that includes defence manufacturing as well. Under the Make in India programme, the government has undertaken a series of reforms across various sectors. The MoD has, on its part, undertaken a host of reform measures. These pertain to industrial licensing, foreign direct investment (FDI), exports, and the creation of a level-playing field among various players and the DPP. Additionally, the new government has also shown definite inclinations towards indigenisation, and is encouraging increased participation by the local industry including the private sector.

The major reform in the domain of industrial licensing is the simplification and codification of rules and process regulating the private sector's entry into defence production. Among other things, the government has published a list of items against which licences would be given to the industry; increased the validity of the licence from three years to 18 years; removed the annual capacity norms as a condition for the grant of licences; and allowed licence holders to sell their products to government agencies and other licence holders without prior approval of the government. Moreover, the government has been quite liberal in granting licences in a timely manner. This has created a positive atmosphere in an industry that was earlier struggling to obtain licensing rights, the minimum requirement to commence production of defence items.

The reform in the defence FDI cap was in the form of increasing the equity that can be invested by the foreign companies in an Indian joint venture. Within few months of coming to power, the Modi government decided to increase the cap from 26 per cent to 49 per cent. The cap on 49 per cent was subsequently increased to 100 per cent with the provision that equity investment up to 49 per cent is permitted through the automatic route and beyond 49 per cent through the government approval route, "in cases resulting in access to modern technology in the country or for other reasons to be recorded".[27] Moreover, the Modi government has also permitted FDI in the production of small arms and ammunition covered under the Arms Act 1959.

After unveiling the reforms to promote defence exports, the government came out with a strategy and a detailed set of standard operating procedures (SOPs) for granting export licences. While the former talks of various options such as the inclusion of industry representatives in the official delegations for bilateral meetings with a foreign country and the provision of soft loans to external buyers, the SOPs aim to bring in elements of transparency, objectivity and predictability to the process of regulating of export licences. The measures attempt to meet a long-standing demand of the industry – especially the private sector companies – which had thus far, been constrained to explore the external market without any governmental supervision/advice.

In addition to the demand for an export promotion measure, the private sector has also long complained about the lack of a level playing field with respect to certain aspects of taxation and payment terms. The complaint was that while DPSUs and OFs are exempted from paying taxes (customs duty and excise duty) and insulated against exchange rate fluctuations, the same benefits were not extended to them. In order to allay these concerns, the government has subjected all the industry players (both private and public) to the same duty/tax structure. They have also provided exchange rate variation benefits to the private sector.

Apart from the aforementioned reforms, the government has also reformed its capital procurement procedures. The new procedures, i.e., the DPP-2016, which have come into effect from April 2016, have brought in several new features while also reforming some existing ones.[28] Among the new features, the DPP-2016 has introduced a brand-new procurement category – "Buy Indian-Indigenously Designed, Developed and Manufactured (Indian-IDDM)". The category, which has been given top-most priority for the purposes of acquiring capital items, is intended to promote in-house design and increase localisation efforts. The crucial "Make" procedure (intended to promote design, development efforts by the industry), which had been in limbo since its inception in 2006, has also been given a wholesome overhaul. Instead of 80 per cent funding, which was the norm earlier, the new procedure allows up to 90 per cent finance provision by the government. Furthermore, to bring in an element of accountability, a provision has also been made wherein the tender is to be issued within two years of successful development of the prototype, failing which the government would reimburse the balance 10 per cent to the industry. Moreover, the government has also articulated a list of "Make" projects, thereby providing an increased degree of visibility to the industry as far as the future requirements of the armed forces are concerned.

The DPP-2016 also talks about introducing a new provision in order to select few private companies as strategic partners (SPs). These SPs would be responsible for the execution of high-value defence items on a preferential basis. If and when they are selected, these SPs would be at par with the DPSUs which have retained an uncontested monopoly over major domestic projects thus far. The creation of SPs is also a step in the direction of bridging the trust gap that exists between the MoD and the industry over the long practice of nominating PSUs for the execution of mega projects.

If the all the above-mentioned steps are in the direction of providing

Table 2: Category-wise AoN[30]

Year	'Buy Indian' & 'Buy and Make Indian'		'Buy Global'		Total
	Value (Rs in Crore)	%	Value (Rs in Crore)	%	
2010-11	77546	50.55	40547	26.43	1,53,388
2011-12	30593	54.16	20500	36.29	56480
2012-13	19074	31.44	27114	44.7	60652
2013-14	23736	85.96	371	1.34	27611
2014-15	1,11,070	94.26	6760	5.73	1,17,830

an enabling framework for the greater involvement of local industries in defence production, the new government has also taken a further step in deepening its role. The concrete step that has been taken is the government's resolve to earmark more and more big-ticket projects for the local industry. An early sign to this effect is clearly visible from the value of the Acceptance of Necessity (AoN) given in 2014-15, much before the articulation of the "Buy Indian-IDDM" category, which has now been given the top-most priority. This can be seen in Table 2, that demonstrates the value of projects falling under the two most domestic industry friendly procurement categories – "Buy Indian" and "Buy and Make Indian". Projects under these two categories combined make up for more than 94 per cent. Furthermore, when taken together with "Buy and Make (ToT)", the value of the AoNs amounts to a staggering Rs 1,60,362 crore during 2014-15 and 2015-16.[29] The AoNs include some big projects such as submarines, landing platform docks, howitzer guns and transport aircraft in which the private sector has an important role to play. If these projects are executed in a time-bound manner, it will provide a huge boost and lend credibility to localisation efforts.

Effectiveness of Make in India on Indian Industry

The reform measures undertaken under the umbrella of Make in India have undoubtedly have had a salubrious impact on the local industry, particularly on the private sector, which now sees itself playing a major role in defence production. The streamlining of the licensing process has given the Indian private sector a strong indication of the government's seriousness in engaging this nascent player; whereas, the articulation of export promotion measures has provided an excellent platform for the industry to explore the international market. As demonstrated by Figure 1, total deference exports (which although meagre in comparison to

Figure 1: Defence Exports[31]

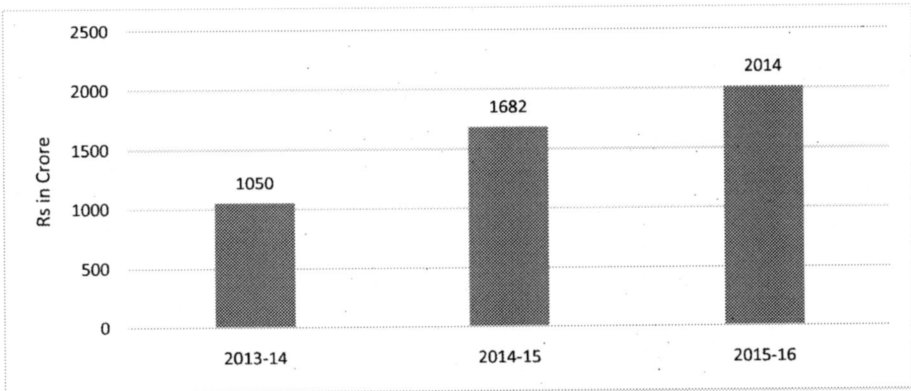

Note: The export figures are based on the no-objection certificate (NoC) given by the MoD.

international standards) have nonetheless nearly doubled since 2013-14, with the private sector contributing to the bulk of the increase. The involvement of the industry is also likely to deepen further as and when the all the domestic industry-centric AoNs fructify.

Above trends notwithstanding, there remains a bit of frustration within the domestic industry as well as the potential foreign investors. Major foreign companies do not seem to be enthused with the liberalised FDI policy. They have raised complaints stating that the policy gives scant respect to the risk factors associated with investment inflows. They have pointed out that unlike in other sectors that are abound in buyers, when it comes to the defence industry, the investments cater primarily to one customer (i.e., the MoD) whose purchase assurance is a minimum prerequisite for any commercial success. Since the FDI policy is not linked to any procurement project, the foreign investors have no assurance that their investment will meet commercial success. This has been the primary reason why the new policy has not attracted any worthwhile investment.

The private sector is also frustrated with some of the government's actions. It is increasingly seeing a disjuncture between the government's policy talk and actual action effected on the ground. Its major complaints are about the slow decision-making process in awarding contracts and the government's old mind-set of giving contracts to the PSUs through nominations. It is a fact that despite the new government having been in power for close to four years, not a single major contract has been awarded to the private sector. At the same time, the PSUs are being awarded major contracts through the traditional route of nomination. The list of the contracts awarded in this manner to the PSUs was further extended when the Modi government decided to award two big shipbuilding projects to Goa Shipyard Ltd (GSL) and Hindustan Shipyard Ltd (HSL). The GSL received a mammoth contract worth Rs 32,000 crore for building 12 Mine Counter Measure Vessels (MCMVs), whereas the HSL has a received a contract worth Rs 10,000 crore for five Fleet Support Vessels (FSVs).[32] The HSL is also all set to bag a contract for building two Landing Platform Docks (LPDs) through nomination. Interestingly, the HSL will get the contract after one of the two private sector shipyards (Reliance and L&T) wins the bid to execute two LPDs based upon their technical and financial capabilities.[33] The differing principles – one of competition for the private sector and the other of nomination for the PSUs – seems hypocritical and does not inspire the private sector's confidence in the industry.

Additionally, the way the government intends to operationalise the revamped "Make" procedure also does not inspire much confidence. The disappointment stems mainly from the emphasis on low-value- and import-substitution-oriented projects identified for execution under revised procedures. Of the 23 potential "Make" projects (of which 13 belong to the army, six to the navy and four to the air force), there is hardly any project that merits the hype and dignity of the revamped procedure. It suffices to mention that the list includes projects such as gun barrel, auxiliary power unit for tank, aircraft refuelling pump, diesel engine for boats and rotor blades, to name a few.[34]

A Reform Agenda for the Indian Defence Industry

Despite the numerous reform measures undertaken under the ambit of the Make in India programme, the Indian defence industry still suffers from several legacy issues which need to be addressed in order to establish an efficient and credible defence industrial base. The reform agenda that needs to be pursued is a multi-pronged one and it needs to be implemented systematically. It should begin with an overarching and integrated institutional structure that would be responsible for the three critical but inter-related functions of procurement, production and R&D. The absence of such a structure thus far, has led to a lack of synergy and a dilution of accountability, that has resulted in the poor industrial base we see today, which is incapable of meeting some of the most basic requirements of the armed forces. Bringing them under one head will eliminate this critical gap in India's defence industrial efforts and provide a thrust to the indigenous defence manufacturing sector.

The DPSUs, OFs and DRDO, which have been the pillars of the Indian defence industry so far, have exhibited a great deal of inefficiency, and need to be reformed in order to contribute to self-reliance efforts in a meaningful manner. For DPSUs, the ultimate reform path lies in changing the very model they have been operating under since their existence. Since defence production is no longer a state monopoly, there is very little justification for keeping the hugely inefficient DPSUs and OFs under government control. In other words, they need to be privatised at the earliest. The government's recent plan for BEML's equity sale to a strategic partner, could provide a future roadmap for the rest of the DPSUs. For this to happen, all the unlisted DPSUs need to be listed in the stock exchange first. For the OFs, the first step for privatisation is corporatisation by converting them from a departmentally run organisation to a corporate structure. Post-corporatisation, they can be privatised as well.

For India to establish a credible defence industrial base, improved R&D will play a vital role. Unfortunately, its role so far has been marginal due to the inefficiency of the DRDO, its lack of synergy with production centres and the industry's miserly attitude towards R&D as a whole. This needs to be corrected by making the DRDO accountable, bringing the R&D labs and the industry together as a team and encouraging the industry to spend far greater resources on in-house technology development.

The Make in India programme needs to go a little further, beyond mere policy announcements. The government needs to walk the talk by expediting procurements, particularly those pertaining to the private sector, which still hasn't been able to bag a big contract, even three-and-a-half years after the Modi government came to power. The award of a big contract to the private sector will be the ultimate test of Make in India's success. The government also needs to ensure a degree of fairness in the awarding of contracts, either by sticking to the competitive approach or by doing away with the nomination practice. The revamped "Make" procedure also needs to be operationalised at the earliest and given due importance by including some major platforms under its purview. The opening up of companies to FDI could be a game changer in spurring production within the country. For this to happen the government needs to link the policy to a set of projects for which foreign investment is desirable. Last, but not least, the government needs to find a way out to give ownership to users in domestic armament projects. Indigenous projects have suffered so long primarily because of the users' reluctant participation among other reasons.

NOTES

1. According to the Stockholm International Peace Research Institute (SIPRI), India is the largest arms importer during 2011-15, with a 14 per cent global share. During 2006-10, India was also the largest arms importer, with a share of 8.5 per cent. See Aude Fleurant, Sam Perlo-Freeman, et al., "Trends in International Arms Transfers, 2015", *SIPRI Fact Sheet*, February 2016.
2. For a recent survey of Indian defence industry, see Laxman Kumar Behera, *Indian Defence Industry: An Agenda for Making in India*, Pentagon, New Delhi, 2016.
3. "Key Achievements in the Defence Sector under the Narendra Modi Government", Ministry of Defence, Government of India, July 2016.
4. See Laxman Kumar Behera, "Indian Defence Industry: Issues of Self-Reliance", *IDSA Monograph Series*, No. 21, July 2013, pp. 46-56.
5. "Import of Defence Equipment", Unstarred Question No. 4110, Lok Sabha, December 09, 2016
6. For a stimulating discussion on the reforms undertaken by the Narasimha Rao government, see Vinay Sitapati, *Half-Lion: How P.V. Narasimha Rao Transformed India*, Penguin, Gurgaon, 2016; Sanjaya Baru, *1991: How P. V. Narasimha Rao Made History*, Aleph, New Delhi, 2016.
7. "Statement on Industrial Policy", July 24, 1991, at http://dipp.nic.in/English/Policies/Industrial_policy_statement.pdf.
8. Strategic sale is part of the disinvestment strategy in which the government transfers the management control to a buyer.
9. Bombay Stock Exchange (BSE). The shareholding pattern is as of September 2016. Institutions include mutual funds, foreign portfolio investors (FPI), financial institutions/banks and insurance companies. Non-institutions include individual shareholders, Non-banking Financial Companies (NBFCs) registered with the Reserve Bank of India (RBI), corporate bodies, non-resident Indians (NRIs), trusts, etc.
10. Dheeraj Tiwari and Deepshikha Sikarwar, "Decks Cleared for Strategic Sale! Government Okays Plan to Exit Sick Psus, Subsidiaries", *The Economic Times*, October 28, 2016.
11. It may be noted post-disinvestment the government with a 28 per cent equity stake, would still have the single largest equity stake in BEML. But that would not give the government the management control over the company as the said control would be transferred to the strategic buyer post sale. It is also worth noting that a government company will also lose its PSU status once the government's equity falls below 51 per cent. The loss of PSU status will also necessitate a change in Articles of Association that govern the functioning of a company. See, "Understanding the Strategic Sales Agreement", Department of Investment and Public Asset Management, at http://dipam.gov.in/Understand_Strategic_Sale.asp.
12. *Of Beat*, Ordnance Factory Board, October 2015, p. 6.
13. *Union Government (Defence Services): Army, Ordnance Factories and Defence Public Sector Undertakings*, Report No. 19 of 2016, Comptroller and Auditor General (CAG), p. 75.
14. Ibid., p. xi.

15. *Union Government (Defence Services): Army, Ordnance Factories and Defence Public Sector Undertakings*, Report No. 44 of 2015, CAG, p. 134.
16. For a critical analysis of DRDO and India's overall R&D performance, see Laxman Kumar Behera, "Defence Innovation in India: The Fault Lines", IDSA Occasional Paper No. 32, January 2014.
17. For a detailed overview of Krishna Menon's contribution to the defence research and production, see Major General B.D. Kapur, *Building a Defence Technology Base*, Lancer International, New Delhi, 1990; and Major General Partap Narain (retd.), *Indian Arms Bazaar*, Shipra, Delhi, 1994.
18. The DSO was created in June 1949 with an initial strength of 140 scientists. At present, the DRDO has a manpower strength of over 25,000.
19. Major General Pratap Narain (retd.), No. 16, pp. 52-53.
20. The DPP-2013 for the first time brought in a preferred order of categorisation of procurement categories, in which 'Buy (Indian)', 'Buy and Make (Indian)' and 'Make (Indian)' were given preference over 'Buy and Make' and 'Buy (Global).
21. The committee was initially set up under the chairmanship of Vivek Rae, former DG (Acq.). However, owing to difference of views among the members, Rae resigned mid-way during the committee's deliberations, and another member, Pritam Singh, was appointed as chairman. Rae was believed to have supported a US-like system, whereas others members were inclined towards a more centralised system like that exists in France. See Manu Pubby, "Vivek Rae Resigns after Differences over Basic Concept of New Procurement Wing", *The Economic Times*, November 03, 2016.
22. Sushant Singh, "Create Unit outside Defence Ministry to Fast-track Defence Deals: Panel to Tell Govt", *The Indian Express*, February 03, 2017.
23. Major General B.D. Kapur, No. 16, p. 5.
24. Ibid., p. 65.
25. *Union Government (Defence Services): Army, Ordnance Factories and Defence Public Sector Undertakings*, Report No. 35 of 2014, CAG, p. 163.
26. *Design, Development, Manufacture and Induction of Light Combat Aircraft*, Report No. 17 of 2015, CAG, pp. 27-28.
27. Press Information Bureau, Government of India, "FDI in Defence Sector", March 31, 2017.
28. The document is available at the official website of the MoD. For a comprehensive review of the DPP-2016, see Laxman Kumar Behera, "DPP-2016: An Analytical Overview", *IDSA Special Feature*, April 12, 2016.
29. "Projects under Make in India Programme", Unstarred Question No. 348, Lok Sabha, February 03, 2017.
30. A. K. Gupta, "Make in India: The Way Ahead for Indigenous Defence Production in India", Y.B. Chavan Memorial Lecture, IDSA, December 07, 2015.
31. Ministry of Defence, "Key Achievements in the Defence Sector under the Narendra Modi Government", July 2016.
32. "HSL to to Build 5 Navy Fleet Support Ships from 2017", *The Times of India*, April 09, 2016.
33. Piyush Pandey, "Reliance, L&T in Last Leg to Bag $2 Billion Defence Deal", *The Hindu*, September 17, 2016.
34. "Updated List of Potential 'Make Projects'", Ministry of Defence, May 26, 2016.

SECTION IV

EDUCATION AND COMMUNICATION

13

Professional Military Education: Agenda for Reform

P.K. Mallick

"The society that separates its scholars from its warriors will have its thinking done by cowards and its fighting done by fools."

– Thucydides

Introduction

Professional Military Education (PME) has always been a critical component in the process of developing military leaders. It is based on two key principles: train for certainty (so that military personnel gain and master the skills needed for known tasks); and educate for uncertainty, (so that they have the broad-based knowledge and critical thinking skills required to handle unanticipated and unpredictable situations.)

The role of PME is to provide the education needed to complement individual training, operational experience and self-development in order to produce the most professionally competent individuals possible.

The Indian Army has a very large number of educational and training institutions. It has a strong, established PME programme that seeks to provide the right soldier with the right education at the right time. For the officer corps, this PME programme is ingrained from their pre-commissioning days, right up until their promotion to General Officer. This chapter will critically look at PME in the Indian Army. At the macro level, most of the issues are similar for the Indian Navy and Indian Air Force.

Historical Background

After the catastrophic defeat of Prussia in 1806 by Napoleon, the Prussian senior military leadership created a programme that would educate a small group of officers who could provide a systematic and coherent approach to war. This was the start of PME as we understand it today. The Prussian system proved its worth in 1866 and 1870 when Austria and France were defeated under the leadership of Helmuth Von Moltke, the Chief of General Staff at the time. The Prussian model was subsequently copied by all major European Armies and Staff Colleges proliferated across the continent.[1,2]

However history records victory in the strategic column. The Germans for all their battlefield success in the initial stages of World War II ultimately failed in strategy and achieving national objectives. The same happened to the US in Vietnam.[3]

Training Vs Education

The term Training is used when the goal is to prepare a leader to execute specified tasks, often includes repetition of tasks. Education has more to do with how to think about problems and how to deal with those things that may not lend themselves to outright solutions. It is a matter of intellect, thought, indirect leadership, advice and consensus building. Training is useful, as it prepares students for the unknown.

Military operations are divided into three levels of warfare – Tactical, Operational and Strategic. Figure 1 depicts these levels and the associated training establishments that an Indian Army officer has to go through in order to prepare for his professional tasks.

The initial portion of an officer's development during the course of his career, must focus on training in order to inculcate characteristics such as physical strength, courage, direct leadership, etc. As the officer progresses through the ranks, the educational demands of the profession grow and the intellectual component increases. The cross over point is profile when he completes the Defence Services Staff College (DSSC) at Willington.

Figure 2 shows the differences in training and education as well as the change in emphasis during an officer's career.[4]

It is important then to examine how the lessons in the above figure are reflected in the current practices and culture of the Army. While one former US Army War College (USAWC) Commandant noted that the Army was "too busy to learn" the issue is more insidious.[5]

Figure 1: Levels of War and Associated Training Establishments

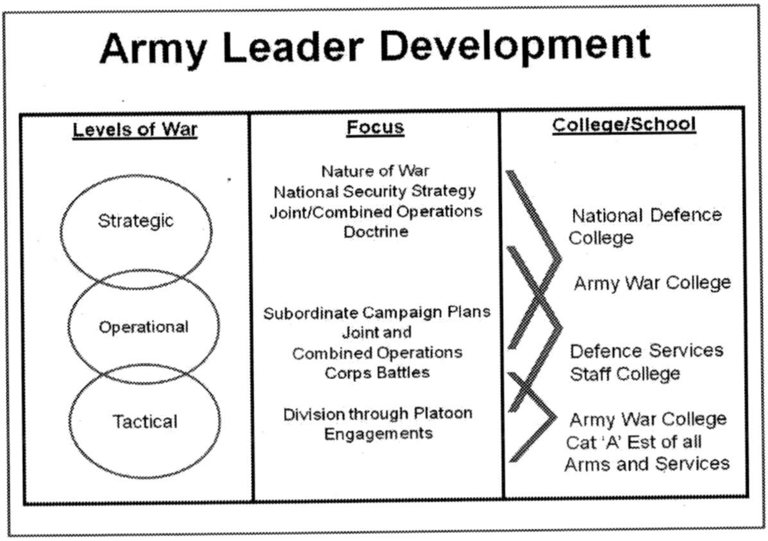

Figure 2: Training and Educational Development during an Officer's Career

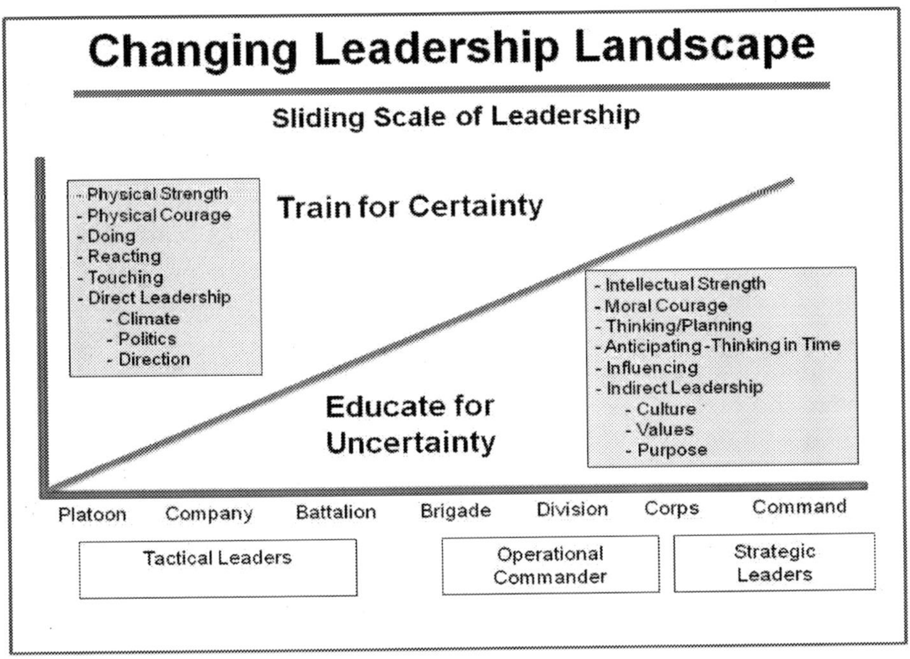

Strategic Corporal/Counter-Insurgency/Counterterrorism Operations (CI/CT OPS)

The term strategic corporal refers to the devolution of command responsibility to lower rank levels in an era of instant communications and pervasive media images.[6] The level of responsibility for critical decision making in the services continues to drift downward. Today, Junior Commissioned Officers (JCO) and Non Commissioned Officers (NCO) make strategic decisions in CI/CT Ops, areas that used to be done by officers in earlier days. The JCOs and NCOs must be educated as well as trained for this new kind of war. Young officers leading tactical units, deployed far from higher headquarters, are making decisions that have far reaching strategic implications. We teach soldiers to shoot, but do we teach them when to shoot and when not to?[7]

Consider the following scenario: An officer gets critically wounded while leading operations against the most wanted terrorist in the Kashmir Valley. Women and Children come out on the road and prevent the medical evacuation of the officer. Or while the operation is in progress a mob collects and starts stone pelting and hinders the operations of the Army and helps the terrorists to get away. What does the Army do? Does it open fire to evacuate the injured soldier where women and children would be casualties? Is it time to consider use of Non-Lethal Weapons especially by forces like Rashtriya Rifles? Are we discussing such issues in our training establishments?[8]

Educating the Strategic Leader

By definition, nearly all the officers who are promoted to one-star rank have excelled at some level of operational responsibilities. Many flag officer appointments demand not operational skills, but the rather different talents required to manage a massive and complex defence bureaucracy. Many of the officers who serve in such positions simply do not possess the educational background or practical experience required to effectively manage the highest levels of the defence enterprise and the sometimes peculiar economics involved.[9]

Those who demonstrate exceptional brilliance and whose capacity for higher level strategic leadership is exemplary should be afforded the opportunity to expand their knowledge. Staff and War Colleges should focus on intellectual merit. A specialist course should be based on an examination as vacancies would be limited. The pedagogical model for such courses could be based on already existing models of School of

Advanced Military Studies at the intermediate level and the Advanced Strategic Art Programme at the senior level at US Army War College.

Analysis of Present System

"Never let your schooling interfere with your education."

– Mark Twain

To successfully develop strategic leaders, the army cannot wait until the 25 years of service to educate them in security studies at Army War College. Such studies should be a part of the PME programme from pre-commission education days, building continuously at each formal school, unit officer education and through continuing education. There is a requirement for lifelong learning.

Some of the criticisms of the present system of PME are as follows:

> Those selected for the Higher Command, Higher Defence Management and National Defence Courses are chosen based solely on job performance rather than for the excellencies of their intellect. Central elements that are necessary to gain a deeper understanding of the nature and character of war, military history along with war games and military psychology and leadership, are often overlooked, in an effort to teach every subject to every conceivable constituency to the lowest common denominator. The standard staff college curriculum is busy mass producing graduates thoroughly versed in staff processes and broadly acquainted with tactical doctrine. With officers representing all arms and services, the course work is aimed at the median group. Training is useful. It prepares students for the known. But the task of Staff College is education, which prepares students for the unknown through the development of improved critical and creative thinking.[10]

The AWC tries to combine the contradictory goals of getting officers quickly trained and back into the system while also developing them as well educated strategic thinkers. There is no prescribed academic standard for doing the course, no examination. No one fails, there is almost 100 percent success rate. Officers get a Masters' degree and certificate for completing the course which gives them additional points for promotion. Any programme with a 100 per cent success rate will raise questions regarding its academic rigour and value. What it takes to be operationally successful can be different from what it takes to be a strategic, critical thinker.

The reason given for doing away with grading at Army War College

(AWC) and National Defence College (NDC) is that it is for injecting more academic rigour. The intent is to mitigate the ill effects of competitiveness within small groups of students. The policy recognises that students arrive with different levels of preparedness for graduate education. The rationale is that military officers are different and should not be bothered about trivialities like grades. The pool of military students is better on an average than the pool of students attending civilian institutions. Military students are more motivated to work hard than their civilian peers.[11]

There is another school of thought. Doing away with grades and passing every officer does nothing for academic rigour. There are two different curricula for the professional requirement of the armed forces and getting a Master's Degree. The AWC and NDC design their curricular for both these requirements in a manner that these can be taught by anyone. Skills such as writing could be taught and tested. Including academic study in professional development can also create institutional tensions, but these tensions can be creative. Education requires time to read, time to absorb readings, time for follow-on discussions and time contemplating different views. Analytical writing, something students are often uncomfortable with, requires uninterrupted blocks of time.[12]

Institutional culture is a cause of concern. Officers from the same group are selected for Higher Command/Higher Defence Management Course. Both are equally prestigious for career enhancement and both award degrees. But there is no comparison of academic rigour between the two courses. Officers undergoing the HDMC are put through very demanding academic curricula. However, when officers from both the groups attend the National Defence College course, the culture of the AWC prevails.

The point should be reinforced at the War Colleges and NDC expecting that the year spent on the course should be of hard and necessary study and not an exercise in building self-esteem. Many PME students approach these courses to be a year off to relax, network and reconnect with family after long operational assignments. Apparently, this is what they are told by detailers and senior officers who themselves attended these courses in the past. It will be an interesting study to see how much of the spare time given to student officers for studies and professional development has been utilised for the same.

Although there is a general consensus on the range of topics that should comprise PME, there is no consensus regarding the relative weighting of those areas. It is important to remember that not every good officer will be a good academic. There is a need to shape education so that it provides the right mix for those who are not academically oriented.

Indian Scenario

The Indian Army has a variety of training establishments. These may be classified as Category "A" and Category "B" establishments. Category "A" establishments are:

- *Army Training.* The training schools/colleges/establishments of Army Air Defence, Army Aviation, Armoured Corps, Combat Army Aviation Training School (CAATS), Infantry, Artillery and Counter Insurgency and Jungle Warfare School, High Altitude Warfare School, Junior Leader Wing, Special Forces Training School.
- *All Arms Training.* Army Education Corps Training Centre and College, Army Institute of Physical Training, AWC, Junior Leader Academy, Military Intelligence School, NCO Academy, Institute of Military Law and Institute of National Integration.
- *Services Training.* Army Medical College & Centre (Armed Forces Medical College is a Joint Services Organisation), Army Service Corps College, College of Modern Management, Corps of Military Police School, Remount and Veterinary College.
- *Technical Training.* College of Military Engineering (CME), Electrical and Mechanical Engineers School, Military College of Electrical and Mechanical Engineers (MCEME) and Military College of Telecommunication Engineers (MCTE).
- *Pre-Commission Training.* Indian Military Academy (IMA), Officer Training Academy (OTA), Gaya and Chennai.

Category "B" establishments are primarily regimental training centres where recruits are trained. They provide limited training to JCOs and NCOs as well.

Joint Defence Training is also imparted at three levels across different training establishments in the country. These are the National Defence Academy (NDA), College of Defence Management (CDM) and the National Defence College (NDC). The Indian Navy has also started providing engineering degrees to its trainees at the NDA.

Pre-Commission Training

There are 19 different types of entries for commission into the Indian Army from which approximately 1,800-2,000 officers get commissioned each year from different entries schemes. It is extremely difficult to get everybody on the same level after going through different training establishments and time periods.

The Military/Sainik Schools were created with the main aim of preparing potential young recruits for the NDA. The number of people entering the NDA from these schools is alarmingly low when compared to the tremendous infrastructural costs of these schools. Compared to them, some private coaching institutes are doing a far better job of preparing their students with much fewer resources. In light of the above, this establishment should be subject to de novo consideration.

The Technical Entry Scheme (TES) has proved to be very successful. The three Cadet Training Wings (CTWs) at the CME, Pune, MCTE, Mhow, and MCEME, Secunderabad, are being run on an ad hoc basis. For centralised conduct of training of all TES cadets, it is recommended that one establishment like the OTA, Gaya, be earmarked or one of the CTWs be enlarged so that the CTWs have an identity of their own.

Professional Training at Junior Officer Level

After commissioning officers are trained by their respective arms and services in their training establishments. Thereafter, officers go through a competitive examination for the DSSC/Technical Staff Officers Course (TSOC). Artillery, for example, has an entrance examination for Long Gunnery Staff Course (LGSC) and Engineers/Signals/EME have an exam for selection to M-Tech or equivalent courses. Officers who pass the examination, are selected for these courses, on the basis of merit. Moreover, there are provisions for study leave, resettlement courses, foreign language courses and others.

Middle Level

After 14 to 16 years of service, selected officers at the rank of Lieutenant Colonel are sent for the Senior Command Course at the AWC. These are followed by courses at their respective arms and services as well. After command of a unit at around 25 years of service officers are shortlisted and selected for the Higher Command Course (HCC) at the AWC and the Higher Defence Management Course (HDMC) at the College of Defence Management (CDM). The CDM is a joint service training organisation where officers of all the three services of around the same professional and age profile are trained.

Higher Level

After command of brigade or equivalent officers of the rank of Brigadier and equivalent are selected for a course of 11 months at the NDC once they have completed around 30 years of service. Ten officers of the Army are also selected for the Advanced Professional Programme for Public

Administration (APPPA) course which is a 10 month programme at the Indian Institute of Public Administration.

NDC

The NDC, New Delhi, conducts an 11-month course for around 100 officers of the rank of Brigadier or its equivalent. After a very strict selection procedure by the respective services, 40, 12 and 6 officers from Indian Army, Air Force and Navy are nominated for the course. In addition, around 25 officers from countries all over the world also participate in this prestigious course. The remaining 17 participants are nominated from the Indian Administrative Services (IAS), Indian Police Services (IPS), Indian Revenue Services (IRS) and other Central Services (CS), along with those from the Defence Research and Development Organisation (DRDO) and Ordnance Factory Board (OFB).

The instructors for this course are senior officials from the three services, as well as the Indian Administrative Services (IAS) and Indian Foreign Services (IFS) cadres. Unlike students, there are no specified selection criteria for instructors.

There are six studies in the course curriculum. These are Socio-Political Study of India, Economy and Science and Technology, International Security Environment, Study of Global Issues, India's Strategic Neighbourhood and Strategies and Structures for National Security. In each study, Integrated Analysis Groups are formed to critically analyse the issue relevant to the particular study. Each study is conducted in the form of group discussions, presentations and written assignments.

Institutes like the Royal College of Defence Studies (RCDS) also run similar courses. The course is divided into the following parts:

- Term 1: Current and Future Strategic Context
- Term 2: Conflict and Strategy in the Modern World
- Term 3: Contemporary International Issues

The role of the NDC is to educate the future strategic leaders of the country in terms of strategy making, strategic leadership and civil military relations. The emphasis has to be on national military and defence strategies. The strategy and leadership issues should be conjoined under a common thread as is being done at the RCDS. Presently, the most important study of the course, Strategies and Structures for National Security, is undertaken towards the end of the course, which has its disadvantages in terms of diminishing interest due to posting, thesis submission and viva voce, end-of-term activities and increased socialisation.

An independent body of experts outside the preview of the NDC should evaluate the curriculum, method of instruction, compare the course structure, etc., against that of similar international institutions and suggest measures for further improvement.[13]

Indian National Defence University (INDU)

The idea of the INDU was first conceived by the Chiefs of Staff Committee in 1967. After the 1999 Kargil War, this idea was taken seriously when the government created a Committee on the National Defence University (CONDU) headed by the late K. Subrahmanyam in 2002. It was to be established in seven years' time (by 2008). [14]

In 2010, the Cabinet gave an "in principle" approval for setting up the Defence University. Subsequently, a public sector undertaking, EdCIL (India) Limited was tasked with preparing a detailed project report (DPR), a blueprint explaining the physical construction of the university, its act and statutes, plans for faculty development and the overall intellectual approach. In 2013, the then Prime Minister, Manmohan Singh, laid the foundation for the nation's first defence university at Binola in Gurgaon. The fact remains, however, that since then there has been no progress and even the basic bill for the establishment of the University has not been put up in the Parliament. There is no informed discussion in the open domain about the INDU. The CONDU Report and the report of EdCIL (India) Limited remain classified. Security remains the biggest bugbear of Indian military education system.[15]

A military university faces challenges at three levels:[16]

- The first level involves its place as an institution of national governance and civil-military relations, including the preparation of national leaders.
- The second challenge involves its place in the armed forces and within the Ministry of Defence, including the preparation of military leaders as part of a force generation plan and a personnel development strategy. As a national government becomes well-established, and the military instrument is regularised and subordinated to civil authority, the focus of PME shifts from the first to the second level.
- The third challenge involves preserving capacity as a university and this extends to external relations within the university community, academic governance and faculty-management relations.

There are justifiable reasons for clamouring for civilian faculties in NDU. There are 29 Universities in India which have a department for defence studies, and the research output, faculty and profile of students of these academic institutions are poor. Retired military officers with proper education, well developed critical intellectual abilities, and experience in teaching and writing on professional matters are a good alternative. In effect, there has to be a judicious mixture.

Considering the delay and interference from various stakeholders, it is high time to consider the establishment of an Army University, as has been done in the US like Army University, Air University, Naval Post Graduate School and Marine Corps University.

Recommendations

> *"War is not an affair of chance. A great deal of knowledge, study and meditation is necessary to conduct it well."*
>
> – Fredrick the Great

There should be a fundamental core curriculum programme which should be taught at each level but adjusted appropriately for the level of education and experience of the military personnel who attend the PME continuum. This core curriculum should consist of the following "Fundamental Five":[17]

- History – Military, Civilisational, Cultural and Political History
- Theory – Military, Political and International Relations
- Geography
- Operational Art
- Strategy

JCO/NCO Education

For a 1.3 million strong army, there is only one Junior Leader Academy (JLA) for JCOs and one NCO Academy for NCOs. This is grossly inadequate. More emphasis should be given to the NCO PME. NCOs should be encouraged to complete their graduate degree through the distance education programme. Ex-servicemen from the Navy and Air Force get a disproportionately larger share of the jobs reserved for ESM compared to army personnel.

The National Skill Development Agency (NSDA) is an autonomous body under the Ministry of Skill Development and Entrepreneurship, Government of India. The NSDA coordinates and harmonises the skill development efforts of the Indian Government and the private sector to achieve the skilling targets of the 12th Plan document and beyond.[18] The

Indian armed forces must closely co-ordinate its training activities with NSDA.

The Government of India has enunciated its National Policy for Skill Development and Entrepreneurship 2015.[19] With the vast and extensive training infrastructure, trainers, human resources the quantification and benchmarking of its training in line with that of standards set by NSDA would give wonderful opportunities to approximately 60,000 army personnel who retire every year.

Use of Technology

Very useful technologies are now available for improving education methodology. Though the armed forces have excellent infrastructure, these technologies are not being utilised effectively. The use of war gaming, simulation, blended learning; massively open online courses (MOOCS), flipped classrooms, learning analytics and distributed learning should be encouraged.[20]

Distance Education

Out of 1,800 to 2,000 officers who are commissioned in the army every year, only about 280 officers are selected for the DSSC course. Similarly, there are only 58, 92 and 11 vacancies for the Higher Command Course, Higher Defence Management Course and Higher Air Command courses, respectively. There are a considerable number of officers who are left out of the orbit of PME, and the selection for the next ranks becomes very narrow. Officers should be given the opportunity to complete these courses through distance learning. The duration of these courses may be double the period of residential programmes. However, infrastructure needs to be created for content management, facility, training aids, examination methods, instructors, etc., before starting such a programme. Existing infrastructure is not adequate for such a venture. Shifting to a purely distance education system isn't advisable since it would lead to a loss of the bonding and network building that takes place in a residential programme. It is also more challenging to recruit and retain a world-class faculty for a purely distance education programme. And while a large proportion of educational resources are now online, not having access to a library or archives can be an obstacle in distance education, albeit a declining one as more library and archive resources are going online.[21]

Enterprise Management

The Army is a huge enterprise. To manage such a big organisation such as the Indian Army, officers with expertise on financial and project management, human resource development, acquisition process, works procedure, land management, law, information technology and cyber technologies, etc., are required. Specific training modules for respective ranks and appointments need to be developed. To this effect, the Indian armed forces should look into organisations like the Dwight D. Eisenhower School for National Security and Resource Strategy (Eisenhower School), formerly known as the Industrial College of the Armed Forces (ICAF), which is a part of the US National Defense University. Alternatively, the CDM may be used for such courses, duly augmented by faculties from reputed business schools like the Indian Institutes of Management.[22]

Education at Unit and Formation Level

Commanders focus energy on what their higher level Commanders deem to be most important. Presently, the responsibility of learning has been relegated to military learning institutions. To fight future wars, the responsibility for learning should be shifted to the unit commanders. Several training activities are undertaken at unit and formation levels. The education component has to be increased at these levels. The onus of education has to be taken by unit/formation commanders.

Knowledge Management

The following should be available via the Internet for officers to access:

- Lectures, presentations given at different PME Institutions.
- Theses submitted by student officers.
- All the papers presented at seminars organised at the behest of the Army Training Command (ARTRAC) at different Category "A" establishments.
- Course-wise relevant reading material.
- Professional journals published by the ARTRAC and Category "A" establishments.

Since more than 95 per cent of the above are unclassified, they should be put on the Internet. There are problems of accessibility with the Army Intranet at home, downloading media and other security issues; these need to be rectified.

Army University

Even after four years of the Prime Minister laying the foundation stone of INDU, the basic action of passing the bill in the Parliament has not yet taken place. Within the ARTRAC, the army's colleges, institutes, schools and training centres provide high-quality education and training to soldiers from across the world. This system, however, is not optimal to developing the critical and creative thinkers the army requires in the future. To cater for its educational needs and accreditation, the army must initiate the process of creating an Army University. Since most of the infrastructure is already available, this would be cost-effective. The organisation of US Army University is given at Appendix "A".[23]

Academic Research and Scholarly Publications

The research activities in army educational institutes are poor. Every Category "A" establishment has a Faculty of Studies. These faculties need to be made accountable. Suitable personnel may be employed permanently or on a contract basis. The Indian Army should create a publishing house for the publication of its research papers and journals, which conforms to established standards of professional journals.[24]

Permanent Civilian Faculty

Category "A" establishments may think of employing appropriate subject matter experts in the form of permanent civilian faculty. Employing experts on deputation or getting retired defence service officers with expert knowledge and experience is also an alternative that may be explored.

Study of Military History, Social Sciences, Ethics, Geography, etc.[25]

More emphasis should be placed on the study of military history, social science, ethics, values, geography, leadership, strategy, etc.

Language

Instead of emphasizing the importance of learning languages like French, Spanish, German, etc. Due impetus must be given forthwith to Chinese, Pashtu, Balti, etc., for strategic reasons. Languages used in J&K and the insurgency areas of the North East should also be added to the curriculum. The human resource management related issues of learning, posting, career interests, etc., should also be taken care of.

Selection of Top Echelons

Commandants of prestigious institutes like the NDC, DSSC, CDM and AWC should be chosen deliberately. Being a three star general does not necessarily make one a good Commandant automatically.

Jointmanship

Though some importance is now being given, much more is required to be done in today's era of joint operations.[26]

Competencies of Officers

There is no identified set of competence criteria for officers. The Army should lay down what competencies it expects of its officers during the various stages of their careers. The PME institutes need to evaluate and assess proper course lengths for these competencies. The US Navy and US Marine Corps have identified the competencies expected out of officers.

Lessons Learned

Lessons Learned is an important aspect of capturing the knowledge and experience gained in the ongoing conflicts and CI/CT Ops scenario. There is a need to translate "lessons learned" more quickly from the battlefield to the classroom. The Lessons Learned Cell at ARTRAC can do this. However, what is more important is to quickly send back the lessons learned in a particular operation in CI/CT environment in a time frame of, say, 72 hours in order to ensure that the valuable lessons are not lost. The lessons of ongoing operations should be internalised in a systematic manner.[27]

Explore models of School of Advanced Military Studies and Advanced Strategic Art Programme at the US AWC

A small portion of each DSSC course may be selected and ten-month graduate degree level education programme on how to think about military art.[28]

Entrance Test

For entry into the DSSC there is a competitive examination. Officers are nominated for all except M Tech/LGSC courses. The requirement of entrance examinations for HCC/HDMC and NDC courses is a possibility that needs to be evaluated and implemented.

Cost

No cost-benefit analysis of training is carried out at present. A method should be found to discern the return on investment. Though there will be obstacles to doing this, a beginning still needs to be made.

Train the Trainer

There should be a formalised "train the trainer" programme before an instructor starts talking classes. Trainers can be sent to professional organisations to enhance their knowledge and skill for imparting better instructions.

Conclusion

> *"The enormous irony of the military profession is that we are huge risk takers in what we do operationally – flying airplanes on and off a carrier, driving a ship through a sea state five typhoon, walking point with your platoon in southern Afghanistan – but publishing an article, posting a blog or speaking to the media can scare us badly. We are happy to take personal risk or operational risk, but too many of us won't take career risk."*
>
> – Admiral James Stavridis, Commander US European Command and Supreme Allied Commander Europe

Training and education are not mutually exclusive. Education complements training and experience, enabling officers to apply appropriate judgement in complex strategic environments. The general model for developing military leaders consists of a combination of PME, training and experience along with mentoring and self-development. PME should be stimulating, interesting and thought-provoking. The Army should try to be a learning organisation. Competing demands make it difficult to accommodate the need for the requisite PME, training and experience.

Senior officers today should try to acquire a more sophisticated understanding of the integration of all elements of national power (military, diplomatic, economic and informational) in the pursuit of national objectives. A habit of reading, writing and speaking must be inculcated in the officers' education programme.

PME is a well-established system in our armed forces. The Indian Army's current approach to educational training has many strengths. It delivers excellent training to its people, has good quality instruction, and its infrastructure in support of training is excellent. However, the global security environment, situation in strategic neighbourhood and internal security situation are experiencing rapid changes. There are a large number of new technologies available today for educational purpose. There is a need to review the entire PME system for holistic effectiveness.

NOTES

1. Walter Goerlitz, *History of the German General Staff, 1657-1945*, New York: Praeger, 1953; Hajo Halborn, "The Prusso-German School: Moltke and the Rise of the General Staff", in Peter Paret (ed.), *Makers of Modern Strategy: From Machiavelli to the Modern Age*, Princeton University Press, Princeton, 1986, pp. 281-95.
2. Halborn, Hajo, "The Prusso-German School: Moltke and the Rise of the General Staff." In Makers of Modern Strategy: From Machiavelli to the Modern Age, ed.

Peter Paret, 281-95. Princeton: Princeton University Press, 1986.

3. Fitzsimonds, James R. and Manhken, Thomas G, "Exploring Institutional Impediments to Innovation.", *Joint Forces Quarterly*, 56, Third Quarter, 2007, pp. 96-103. http://www.ndu.edu/inss/Press/jfq_pages/editions/i46/15.pdf
4. Col. P.K. Mallick, "Challenges of 21st Century Military Leadership – How Do We Train? "*Defence Management Journal*, October 2002.
5. Robert H. Scales, "Too Busy to Learn", Proceedings 136, no. 2/February 2010, p. 284, at www.usni.org/ magazines/proceedings/story.asp? STORY_ID=2195.
6. Gen. Charles C. Krulak, "The Strategic Corporal: Leadership in the Three Block War", *Marines Magazine*, January 1999, at http://www.au.af.mil/au/awc/awcgate/usmc/strategic_corporal.htm.
7. Special Edition, International Relations in Professional Military Education, *Infinity Journal*, January 2016 .
8. Brig. P.K. Mallick, "Asymmetric Wars – Lessons from Recent Conflicts and Its Relevance to India", *Pinnacle*, 8, June 2009; Col. P.K. Mallick, "Combat Leadership in 21st Century", *USI Digest*, March 2006-August 2006 and September 2006-February 2007.
9. Admiral James Stavridis gave his take on the difference in his College, at http://www.aco.nato.int/saceur/read-think-write.aspx.
10. Jeffrey D. McCausland and Gregg F. Martin, "Transforming Strategic Leader Education for the 21st-Century Army", *Parameters*, Autumn 2001, pp. 17-33.
11. Joan Johnson-Freese and Kevin Kelley, "Meaningful Metrics for Professional Military Education", *Joint Force Quarterly*, 84, January 26, 2017.
12. Steven Metz, "Strategic Horizons: U.S. Profession Military Education on the Chopping Block", *World Politics Review*, April 17, 2013 at http://www.worldpoliticsreview.com/articles/12879/strategic-horizons-u-s-professional-military-education-on-the-chopping-block.
13. Prakash Menon, "Military Education in India: Missing the Forest for the Trees", *Journal of Defence Studies*, 9 (4), October-December 2015, pp. 49-69.
14. Anit Mukherjee and Devesh Kapur, "A fleeting Opportunity", *The Hindu*, August 10, 2016 at http://www.thehindu.com/opinion/op-ed/Afleeting-opportunity/article14562307.ece;Harsh V. Pant, "The Art of War, We Need to Think Creatively about the Proposed Defence University", *The Indian Express*, August 19, 2016.
15. Prakash Katoch, "Defence University: Why INDU Might End up as Just Another Bureaucratic Coup", August 16, 2016 at http://www.firstpost.com/category/india;
16. *Report of the Panel on Military Education of the One Hundredth Congress*, 101st Congress, 1st session, US Congress, House of Representatives, Committee on Armed Services, US Government Printing Office, Washington, DC, 1989, p. v.
17. *The Ryan Review, A Study of Army's Education, Training and Doctrine Needs for the Future*, Department of Defence, Australia, 2016, athttp://hdl.voced.edu.au/10707/404547.
18. "National Skill Development Corporation", Ministry of Skill Development and Entrepreneurship, Government of India, at http://www.skilldevelopment.gov.in/nationalskilldevelopmentcorporation.html.
19. National Policy for Skill Development and Entrepreneurship 2015, Ministry of Skill Development and Entrepreneurship, Government of India, 2015, at http:/

/www.skilldevelopment.gov.in/assets/images/Skill%20India/policy%20booklet-%20Final.pdf.

20. Brig. P.K. Mallick, "Leveraging Technology in CI Ops", *Pinnacle*, June 2008.
21. *Another Crossroads? Professional Military Education Two Decades after the Goldwater-Nichols Act and the Skelton Panel*, US House of Representatives, Committee on Armed Services, Subcommittee on Oversight & Investigations, April 2010, athttp://www.au.af.mil/au/awc/awcgate/congress/hasc_pme_report_6may2010.pdf.
22. "Dwight D. Eisenhower School for National Security and Resource Strategy", *Wikipedia*, at https://en.wikipedia.org/wiki/Dwight_D._Eisenhower_School_for_National_Security_and_Resource_Strategy.
23. Strategic Business Plan for the Army University, at http://armyu.army.mil/sites/default/files/documents/20150331_SIGNED_FINAL_Strategic_Business_Plan_for_ the_%20Army_University(Unrestricted).pdf.
24. Joan Johnson-Freese and Kevin Kelley, No. 12, Meaningful Metrics for Professional Military Education JFQ 84, 1st Quarter 2017.
25. Brig. P.K. Mallick, "Ethics, Values, Morality and 21st Century Warfare", *Trishul Journal*, 2, Spring 2008.
26. Statement of General James N. Mattis, USMC, Commander, United States Joint Forces Command, Before the House Armed Services Committee, March 18, 2009;
27. S. Moore, "USMC Approach to Professional Military Education, Briefing for Director General Training", March 11, 2016.
28. Brigadier General HubaWass de Czege, US Army, Retired, "The Need for Advanced Military Study", *Military Review*, July-August 2009.

REFERENCES

1. Judith Hicks Stichm, US Army War College, *Military Education in a Democracy*, Temple University Press, Philadelphia, 2002.
2. Alvin and Heidi Toffler, *War and Anti-War* (Boston, Mass: Little, Brown, and Co, 1993).
3. Study Report on Professional Military Education (PME) and Development of Enhanced Competence in the Indian Army, Army Training Command, October 2011.
4. Draft Notes on the January 1998, Naval Postgraduate School – Office of Naval Research Conference on Professional Military Education for the 21st Century Warrior For NPS Presentation at the Military Education Coordinating Committee (MECC).
5. U.S. Congress, House of Representatives, Committee on Armed Services, Report of the Panel on Military Education of the One Hundredth Congress, 101st Cong., 1st sess. (Washington, DC: U.S. Government Printing Office, 1989).
6. Anit Mukherjee (2016): Fighting Separately: Jointness and Civil-Military Relations in India, Journal of Strategic Studies, DOI: 10.1080/01402390.2016.1196357.
7. Prakash Menon (2015): Military Education in India: Missing the Forest for the Trees, Journal of Defence Studies, Vol. 9, No. 4 October-December 2015, pp. 49-69.
8. Joan Johnson-Freese and Kevin Kelley, Meaningful Metrics for Professional Military Education, Joint Force Quarterly 84 (1st Quarter, January 2017).

9. Lewis, S. J. "Reflections on German Military Reform." Military Review, (August 1988), 60-69. Reprinted in H200: Military Innovation in the Interwar Period, 187-93. Fort Leavenworth: US Army Command and General Staff College, September 2007.
10. Jason M. Bender, Non-Technical Military Innovation: The Prussian General Staff and Professional Military Education, Small War Journal, 14 Sep 2016, Available online at: http://smallwarsjournal.com/jrnl/art/non-technical-military-innovation-theprussian-general-staff-and-professional-military-educ
11. Knox, MacGregor. "Mass Politics and Nationalism as Military Revolution: The French Revolution and After." In The Dynamics of Military Revolution, 1300-2050, eds. MacGregor Knox and Williamson Murray, 57-73. Cambridge: University Press, 2001.
12. *Report on the Proceedings: Conference on Professional Military Education, Rebuilding America's Intellectual Arsenal, March 25, 2006, US Merchant Marine Academy, New York, Sponsored by Congressman Steve Israel.* Available at: http://smallwarsjournal.com/documents/housepmeconference.pdf
13. Matthew F. Cancian, Officers Are Less Intelligent: What Does It Mean?, *Joint Force Quarterly*, March 29, 2016.
14. S Thomas P. Galvin, Enhancing Identity Development at Senior Service Colleges, Strategic Studies Institute and U.S. Army War College Press, December 2016.
15. Williamson Murray, "Grading the War Colleges," The National Interest, no. 6 (Winter 1986–87), pp. 12–19.
16. Maj Gen Robert H. Scales, Are You A Strategic Genius?: Not Likely, Given Army's System for Selecting Educating Leaders available at: http://strategicstudyindia.blogspot.in/2016/11/are-you-strategic-genius-not-likely.html
17. Building Better Generals By David Barno, Nora Bensahel, Katherine Kidder and Kelley Sayler, October 2013, Center for New American Security.
18. Linda Robinson, Paul D. Miller, John Gordon IV, Jeffrey Decker, Michael Schwille, Raphael S. Cohen, Improving Strategic Competence: Lessons from 13 Years of War, RAND Corporation, Santa Monica, Calif. 2014 available at http://www.rand.org/content/dam/rand/pubs/research_reports/RR800/RR816/RAND_RR816.pdf
19. Celestino Perez, Strategic Discontent, Political Literacy, and Professional Military Education, January 14, 2016. Available at: http://thestrategybridge.org/the-bridge/2016/1/7/strategic-discontent-political-literacy-and-professional-military-education
20. Celestino Perez, Jr., Strategic Discontent, Political Literacy, and Professional Military Education, January 14, 2016 available at: http://thestrategybridge.org/the-bridge/2016/1/7/strategic-discontent-political-literacy-and-professional-military-education#_ftn3
21. B. H. Liddell Hart, Why Don't We Learn from History? (New York: Hawthorn Books, 1971), p. 15.
22. Michael Howard, "Military History and the History of War," in The Past as Prologue, 12.
23. Milan Vego, Military History and the Study of Operational Art, Joint Forces Quarterly, issue 57, 2d quarter 2010.

24. Frank G. Hoffman, "Embracing a Full Spectrum Profession," Keeping the Edge: Revitalizing America's Military Officer Corps, Center for a New American Security, February 2010.
25. Johnson, L., Adams Becker, S., Estrada, V., and Freeman, A. (2015). NMC Horizon Report: 2015 Higher Education Edition. Austin, Texas: The New Media Consortium.
26. Anderson, J., Boyles, J. & Rainier, L. (2012). The Future of Higher Education. Available at: http://www.pewinternet.org/2012/07/27/the-future-of-higher-education/
27. http://www.benning.army.mil/mcoe/maneuverconference/2012/presentation/ppt/GENCone.ppt
28. See http://www.benning.army.mil/mssp/ for this very comprehensive approach to providing online resources for soldiers and officers to continue their professional development in their own time.
29. The Ryan Review A study of Army's education, training and doctrine needs for the future Brigadier Mick Ryan. Australian Army, April 2016.
30. Michael G. Shanley, James C. Crowley, Matthew W. Lewis, Susan G. Straus, Kristin J. Leuschner, John Coombs, Making Improvements to The Army Distributed Learning Program. 2012 RAND Corporation.
31. David Last, Picking Leaders for Professional Military Education, SSR 2.0 Brief, Issue NO. 6 | October 2016 Centre For Security Governance.
32. Michael C. Sevcik, Army Learning Concept 2015: These are not the droids you are looking for Small Wars Journal available at: http://smallwarsjournal.com/printpdf/10812 .
33. TRADOC Pamphlet 525-8-2, The US Army Learning Concept for 2015, released 20 Jan 2011.
34. U.S. Department of the Army, Training and Doctrine Command, Combined Arms Center, Power Point Briefing: Non-commissioned Officer Education System Transformation (Fort Leavenworth KS, Combined Arms Center, November 2005).
35. The Army wants to pay for your civilian electrician, mechanic or any other credential, Myers, January 19, 2017, https://www.armytimes.com/author/meghann-myers.
36. http://www.skilldevelopment.gov.in/nationalskilldevelopmentcorporation.html
37. http://www.skilldevelopment.gov.in/assets/images/Skill%20India/policy%20booklet-%20Final.pdf
38. http://www.nsdcindia.org/sites/default/files/files/pdf/Indias_Emerging_Security_Landscape_Pinkerton_8-2014.pdf
39. Maj Gen Robert Scales, Too Busy to Learn, Available at: http://www.usni.org/magazines/proceedings/2010-02/too-busy-learn
40. Dave Maxwell, Thoughts on Professional Military Education: After 9-11, Iraq, and Afghanistan in the Era of Fiscal Austerity, Small Wars Journal, Jan 1 2012, Available online at: http://smallwarsjournal.com/jrnl/art/thoughts-on-professional-militaryeducation-after-9-11-iraq-and-afghanistan-in-the-era-of-f
41. Ah, memories of the Air War College, By June 24, 2011, http://foreignpolicy.com/2011/06/24/ah-memories-of-the-air-war-college/
42. John A. Nagl. Knife Fights: A Memoir of Modern War in Theory And Practice (New York: The Penguin Press 2014), p 37.

43. Nicholas Murray, "Finally, Official Recognition That CGSC Is Broken, Bust and in the Ditch," Foreign Policy, September 25, 2015, available at http://foreignpolicy.com/2015/09/25/finally-official-recognition-that-cgsc-is-broken-bust-and-in-the-ditch/
44. Joan Johnson-Freese, "The Reform of Military Education: Twenty-Five Years Later," *Orbis* 56, no. 1 (Winter 2012), 135–153; and John T. Kuehn, "The Goldwater-Nichols Fix: Joint Education Is the Key to True 'Jointness,'" Armed Forces Journal (April 2010).
45. Thomas E. Ricks, "Need Budget Cuts? We Probably Can Start by Shutting the Air War College," Foreign Policy, April 22, 2011, available at http://foreignpolicy.com/2011/04/11/need-budget-cuts-we-probably-can-start-by-shutting-the-air-war-college/.
46. Christopher J. Lamb and Brittany Porro, "Next Steps for Transforming Education at National Defense University," Joint Force Quarterly 76 (1st Quarter 2015), available at http://ndupress.ndu.edu/JFQ/Joint-Force-Quarterly-76/Article/577587/next-steps-for-transforming-education-at-national-defense-university/
47. Nicholas Murray, "The Role of Professional Military Education in Mission Command," Joint Force Quarterly 72 (1st Quarter 2014), available at http://ndupress.ndu.edu/Portals/68/Documents/jfq/jfq-72/jfq-72_10-13_Murray.pdf.
48. Cuccolo and Betros; Charles E. Wilhelm et al., U.S. Marine Corps Officer Professional Military Education 2006 Study and Findings (Quantico, VA: Marine Corps University, 2006), available at www.mcu.usmc.mil/SACS1/PME/U.S.%20Marine%20Corps%20Officer%20Professional%20Military%20Education%202006%20Study%20and%20Findings%20(Wilhelm%20Study).pdf.
49. Thomas E. Ricks, 10 things I don't get about PME, Foreign Policy, January 31, 2013 available at: http://foreignpolicy.com/2013/01/31/10-things-i-dont-get-about-pme/
50. Dr. Leonard Wong, Dr. Stephen J. Gerras, Lying to Ourselves: Dishonesty in the Army Profession, Strategic Studies Institute and U.S. Army War College Press, February 17, 2015 available at: http://www.strategicstudiesinstitute.army.mil/pdffiles/PUB1250.pdf
51. Future Strategic Priorities For Professional Military Education: A Practitioner Perspective
52. Georgia, Japan, Kuwait, Nigeria, Norway, Pakistan, Qatar, Singapore, and the UK available at: https://www.kcl.ac.uk/sspp/departments/dsd/research/researchgroups/cmeo/index.aspx
53. In 1989, then–House Armed Services Committee Chairman Les Aspin appointed then-Congressman Ike Skelton to lead a panel to conduct an assessment of military education. This panel developed the key recommendations that later became the requirements, standards, and learning areas set in the Chairman's policy for officer joint professional military education. 6 1. U.S. Congress, House of Representatives, Committee on Armed Services, Report of the Panel on Military Education of the One Hundredth Congress, 101st Cong., 1st sess., 1989, no. 4, available at http://catalog.hathitrust.org/Record/007602201. Hereafter, the Skelton Report.
54. Ike Skelton, "JPME: Are We There Yet?" *Military Review* 77, no. 1 (January–February 1997), pp 6-7.

55. Joan Johnson-Freese, Teach Tough, Think Tough: Why Military Education Must Change, June 15, 2011 available at: http://breakingdefense.com/2011/06/teach-tough-think-tough/v
56. David Last, Picking Leaders for Professional Military Education, Centre For Security Governance, SSR 2.0 Brief Issue No. 6, October 2016.
57. Thomas E. Ricks, Slightly 'steamed,' Gen. Scales explains his criticism of the military's war colleges, Foreign Policy, May 11, 2012 available at: http://foreignpolicy.com/2012/05/11/slightly-steamed-gen-scales-explains-his-criticism-of-the-militarys-war-colleges/ .
58. Charles D Allen, Redress of Professional Military Education: The Clarion Call, issue 59, Joint Forces Quarterly, 4th quarter 2010.
59. Steven Metz, Strategic Horizons: U.S. Professional Military Education on the Chopping Block, 17 Apr 2013.

Appendix 'A'

The Structure of the US Army University

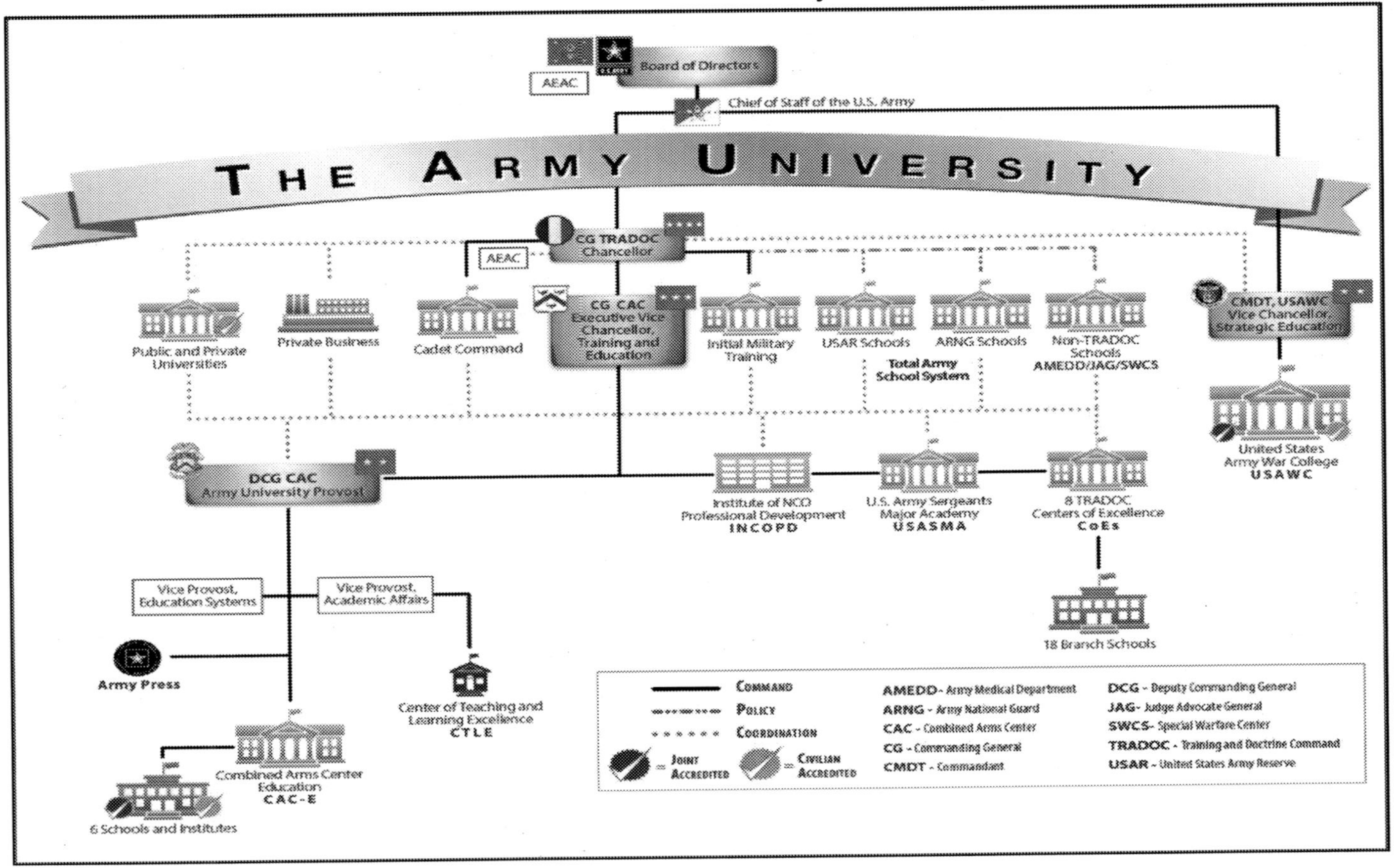

14

Rethinking Strategic Communication in the Age of "Instant" Warfare

Shruti Pandalai

Introduction

Conflict in the 21st century is largely asymmetric, re-defined primarily by the presence of an all-pervasive media ecology where even local operations acquire a global context. In this multidimensional theatre of conflict, managing public opinions, and building consensus on strategic responses adopted by the state become essential. It is central to the idea of providing legitimacy to military action in contemporary conflicts.

This is especially true for conflicts where pre-existing sensitivities are in play and public opinion is susceptible to quick polarisation and mobilisation, amplified by the presence of many dissenting narratives. In the case of protracted operations, if not catered for, this may have ramifications on both the conduct of military operations and the image of the military as well as troop morale. Strategic communication therefore becomes an indispensable pillar of modern military planning that requires thought at the operational level and is no longer an adhoc exercise. This means increasing investment in the building of messages and communication strategies that support military actions aimed at the local, domestic and international audience. It requires circumventing hierarchies to ensure that those responsible for planning, executing and communicating these strategies are empowered to do so in real time, responding to situations on the ground and adapting to emerging counter-narratives. This is imperative to retaining credibility in a 24/7 media environment.

The Indian state has often been criticised for a lack of strategic coherence in communicating the larger message that underpins its strategy; weighed down due to shifting policy goal posts or other compulsions. This often gives way to ambiguity and confusion in the public sphere. The skirmishes between the Chinese and Indian troops over differing perceptions of the Line of Actual Control on the disputed border is a case in point. In most of these cases, the approach adopted is to subdue media frenzy till the next incident occurs. Instead, an inordinate amount of attention is paid to the co-ordination and tools of the message, as opposed to the message itself.

This paper aims to grapple with these issues, and analyse the success or setbacks of existing strategic communication operations conducted by the Indian military. It primarily focuses on the Indian Army and recommends possible reforms to existing practices. It argues strongly for the need to institutionalise strategic communication as a key part of the military planning and implementation process.

Defining Strategic Communication

Strategic Communication as a concept finds its origin in the Western military's narrative of winning hearts and minds, and the war of ideas. The underlying strategy was based on "*jus ad bellum* and *jus in bello*"[1] justifications of the US-led global war on terror. In the 2006 *Quadrennial Defense Review Execution Roadmap for Strategic Communication*, the US Department of Defence defined strategic communication as "focused governmental processes and efforts to understand and engage key audiences to create, strengthen or preserve conditions favourable to advance national interests and objectives using coordinated information, themes, plans, programs, and actions synchronised with other elements of national power".[2]

The US with its *National Strategy for Strategic Communication and Public Diplomacy* (2007) and UK with its draft Joint Doctrine Note, *Strategic Communication: The Defence Contribution* (2012) have long since been thinking ahead, improvising structures and investing in manpower and resources to address this issue.[3] The idea is to identify the core political objective, craft a strong policy narrative and align all diplomacy and communication programmes to target specific audiences using the most appropriate and effective media available. They argue that this is only possible, if "consideration of communication and its effects (is) integrated into operational planning, decision-making, and execution cycles, [and] not considered as an afterthought".[4]

Even the North Atlantic Treaty Organisation (NATO) echoes this vision as part of the overarching political-military approach to strategic communications. NATO's doctrine seeks to put "Strategic Communications at the heart of all levels of military policy, planning and execution, and then, as a fully integrated part of the overall effort, ensure the development of a practical, effective strategy that makes a real contribution to success".[5]

While many would argue that despite the most sophisticated strategic communication operations by the NATO alliance partners, the results of the Iraq and Afghanistan experiences were not favourable, we still need to take a leaf out of their book. There is a necessity to craft our own approach regarding the framing of the military narrative in India. This strategic exposition needs to be placed within the framework of our national policy interests, and it should acknowledge existing lacunae and project our military capabilities.

Winning Wars, but Not Always the Public

The Indian military has fought protracted insurgencies, cross-border terrorism, prepared for a two-front war on its borders, handled border intrusions and managed humanitarian and disaster relief operations valiantly. Yet the overall standing of the military as a national institution has suffered criticism in the public sphere on various issues. For the army, particularly, the controversy around the "misuse of the Armed Forces Special Powers Act" and accusations of opacity/lack of transparency in dealing with issues of human rights violations in counter-insurgency operations in Kashmir and the Northeast, have been particularly damning. Lt General Ata Hasnain (Retd.), a veteran officer and vocal critic of the Indian Army's image projection, stated the facts as they are when he wrote,

> The Army's strategic communication machinery remains mute and has no intellectual approach to educate Indian citizens [on the Indian army's point of view on AFSPA]. The battle of perception was lost many years ago. This is why I now believe that AFSPA is almost a liability being used by all shades of adversaries to beat the Army and the Government. It should be replaced by a legislation which empowers and projects the Army as a rights friendly organisation. It is not difficult if the Army applies its mind and convinces the Government that strategic communication is part of its General Staff responsibilities.[6]

Essentially, the army needs to institutionalise a Strategic Communication Policy, at the higher most levels and ensure its implementation by empowering leadership down the chain of command and replace adhoc mechanisms used to douse fires in the public square.

Take for instance, the complete lack of military and state leadership interface in controlling the narrative in the Valley post the death of the Pakistani terrorist group Hizbul Mujahideen Commander Burhan Wani. The self-styled, social media face of the Kashmir rebellion, Wani was killed in an encounter with security forces in Anantnag. Wani's death plunged the state into deep turmoil, pitting Indian security forces against a large section of the disenfranchised Kashmiri youth that was sympathetic to Wani's easy social media narrative of an anti-India resistance. Wani changed the public face of militancy in Kashmir by crowd sourcing support in a manner that was popularised by the agitators of the Arab Spring and the Islamic State. In the absence of an effective counter-narrative from authorities representing the Indian state, Wani's popularity grew unchecked. A full-blown confrontation between incensed youth and Indian security forces, that followed post his funeral, resulted in 68 civilian deaths and over 2,000 injured protestors, leaving an embarrassed Indian state facing a crisis of governance, and the army once again filling in the absence of the civilian administration.[7] While the army was not as involved in the post-Burhan Wani operations as the state police and the Central Reserve Police Force (CRPF) were, the literature fuelling jihadi sentiment and recruitment in Kashmir largely focuses on revenge against the Indian Army.[8]

This episode raised troubling questions for the Indian state. Several analysts asked, "Why is the rhetoric of terrorist groups such as Hizbul Mujahideen gaining alarming popularity among Kashmiri youth, mobilising them in thousands? Can a larger military presence bring stability and return the Kashmir valley to normalcy?"[9] Who is responsible for answering these tough yet pertinent questions, all of which have a tremendous impact on military planning and operations? Is the military supposed to respond independently or as an arm of the government? More importantly, how are government agencies equipped to deal with the social media challenge that has complicated the battle of perceptions and the theatre of 21st century conflict?

This is not to say that the top brass of the Indian military is unaware of the scale of change and the increase in media intrusion in its arena of operations. In a seminar titled "Social Media and the Armed Forces", held in New Delhi, the heads of various arms of the military acknowledged that "the armed forces have been slow and conservative in adopting the use of social media largely due to traditional and dated concepts of security".[10] There was consensus among senior officers that "forces must harness its strengths and exploit it as a force multiplier – to be able to do this we need to remove protocols of time and space barriers and decentralise responsibilities".[11]

While these aspects of strategic communication are a work in progress with the Indian military, it is disheartening to see that public diplomacy efforts conducted by the army like Operation Sadbhavna have also had a very limited impact on public perception. Operation Sadbhavna, launched in rural Jammu and Kashmir (J&K) in 1998 (and revitalised for towns and cities in 2006), was an attempt at acting on a counter-insurgency doctrine that was more people centric and argued for minimum use of force. According to an Institute for Defence Studies and Analyses (IDSA) study, "Rs. 276.08 crore, allocated by the Ministry of Defence (MoD), between 1998-2008, was spent by the army on running schools, orphanages, improving the living standard of the locals by constructing roads and bridges, installing hand pumps and electrifying villages and giving them free medical services."[12] The Operation generated tremendous goodwill between the army and the locals, but was often targeted by the local administration as a de-legitimisation of the state machinery, making the army indispensable to the region. Even though YouTube videos of the good work done by the forces have been shown by channels like DD-Kashmir, they seem to have very few takers and even lesser hits online.[13] This shows that little or no thought has been given to engaging with stakeholders who can help re-invent the armed forces image in the battle against insurgency. Most of these efforts are individual driven and not institution led.[14] The next section examines the institutional challenges facing the Indian military in greater detail.

The Indian approach to Strategic Communication: A Grudging Embrace[15]

An overarching structure for media engagement and communication planning is in place in India, however, its functioning leaves much to be desired. The organisations described below, are geared towards media engagement and not focused on strategic communication – which is the more important operational exercise – despite being manned by senior officials of the civilian and military establishment.

All ministries or departments under the Government of India have high-ranking joint secretary-level officers in charge of public relations or media affairs. The Ministry of Defence is no different. The Defence Public Relations (DPR) is headed by Additional Director General (ADG) Media and Communication. Under him/her are three senior Public Relation Officers (PROs) representing the three Services, and 24 staff-level PROs spread across the country selected from all the three forces and the Indian Information System/Service. This department also includes the services of the editor of *Sainik Samachar* and the Films Division.

Additionally, each service also has its own set of media liaison officers. The army hosts the office of the ADG Public Information (ADGPI) that deals closely with the media interactions of the Chief of Army Staff (COAS) on a day-to-day basis, while also planning for information and psychological warfare, for the organisation as a whole. The ADGPI is an adjunct office to the Director General Military Intelligence (DGMI) and comes under the Directorate of Military Intelligence, and not the DPR. The ADGPI does not have financial sanctions and remains an advisory post without empowerment, despite its proximity to the corridors of power. This, despite the fact that according to the ADGPI's functions and mandate, it is the most equipped to carry out strategic communication operations. Ironically, since the ADGPI does not come under the DPR, the interface with PROs outside its service, is often strained due to an incongruent agenda.

Reforms thus far are underway, but they have been slow. Each command, especially the Northern and Eastern Commands manning borders with hostile neighbours, has an Information Warfare (IW) branch. Each command branch is headed by a Major General Staff (MGGS), along with appointments of Brigadier General Staff (BGS) (IW) and Colonel (IW) down the order. An effective strategic communication strategy would harness the work being done by the IW branches at the tactical level and leverage it at the national level. However, since the services have their administrations working in silos, this collaboration is rare.

Usually, in practice, briefings held by Defence PROs are verbatim reproductions of written communiqués which outline bare information and leave room for wild speculation by the media on matters that are considered "classified". The entire process, more often than not, is rendered counterproductive. According to a former Deputy COAS, "The DPR has no credibility with the media; a revolutionary change in the system is required."[16]

In contrast, the navy and air force, being smaller services, are thought to have more efficient systems, with their PROs having a considerably higher degree of empowerment. This is symptomatic of a typically bureaucratic mind-set. The size of the force should not be a determinant in the degree of empowerment of its officers.

In another damning indictment of the Indian Army's approach to information management when compared to its adversary Pakistan, military experts have pointed out:

> Right across the international border in Pakistan exists the most professional PR and strategic communication machinery ever put together by a set of armed forces anywhere in the world ... Over time the ISPR [Inter Services Public Relations] has virtually become the psychological warfare centre of the Pakistan armed forces. It is a force multiplier, managing perception within the Pakistan armed forces, within civil society of Pakistan and most importantly abroad. Its specific task in relation to India is to run the most astute psychological warfare campaign 24x7 with the Indian armed forces the major target...
>
> On our side, PR is grudgingly executed by the three Services making use of organisations which are ad hoc and unauthorised because institutionally they are not supposed to speak to the public or the media. That is only the purview of the Ministry of Defence (MoD) and its archaic PR machinery termed PRO Defence. It has a set of people who may be professional PR persons but know little about modern psychological warfare, perception management or strategic communication. There are a few uniformed people to assist in this too but have little idea about the General Staff requirements of outreach. There are Regional PROs at various stations who once again report to the PRO Defence, are not under the local formation commanders or staff and hence not in sync with the Army's operational needs. To imagine that in today's world a set of armed forces can be without a General Staff oriented PR/Information machinery is actually unthinkable. But, then that is how backward we are in our thinking on as important as subject as information.[17]

Re-wiring Reforms?

Problems in the Current Structure[18]

As identified in the section above, despite having an overarching structure and manpower in place, organisational culture, the lack of clear strategic objectives and systemic and bureaucratic inconsistencies hinder effective strategic communications – both in planning and execution. In current practice, the whole range of strategic communication operations – from the careful curation of the message, to their customisation for targeted audiences through psychological operations/keeping up with counter-narratives, etc. – have been done inconsistently, with a bulk of the focus retained towards maintaining public relations.

Culturally, we have inherited a closed bureaucratic system from the British where information, whether classified or otherwise, comes at a premium. Currently, information sharing is seen as a unidimensional exercise, with a focus on managing the media, and dealing with it when required for "publicity", if it fits "agendas", or for "score-settling".[19] The approach is adhoc, generally under pressure, and often antagonistic, in cases where the media does not toe the "official line". While the explosion in the Indian media space is forcibly effecting a grudging change in the establishment, the reforms being undertaken are at best cosmetic.

For Strategic communication to actually find place in the operation and planning process implemented by military and political planners, there needs to be a top-down cultural shift in mind-set. It is imperative for the top brass to encourage and empower their subordinates to engage the public information space, create awareness, counter misperceptions and work towards aligning public opinion with policy objectives and improving the perception of transparency and good governance. For example, in a state like Kashmir, where there exists a state-on-state proxy war, a purely public relations exercise is ineffective. The need of the hour is to align all instruments of state power to effectively communicate the message of the Indian state and negate any misperceptions fuelled by the adversary that are aimed at delegitimising military-civilian ground action. Therefore, strategic communication operations are extremely necessary in these areas.

There is also a dire need to change the attitude and approach adopted in selecting the appointments made to the office of public relations. Until recently, officers posted in the DPR were often superseded and these billets were considered retirement postings.[20] While this does not imply that the superseded officers are incapable, it is generally understood that– unless motivated by the organisation – they tend to lack the zeal to deal with an aggressive media ecology. The ADGPI has led by example to change this attitude and this mind-set needs emulation.

Furthermore, Military officers, also need to be provided with incentives, to volunteer to train themselves as strategic communication specialists. Language training for field operations, and media capsules covering the handling of print, television and social media need to be inculcated in junior-level courses (Young Officers training) and then revised subsequently during Staff College, Higher Command (HC) and National

Defence College training. Some thought could also go into creating a specialised military cadre of communication planning specialists, depending on the resources available and the types of missions planned.

However, there is no point investing in communication specialists if the MoD does not empower them – as is often the case – since the DPR often works at loggerheads vis-à-vis military spokespersons. For instance, in the case of the army, there is a clear disconnect between the DPR and the ADGPI, which is well-recorded. So much so that at times, the former refuses to release press statements issued by the ADGPI despite being mandated by protocol. Many believe that the DPR only defends the offices of the Defence Minister and Defence Secretary and will not support the armed forces in times of controversy.[21] In contrast, media spokespersons for the Services are accused of furthering the agenda of their respective Chiefs. In short, the turf war that plays out between the MoD and Service Headquarters sends mixed messages to the media. This defeats the larger policy thrust behind the exercise of strategic communication.

In fact, some of the problems identified by the Kargil Review Committee[22] on information management during military operations still remain relevant today. These are:

(a) With some exceptions, media personnel lacked training in military affairs and war reporting and the Armed Services lacked training and preparedness to facilitate the task of the media and counter disinformation.

(b) The DPR, which is routinely handled by the MoD through regular Information Service cadres, is not equipped to handle media relations during a war or even a proxy war.

(c) The army needs improved public relations capabilities even when deployed on counter-insurgency duties. Public relations are presently managed by the MoD at the higher level and by military officers who have no media background at the formation level.

(d) War and proxy war do not leave the civil population untouched. This calls for the creation of a civil-military interface at various levels to deal with a whole range of problems on an emergency basis. Such a liaison was lacking during the Kargil action and points to a deficiency that must be made good.

(e) Negative propaganda needs to be nipped in the bud to ensure a prevention of the escalation of tensions. Quick responses and mechanisms are needed to initiate action.

A Possible STRATCOM Model

If one looks back, the Uri operation in 2016, stood out particularly for the clarity with which information about the surgical strike was presented in the public domain. The narrative was precise, had clarity of purpose and showed a unity of response in the military, political and diplomatic wings of the government. The messaging was clear: this was a limited strike to pre-empt terrorists from entering India, the target were terrorists and not the Pakistan Army, India had acted within its rights and the Indian Army was in constant touch with its Pakistani counterpart to ensure that there was no ratcheting up of tensions. The combined press briefing conducted by the Director General of Military Operations (DGMO) and the spokesperson of the Ministry of External Affairs (MEA) left no ambiguity about the limited scope of the operation and its demonstrative nature, and built upon the official narrative that had shored in international diplomatic capital post the Uri attacks.

The above example proves that a communication model loosely exists within the aegis of the Government of India that comes into prominence during crisis situations. This model includes SOPs for contingencies, but the problem lies solely with implementation. Figure 1 gives a suggested strategic communication structure to handle contingencies.

This suggested structure would not entail the creation of another layered bureaucracy but would instead pool in available resources to ensure efficiency. Obviously, depending on the nature of operations, the apex body would be the Cabinet Committee on Security which would take all decisions on policy and mandate and frame the core narrative for the operation. The core group would change depending on the nature of the operation, but in most cases, it would comprise of an MEA-MoD composition along with military commanders and a media consultant, who would help the group "frame the message", manage press briefings, and gauge audience perception and receptivity.

Further down the chain of command, media cells would be created at the Integrated Defence Staff level and at the Intervening Joint Service Headquarters, to form links with individual Defence PROs from each of the Services and then right down to media cells at the formation level. Each of these media cells would coordinate intelligence, disseminate communiqués, monitor social media and engage with local media to convey our national interest. The already existing IW branches of the Indian Army could also be put to good use. They could ensure that troops on the ground are psychologically prepared for the operation and remain routinely briefed on developments and changing mandates of the operation.

Figure 1

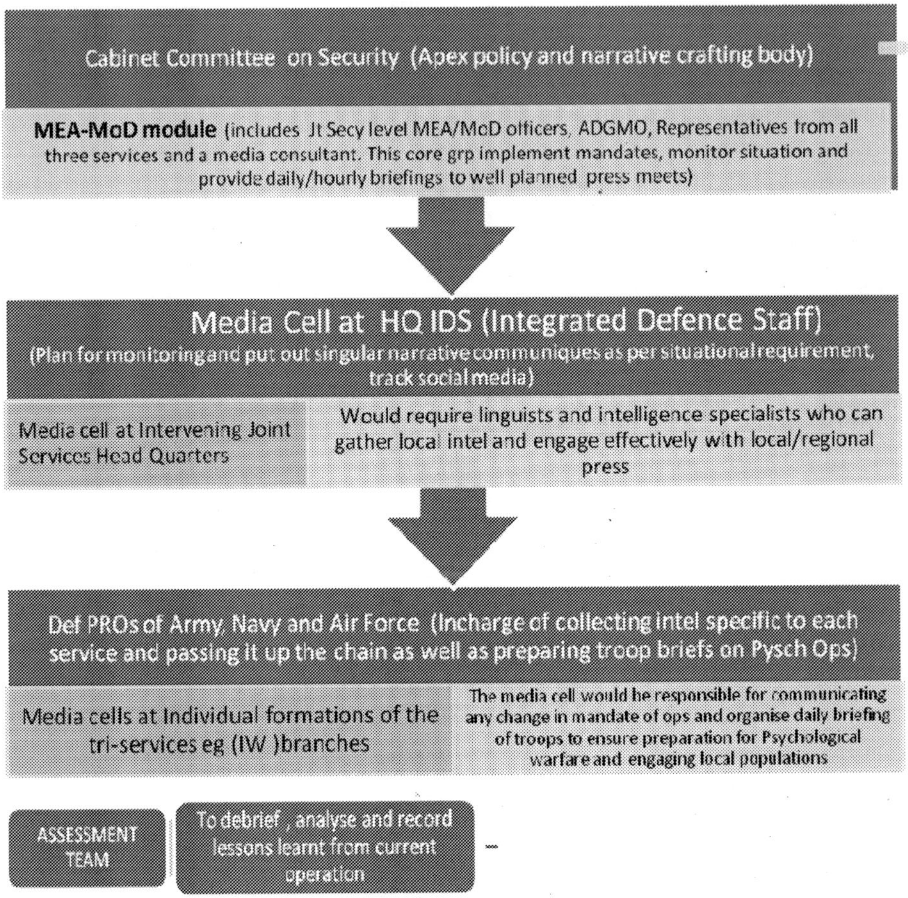

Source: First developed by the author for the IDSA Task Force Report 2012, Net Security Provider: India's Out-of-Area Contingency Operations.

Finally, an assessment cell also needs to be institutionalised at every level to debrief, analyse the operation, record the lessons learnt and imbibe them into plans for future operations. For this model to succeed, it is imperative that strategic communication is included in the policy and strategy planning stages – and not as an afterthought.

Recommendations and Conclusion

While many recommendations have been made throughout this chapter, this section focuses attention on a select few:

(a) A clear political message, crafted in cohesion with all the key departments involved in the operation, is an integral part of the strategy planning exercise and not an ad hoc measure.

(b) A body of SOP (standard operating procedure) narratives or media/social media statements need to be developed for specific exercises or situations that can be passed down the command chain.

(c) As per the suggested Stratcom model, the force commander should have a mandate for "strategic communication" during specific operations. Restrictions and hierarchy in situations that require quick reactions will be counterproductive.

(d) The Services need to invest in training their officers to engage with the media effectively. This includes social media, which can be used to mine intelligence and plant effective counter-narratives. This could be started at the YO-level courses and continued up to HC and NDC.

(e) More resources must be pooled into linguist training, and a specialist cadre of officers should also be created to focus on strategic communication and influencing target audiences.

(f) Postings of Defence PROs should be incentivised and made competitive.

(g) Defence correspondents should be continually targeted with regular briefings, courses and area tours to inform reportage and build transparency. Embedded journalism in some operations could also be beneficial.

(h) The websites of the MoD and the Services need to be overhauled, ensuring accuracy of information as well as positive projection.

(i) Finally, the government and the Services need to institutionalise a cultural shift in mind-set, and begin engaging in the information battlefield as opposed to avoiding it. Training, awareness and a flexible approach are pre-requisites for any successful strategic communications infrastructure.

NOTES

1. For more see: "What are jus ad bellum and jus in bello?", January 22, 2015, accessed on URL: https://www.icrc.org/en/document/what-are-jus-ad-bellum-and-jus-bello-0 February 5, 2017.
2. See *Quadrennial Defense Review Execution Roadmap for Strategic Communication*, US Department of Defence, Deputy Under Secretary of Defence, Washington, DC, 2006, p. 3.
3. *U.S. National Strategy for Public Diplomacy and Strategic Communication*, Policy Coordinating Committee (PCC), June 2007, at http://www.au.af.mil/au/awc/awcgate/state/natstrat_strat_comm.pdf (Accessed February 5, 2017); *Joint*

Doctrine Note 1/12, Strategic Communication: The Defence Contribution, Defence Concepts and Doctrine Centre, UK Ministry of Defence, January 2012, at https://www.gov.uk/government/uploads/system/uploads/attachment_data/file/%2033710/20120126jdn112_Strategic_CommsU.pdf (Accessed February 5, 2017).

4. For more, see Lindsay J. Borg, "Communicating with Intent: Department of Defence and Strategic Communication", Executive Summary, Incidental Paper, Centre For Information Policy Research, Harvard University, 2008, at http://pirp.harvard.edu/pubs_pdf/borg/borg-i08-1.pdf (Accessed February 5, 2017).
5. *NATO Military Concept for Strategic Communications,* NATO, July 27, 2010, at https://publicintelligence.net/nato-stratcom-concept/ (Accessed February 5, 2017).
6. Lt Gen. Syed Ata Hasnain, "Image Challenge for the Indian Armed Forces: Take it by the Horns", *News18.com,* March 15, 2016, at http://www.news18.com/blogs/india/lt-gen-syed-ata-hasnain/image-challenge-for-the-indian-armed-forces-take-it-by-the-horns-14405-1216269.html (Accessed February 05, 2017).
7. Seema Mustafa, "The Army Says It as It Is in Kashmir", *The Citizen,* August 21, 2016, athttp://www.thecitizen.in/index.php/NewsDetail/index/1/8514/The-Indian-Army-Says-It-As-It-Is-in-Kashmir(Accessed February 22, 2017).
8. Rayan Naqash, "Militancy Videos Are Everywhere in Kashmir. But Are They Actually Effective?", *Scroll.in,* February 09, 2017, at https://scroll.in/magazine/828454/militant-videos-continue-to-circulate-in-the-valley-long-after-burhan-wani-introduced-the-trend (Accessed February 22, 2017).
9. Ayesha Ray, "The Case for Revising India's Counterinsurgency Strategy in Kashmir", *War on the Rocks,* September 14, 2016, at https://warontherocks.com/2016/09/the-case-for-revising-indias-counterinsurgency-strategy-in-kashmir/ (Accessed February 22, 2017).
10. Lt. Gen. V.G. Khandare, DG DIA, quoted in "A Compilation of the Deliberations and Takeaways from the Symposium on Social Media and the Military", *Defstrat,* 10 (4), September-October 2016, at http://www.defstrat.com/current-issues/social-media-and-armed-forces (Accessed February 05, 2017).
11. Quoted from "A Compilation of the Deliberations and Takeaways from the Symposium on Social Media and the Military", *Defstrat,* 10 (4), September-October 2016, at http://www.defstrat.com/current-issues/social-media-and-armed-forces (Accessed February 05, 2017).
12. Arpita Anant, "Counterinsurgency and 'Op Sadhbhavana' in Jammu and Kashmir ", IDSA Occasional Paper No. 19, October 2011, at http://www.idsa.in/system/files/OP_CounterinsurgencyKashmir.pdf (Accessed February 06, 2017).
13. As of February 2017, there were less than 200 hits on the YouTube videos of Operation Sadbhavna.
14. Arpita Anant, No. 11.
15. Information in this section is based on the author's previous research paper: Shruti Pandalai, "Strategic Communication and Perception Management for Out-Of-Area Contingency Operations", in *Net Security Provider: India's Out-of-Area Contingency Operations,* IDSA Task Force Report 2012, at http://www.idsa.in/book/NetSecurityProviderIndiasOutofAreaContingencyOperations (Accessed February 06, 2017).
16. Ibid.

17. Lt Gen. Syed Ata Hasnain, No. 5.
18. Shruti Pandalai, No. 14.
19. A senior officer, quoted off the record, in an interview with the author.
20. Ibid.
21. Ibid.
22. The following account of media-military relations during the Kargil War relies on *The Kargil Review Committee Report*. See *From Surprise to Reckoning: The Kargil Review Committee Report*, Sage Publications, New Delhi, 2000, p. 248.

Index